# First World War
### and Army of Occupation
## War Diary
### France, Belgium and Germany

42 DIVISION
126 Infantry Brigade
Manchester Regiment
1/9th Battalion
1 March 1917 - 19 February 1918

WO95/2658/1

The Naval & Military Press Ltd
www.nmarchive.com
**Published in association with The National Archives**

Published by

## The Naval & Military Press Ltd

Unit 10 Ridgewood Industrial Park,

Uckfield, East Sussex,

TN22 5QE England

Tel: +44 (0) 1825 749494

www.naval-military-press.com

www.nmarchive.com

*This diary has been reprinted in facsimile from the original. Any imperfections are inevitably reproduced and the quality may fall short of modern type and cartographic standards.*

**© Crown Copyright**
**Images reproduced by permission of The National Archives, London, England, 2015.**

# Contents

| Document type | Place/Title | Date From | Date To |
|---|---|---|---|
| Heading | 42nd Division 126th Infy Bde 1-9th Bn Manchester Regt Mar 1917-Feb 1918 To 66 Div 199 Bde. | | |
| Heading | WO95/2658 1/9 Manchester R. Mar'17-Feb'18. | | |
| Heading | 1/9 Battalion Manchester Regiment. War Diary 1916. | | |
| Heading | War Diary 1/9th Manchester Regt. March 1st To 31st 1917. Vol II. | | |
| War Diary | Moascar. | 01/03/1917 | 01/03/1917 |
| War Diary | Alexandria. | 02/03/1917 | 02/03/1917 |
| War Diary | H.M.T. Arcadian. | 03/03/1917 | 11/03/1917 |
| War Diary | Orange. | 12/03/1917 | 12/03/1917 |
| War Diary | Montereau | 13/03/1917 | 13/03/1917 |
| War Diary | Pont Remy | 14/03/1917 | 14/03/1917 |
| War Diary | Doudelainville | 15/03/1917 | 30/03/1917 |
| War Diary | Bailleul. | 31/03/1917 | 31/03/1917 |
| Miscellaneous | CMQ 2787/6 App. 1. Entrainment-Embarkation Orders. | 23/02/1917 | 23/02/1917 |
| Miscellaneous | CMQ 2787/6. App 1. | 28/02/1917 | 28/02/1917 |
| Miscellaneous | App 1. | | |
| Miscellaneous | To:- O.C. 1/9th. Manchester Regt. App 1. | 24/02/1917 | 24/02/1917 |
| Miscellaneous | Marching Out State Vol XX App 1. | 15/02/1917 | 15/02/1917 |
| Miscellaneous | Move Orders. App. 1. | 24/02/1917 | 24/02/1917 |
| Miscellaneous | O.C., 9th Manchester Regt. Vol XX App 1. | 20/02/1917 | 20/02/1917 |
| Miscellaneous | Move Orders. 9 Man Regt. App 1. | 20/02/1917 | 20/02/1917 |
| Miscellaneous | Extracts From Embarkation Instructions. Vol XX App 2. | | |
| Miscellaneous | To Lieut Colonel D.H. Wade Commanding 1/9th Manchester Regt. Vol XX App 2. | 24/02/1917 | 24/02/1917 |
| Miscellaneous | O.C. 9th Manchester Regt. Vol XX App 2. | 10/02/1917 | 10/02/1917 |
| Miscellaneous | Embarkation Orders By Brigadier General R.C. Boyle, C.B. Commanding Alexandria District. Vol XX App. 2. | 08/08/1916 | 08/08/1916 |
| Miscellaneous | A Form. Messages And Signals. Vol XX App 2. | | |
| Miscellaneous | Instructions Relating To Entrainment And Embarkation. Vol XX App 2. | 08/02/1917 | 08/02/1917 |
| Miscellaneous | O.C. 1/9th Bn. March R. A. 214/262. Vol XX App 2. | 10/02/1917 | 10/02/1917 |
| Miscellaneous | H.Q. 2nd A. & No Z Army Corps. Vol XX App 2. | 23/05/1916 | 23/05/1916 |
| Miscellaneous | From Commander To O.C. Troops Vol XX Appendix 3. | 11/03/1917 | 11/03/1917 |
| Miscellaneous | Disembarkation Orders By Colonel G.F.N. Tinley. C.B. Base Commandant, Marseilles. Appendix 4. | 18/03/1916 | 18/03/1916 |
| Miscellaneous | To The Disembarkation Staff Officer. 42nd Division. App 4 | | |
| Diagram etc | | | |
| Miscellaneous | Entrainment Orders By Colonel G.F.N. Tinley. Base Commandant Marseilles Appendix 5. | 16/05/1916 | 16/05/1916 |
| Miscellaneous | Trains Moving With Troops. Standing Orders For The Officer i/c Train. App 5. | 27/09/1916 | 27/09/1916 |
| Miscellaneous | Important Notice App. 6. | 23/05/1916 | 23/05/1916 |
| Miscellaneous | Entrainment Orders By A. Pope. Lieut-Colonel. D.A.D.R.T. App 6 | | |

| | | | |
|---|---|---|---|
| Miscellaneous | Special Order Of The Day. Farewell Message From Major General Sir William Douglas, K.C.M.G., C.B., D.S.O. App. 7 | | |
| Heading | War Diary 1/9th Manchester Regt April 1917 Vol XXI. | | |
| War Diary | Bailleul (K 6) | 01/04/1917 | 04/04/1917 |
| War Diary | Bailleul | 05/04/1917 | 07/04/1917 |
| War Diary | Morcourt. | 08/04/1917 | 11/04/1917 |
| War Diary | Feuilleres (Ref Map. Sq. 51) | 12/04/1917 | 13/04/1917 |
| War Diary | Feuilleres. | 14/04/1917 | 17/04/1917 |
| War Diary | Cartigny Sq A2. | 18/04/1917 | 18/04/1917 |
| War Diary | Marquaix Sq A1. | 19/04/1917 | 19/04/1917 |
| War Diary | Marquaix. | 20/04/1917 | 20/04/1917 |
| War Diary | Villers-Faucon. | 21/04/1917 | 21/04/1917 |
| War Diary | Epehy F 1. | 22/04/1917 | 23/04/1917 |
| War Diary | Epehy | | |
| War Diary | Epehy. | 23/04/1917 | 30/04/1917 |
| Diagram etc | Tracing From Sheet 62c NE And Sheet 57a S.E Scale 1/20000. | | |
| Map | Sheet 62 c NE Little Prielle Farm. | | |
| Operation(al) Order(s) | 1/9th. Bn. Manchester Regt. Order No. 2 Appendix 2. | 25/04/1917 | 25/04/1917 |
| Miscellaneous | Attack On Old German Trench 26/4/17. Appendix 3. | 26/04/1917 | 26/04/1917 |
| Operation(al) Order(s) | 1/9th. Battalion. Manchester Regt. Order No. 3. Appendix 4. | 26/04/1917 | 26/04/1917 |
| Miscellaneous | 1/9 Manchester Regt. Casualty Report For April 1917 Appendix 5. | 30/04/1917 | 30/04/1917 |
| Heading | 1/9th Manchester Regt War Diary May 1917 Vol XXII. | | |
| War Diary | Marquaix. | 01/05/1917 | 06/05/1917 |
| War Diary | Marquaix | 05/05/1917 | 05/05/1917 |
| War Diary | F.23.C.0.7 | 06/05/1917 | 07/05/1917 |
| War Diary | F.23.C.0.7. | 06/05/1917 | 10/05/1917 |
| War Diary | Templeux Quarry | 10/05/1917 | 14/05/1917 |
| War Diary | F.23.C.0.7. | 14/05/1917 | 18/05/1917 |
| War Diary | Villers-Faucon. | 18/05/1917 | 19/05/1917 |
| War Diary | Equancourt | 20/05/1917 | 20/05/1917 |
| War Diary | Bertincourt. | 21/05/1917 | 22/05/1917 |
| War Diary | Havrincourt Wood P.18.d.9.6. | 23/05/1917 | 24/05/1917 |
| War Diary | P 18 d 9.6 | 24/05/1917 | 27/05/1917 |
| War Diary | Harincourt Wood Q.14.d.1.9. | 27/05/1917 | 27/05/1917 |
| War Diary | Q.14.d.1.9. | 27/05/1917 | 31/05/1917 |
| Heading | 1/9th Manchester Regt. War Diary-Vol XXII May 1917. | | |
| Operation(al) Order(s) | 1/9th. Battalion. Manchester Regt. Order No. 5. Appendix 1 | 05/05/1917 | 05/05/1917 |
| War Diary | Special Instructions To O.C. 1/9th. Bn. Manchester Rgt. Appendix 2. | 07/05/1917 | 07/05/1917 |
| Operation(al) Order(s) | Special Order No. 1. App 3 | | |
| Operation(al) Order(s) | 9th Bn. Manchester Regt. Orders No. 8. Appendix 6. | 17/05/1917 | 17/05/1917 |
| Diagram etc | Scale 1/20.000 Appendix 7. | | |
| Operation(al) Order(s) | 1/9th Bn. Manchester Regt. (Order No. 6. May 8th 1917) App 34. | 08/05/1917 | 08/05/1917 |
| Operation(al) Order(s) | 1/9 Battn. Manchester Regt. Order No. 7. App 5. | 13/05/1917 | 13/05/1917 |
| Operation(al) Order(s) | 1/9th Bn. Manchester Regt. Order No. 9 Appendix 8. | 18/05/1917 | 18/05/1917 |
| Operation(al) Order(s) | 1/9th Bn. Manchester Regt. Order No. 11 App 9. | 21/05/1917 | 21/05/1917 |
| Map | Ref. 57 C SE 1.20000 Appendix 10. | | |
| Operation(al) Order(s) | 1/9th. Bn. Manchester Regt. Orders No. 11. App II. | 26/05/1917 | 26/05/1917 |

| Type | Description | Date 1 | Date 2 |
|---|---|---|---|
| Operation(al) Order(s) | 1/9th. Bn. Manchester Regt. Orders No.12 Appendix 12. | 30/05/1917 | 30/05/1917 |
| Miscellaneous | 1/9 Manchester Regt Casualty List For May 1917 App. 13. | 01/06/1917 | 01/06/1917 |
| Heading | War Diary 1/9th Manchester Regt. June 1917 Vol. XXIII. | | |
| War Diary | Havrincourt Wood Q.14.d.19. | 01/06/1917 | 02/06/1917 |
| War Diary | Q.15.a.0.7. | 02/06/1917 | 05/06/1917 |
| War Diary | Ruyaulcourt | 06/06/1917 | 06/06/1917 |
| War Diary | Ruyaulcourt P.15.b.98. | 07/06/1917 | 11/06/1917 |
| War Diary | Havrincourt Wood P 18.d.73. | 12/06/1917 | 16/06/1917 |
| War Diary | Ypres P.26.a. | 17/06/1917 | 19/06/1917 |
| War Diary | Ypres. | 20/06/1917 | 22/06/1917 |
| War Diary | Havrincourt Wood Q.18.d.7.3. | 22/06/1917 | 23/06/1917 |
| War Diary | Q.18.d.7.3. | 23/06/1917 | 01/07/1917 |
| Miscellaneous | Special Order, By Lieut.-Colonel, E.C. Lloyd, Commanding, 1/9th. Bn. Manchester Regt. Appendix 1 | 03/06/1917 | 03/06/1917 |
| Operation(al) Order(s) | 1/9th, Bn. Manchester Regt. Order No. 12 Appendix 2. | 05/06/1917 | 05/06/1917 |
| Operation(al) Order(s) | 1/9th. Bn. Manchester Regt. Move Orders No. 13. Appendix 3. | 10/06/1917 | 10/06/1917 |
| Operation(al) Order(s) | 1/9th. Bn. Manchester Regt. Order No. 14. Appendix 4. | 12/06/1917 | 12/06/1917 |
| Operation(al) Order(s) | 1/9th. Bn. Manchester Regt. Order No. 15. Appendix 5. | 16/06/1917 | 16/06/1917 |
| Operation(al) Order(s) | 1/9th Bn. Manchester Regt. Orders No. 15A Appendix 6. | 20/06/1917 | 20/06/1917 |
| Operation(al) Order(s) | 1/9th. Bn. Manchester Regt. Orders No. 16 Appendix 7. | 21/06/1917 | 21/06/1917 |
| Operation(al) Order(s) | 1/9th. Bn. Manchester Regt. Order No. 17 App 8. | 25/06/1917 | 25/06/1917 |
| Map | 57c Scale 1:10000 Appendix 9. | | |
| Miscellaneous | 1/9th. Bn. Manchester Regt. Casualty List For June 1917. Appendix 10. | 30/06/1917 | 30/06/1917 |
| Heading | Cover For Documents. War Diary 1/9th Manchester Regt. July 1917. Vol 6. | | |
| War Diary | Q.10.a.44. | 01/07/1917 | 08/07/1917 |
| War Diary | Barastre. | 09/07/1917 | 09/07/1917 |
| War Diary | Bihucourt. | 10/07/1917 | 11/07/1917 |
| War Diary | Courcelles. | 12/07/1917 | 31/07/1917 |
| Miscellaneous | 1/9th. Bn. Manchester Regt. Casualty List For July 1917 Appendix 5. | 31/07/1917 | 31/07/1917 |
| Operation(al) Order(s) | 1/9th. Bn. Manchester Regt. Order No. 18. Appendix 1. | 05/07/1917 | 05/07/1917 |
| Operation(al) Order(s) | 1/9th. Bn. Manchester Regiment Operation Order No. 20 Appendix 2. | 07/07/1917 | 07/07/1917 |
| Operation(al) Order(s) | 1/9th. Bn. Manchester Regt. (Orders No.21) Appendix 3. | 08/07/1917 | 08/07/1917 |
| Operation(al) Order(s) | Addendum No. 1 To 1/9th. Bn. Manchester Regt. Orders No.21 Appendix 3. | 08/07/1917 | 08/07/1917 |
| Operation(al) Order(s) | 1/9th. Bn. Manchester Regt. Order No. 22 Appendix 4. | 10/07/1917 | 10/07/1917 |
| Heading | 1/9th. Bn. Manchester Regt. War Diary And Appendices August 1917 Volume XXV. | | |
| War Diary | Courcelles. | 01/08/1917 | 21/08/1917 |
| War Diary | Forceville. | 22/08/1917 | 22/08/1917 |
| War Diary | Watou X 18 b 7.2. | 23/08/1917 | 29/08/1917 |
| War Diary | Watou Ypres H 18.0.9. | 30/08/1917 | 31/08/1917 |
| Operation(al) Order(s) | 1/9th. Battalion Manchester Regiment Orders No 23. Appendix 1. | 20/08/1917 | 20/08/1917 |
| Operation(al) Order(s) | 1/9th. Bn. Manchester Regt. Orders No.23 Addendum No. 1 Appendix 1. | 20/08/1917 | 20/08/1917 |

| Type | Description | Date From | Date To |
|---|---|---|---|
| Operation(al) Order(s) | 1/9th. Bn. Manchester Regt. Orders No. 24. Appendix 2. | 21/08/1917 | 21/08/1917 |
| Operation(al) Order(s) | 1/9th. Bn. Manchester Regt. Orders No. 25 Appendix 3. | 22/08/1917 | 22/08/1917 |
| Miscellaneous | 1/9th. Bn. Manchester Regt. Summary Of Casualties For Month Ending August 31st 1917. Appendix 4. | 31/08/1917 | 31/08/1917 |
| Heading | 1/9th. Bn. Manchester Rgt. War Diary Vol XXVI Sept 1917. | | |
| War Diary | Ypres Kit & Kat Jid. | 01/09/1917 | 03/09/1917 |
| War Diary | Ypres South | 04/09/1917 | 05/09/1917 |
| War Diary | Ypres South. | 04/09/1917 | 07/09/1917 |
| War Diary | Railway Wood. | 07/09/1917 | 11/09/1917 |
| War Diary | Kit & Kat Jid | 11/09/1917 | 14/09/1917 |
| War Diary | Ypres South. | 14/09/1917 | 17/09/1917 |
| War Diary | Sheet 28 H 1 B 8.0 | 17/09/1917 | 19/09/1917 |
| War Diary | Winnezeele | 20/09/1917 | 21/09/1917 |
| War Diary | Wormhoudt | 20/09/1917 | 20/09/1917 |
| War Diary | Uxem | 23/09/1917 | 23/09/1917 |
| War Diary | La Panne | 24/09/1917 | 24/09/1917 |
| War Diary | Coxyde-Bains. | 25/09/1917 | 30/09/1917 |
| Operation(al) Order(s) | 1/9th. Battn. Manchester Regt. Orders No. 26 App 1. | 01/09/1917 | 01/09/1917 |
| Map | App 3. | | |
| Operation(al) Order(s) | 1/9th. Battalion. Manchester Regt. Orders No. 27 App. 2. | 02/09/1917 | 02/09/1917 |
| Operation(al) Order(s) | 1/9th. Bn. Manchester Regt. (Orders No.28) App 4. | 07/09/1917 | 07/09/1917 |
| Operation(al) Order(s) | 1/9th. Bn. Manchester Regiment Orders No.30 App 5. | 09/09/1917 | 09/09/1917 |
| Operation(al) Order(s) | 1/9th. Battalion. Manchester Regt. Orders No. 31 App 7. | 16/09/1917 | 16/09/1917 |
| Operation(al) Order(s) | 1/9th. Bn. Manchester Regt. Orders No. 31 Addendum App 7. | 16/09/1917 | 16/09/1917 |
| Operation(al) Order(s) | 1/9th. Bn. Manchester Regt. Orders No. 32 App 8. | 18/09/1917 | 18/09/1917 |
| Operation(al) Order(s) | 1/9th. Bn. Manchester Regt. Orders No. 31 App 8. | 18/09/1917 | 18/09/1917 |
| Miscellaneous | App. 9. O.O. 34. | 21/09/1917 | 21/09/1917 |
| Operation(al) Order(s) | 1/9th. Battalion. Manchester Regt. Orders No. 35. App 10. | 23/09/1917 | 23/09/1917 |
| Map | St Idesbald Sector Scale 1:10.000. | | |
| Operation(al) Order(s) | 1/9th. Battn. Manchester Regt. Orders No. 36 App 12. | 27/09/1917 | 27/09/1917 |
| Miscellaneous | 1/9th. Battalion Manchester Regt. Summary Of Casualties for month ending Sept 30th. 1917. Appendix 13. | 30/09/1917 | 30/09/1917 |
| Heading | War Diary Of 1/9th Manchester Regt From 1/10/17 To 31/10/17 Volume XXVII. | | |
| War Diary | Coxyde. Bains. | 01/10/1917 | 06/10/1917 |
| War Diary | M.36.a.7.4 | 06/10/1917 | 11/10/1917 |
| War Diary | Wulpen. | 11/10/1917 | 14/10/1917 |
| War Diary | | 13/10/1917 | 13/10/1917 |
| War Diary | Wulpen. | 14/10/1917 | 15/10/1917 |
| War Diary | M.36.a.7.4. | 15/10/1917 | 18/10/1917 |
| War Diary | Oost Dunkerke | 18/10/1917 | 21/10/1917 |
| War Diary | Oost Dunkerke | 19/10/1917 | 22/10/1917 |
| War Diary | M.36.A.7.4. | 26/10/1917 | 26/10/1917 |
| War Diary | Wulpen. | 27/10/1917 | 30/10/1917 |
| War Diary | M.36.A.7.4. | 30/10/1917 | 31/10/1917 |
| War Diary | Coxyde Bains. | 02/10/1917 | 06/10/1917 |
| War Diary | M.36.a.7.4. | 08/10/1917 | 10/10/1917 |
| War Diary | Wulpen. | 11/10/1917 | 14/10/1917 |
| War Diary | M.36.a.7.4. | 15/10/1917 | 16/10/1917 |

| Type | Description | Date From | Date To |
|---|---|---|---|
| War Diary | Oost Dunkerke | 18/10/1917 | 18/10/1917 |
| War Diary | M.36.a.7.4. | 23/10/1917 | 25/10/1917 |
| War Diary | Wulpen. | 27/10/1917 | 29/10/1917 |
| Operation(al) Order(s) | 1/9th. Bn. Manchester Regt. Orders No. 37. App. 1. | 05/10/1917 | 05/10/1917 |
| Operation(al) Order(s) | 1/9th. Bn. Manchester Regt. Orders No. 37 Addenda Corrigenda. | 05/10/1917 | 05/10/1917 |
| Operation(al) Order(s) | 1/9th. Bn. Manchester Regt. Orders No. 38 App. 2. | | |
| Operation(al) Order(s) | 1/9th. Bn. Manchester Regt. Orders No. 40. App. 3. | 13/10/1917 | 13/10/1917 |
| Operation(al) Order(s) | 1/9 Bn. Manchester Regt. Orders No. 41. App. 4. | | |
| Map | Ref. Lombartzyde. Sheet No. 5. | | |
| Operation(al) Order(s) | 1/9th. Bn. Manchester Regt. Orders No. 42 App. 6. | 18/10/1917 | 18/10/1917 |
| Operation(al) Order(s) | 1/9th. Battalion. Manchester Regt Operation Order No. 43. App. 7. | 21/10/1917 | 21/10/1917 |
| Operation(al) Order(s) | 1/9th. Bn. Manchester Regt. Orders No. 44 App. 8. | 26/10/1917 | 26/10/1917 |
| Operation(al) Order(s) | 1/9th. Bn. Manchester Regt. (Orders No. 45) App. 9. | 30/10/1917 | 30/10/1917 |
| Miscellaneous | 1/9th Battalion Manchester Regiment. Summary Of Casualties For The Month Of October 1917. App. 10. | 31/10/1917 | 31/10/1917 |
| Heading | War Diary 1/9 Manchester Regt. November 1917 Volume XXVIII. | | |
| War Diary | M.36. A.7.4 | 01/11/1917 | 02/11/1917 |
| War Diary | St. Georges. | 02/11/1917 | 03/11/1917 |
| War Diary | Oost. Dunkerque | 04/11/1917 | 07/11/1917 |
| War Diary | St. Georges. | 08/11/1917 | 12/11/1917 |
| War Diary | Wulpen. | 13/11/1917 | 17/11/1917 |
| War Diary | Wellington Camp. | 18/11/1917 | 18/11/1917 |
| War Diary | St. Pol. | 19/11/1917 | 19/11/1917 |
| War Diary | Wormhoudt | 20/11/1917 | 20/11/1917 |
| War Diary | Rietveld. | 21/11/1917 | 21/11/1917 |
| War Diary | Longue Croix. | 22/11/1917 | 22/11/1917 |
| War Diary | Wittes. | 27/11/1917 | 27/11/1917 |
| War Diary | | 25/11/1917 | 26/11/1917 |
| War Diary | Wittes. | 27/11/1917 | 27/11/1917 |
| War Diary | Robecq. | 28/11/1917 | 28/11/1917 |
| War Diary | Mt Berencon. | 29/11/1917 | 30/11/1917 |
| War Diary | | 01/11/1917 | 29/11/1917 |
| Operation(al) Order(s) | 1/9th. Bn. Manchester Regt. Orders No.46 App. 1. | 03/11/1917 | 03/11/1917 |
| Operation(al) Order(s) | 1/9th. Battn. Manchester Regt. Orders No.47 App. 2. | 07/11/1917 | 07/11/1917 |
| Operation(al) Order(s) | 1/9 Bn. Manchester Regt. Orders No.48 App. 3. | 12/11/1917 | 12/11/1917 |
| Operation(al) Order(s) | 1/9th. Bn. Manchester Regt. Orders No.49 App. 4. | 14/11/1917 | 14/11/1917 |
| Miscellaneous | 1/9th. Bn. Manchester Regt. Working Parties. App 5. | 15/11/1917 | 15/11/1917 |
| Operation(al) Order(s) | 1/9th. Bn. Manchester Regt. Orders No. 50 App 6. | 16/11/1917 | 16/11/1917 |
| Operation(al) Order(s) | 1/9th. Bn. Manchester Regt. Orders No. 50. Addendum 1. | 16/11/1917 | 16/11/1917 |
| Operation(al) Order(s) | 1/9th Battalion Manchester Regt Orders No. 50 Addendum No. 2. | 17/11/1917 | 17/11/1917 |
| Operation(al) Order(s) | 1/9 Bn. Manchester Regt. Orders No. 51 App. 7. | 18/11/1917 | 18/11/1917 |
| Operation(al) Order(s) | 1/9 Bn. Manchester Regt. Orders No. 51 Addendum 1. | 18/11/1917 | 18/11/1917 |
| Miscellaneous | O.C. Coys App. 8. | 20/11/1917 | 20/11/1917 |
| Operation(al) Order(s) | 1/9th Battalion Manchester Regiment Orders No. 52 App. 9. | 20/11/1917 | 20/11/1917 |
| Operation(al) Order(s) | 1/9 Bn. Manchester Regt. Orders No. 52 App. 10. | 21/11/1917 | 21/11/1917 |
| Miscellaneous | 1/9th Bn. Manchester Regt. | 31/03/1917 | 31/03/1917 |
| Operation(al) Order(s) | 1/9th. Battn. Manchester Regt. Orders No.54. App. II | 26/11/1917 | 26/11/1917 |
| Operation(al) Order(s) | 1/9th. Bn. Manchester Regt. Orders No. 55. App. 12. | 27/11/1917 | 27/11/1917 |

| | | | |
|---|---|---|---|
| Miscellaneous | 1/9th Battalion Manchester Regiment. Summary of Casualties for month ending November 30th 1917. App. 12. | 30/11/1917 | 30/11/1917 |
| Heading | War Diary 1/9 Manchester Rgt. Vol XXIX December 1917. | | |
| Miscellaneous | | | |
| War Diary | Mt. Bernenchon. | 01/12/1917 | 10/12/1917 |
| War Diary | Right Bn H.Q. Braddell Point A.21.C.2.8. | 10/12/1917 | 13/12/1917 |
| War Diary | Braddell Point. | 12/12/1917 | 16/12/1917 |
| War Diary | Woburn Abbey A.20.B.6.3. | 17/12/1917 | 22/12/1917 |
| War Diary | Braddell Point. | 23/12/1917 | 28/12/1917 |
| War Diary | Le Preol. | 29/12/1917 | 31/12/1917 |
| War Diary | | 02/12/1917 | 31/12/1917 |
| Heading | 1/9th Battn Manchester Regt War Diary Vol XXX January 1918. | | |
| War Diary | Le Preol. | 01/01/1918 | 03/01/1918 |
| War Diary | Beuvry. | 04/01/1918 | 13/01/1918 |
| War Diary | | 07/01/1918 | 15/01/1918 |
| War Diary | Beuvry. | 16/01/1918 | 17/01/1918 |
| War Diary | A.8.d.8.5 near Windy Corner. | 18/01/1918 | 23/01/1918 |
| War Diary | Gorre. | 24/01/1918 | 28/01/1918 |
| War Diary | A.8.d.8.5 Near Windy Corner. | 29/01/1918 | 31/01/1918 |
| War Diary | | 01/01/1918 | 31/01/1918 |
| Operation(al) Order(s) | 1/9th Battalion Manchester Regiment Orders No. 60. App. 1. | 02/01/1918 | 02/01/1918 |
| Operation(al) Order(s) | 1/9th Battalion Manchester Regiment Orders No. 61. App.2. | 16/01/1918 | 16/01/1918 |
| Operation(al) Order(s) | 1/9th. Bn. Manchester Regt. Orders No. 12 App 3. | 22/01/1918 | 22/01/1918 |
| Miscellaneous | Reference Rebate Orders No. 62. App. | 23/01/1918 | 23/01/1918 |
| Operation(al) Order(s) | 1/9th. Battalion. Manchester Regt. Orders No. 63. App. 4. | 28/01/1918 | 28/01/1918 |
| Map | Givenchy. App. 5. | | |
| Miscellaneous | 1/9th. Bn. Manchester Regt Summary Of Casualties For Month Of January 1918. App. 6. | 31/01/1918 | 31/01/1918 |
| Heading | 1/9 Manchester Rg Vol 13 February 1918. | | |
| Heading | 1/9th. Bn. Manchester Regt. War Diary Vol. XXXI February 1918. | | |
| War Diary | A.8.d.8.5 Right Bn HQ. Givenchy. | 01/02/1918 | 04/02/1918 |
| War Diary | Windy Corner A.14.a.9.9. | 05/02/1918 | 10/02/1918 |
| War Diary | A.8.d.8.8. | 11/02/1918 | 13/02/1918 |
| War Diary | Beuvry. | 14/02/1918 | 19/02/1918 |
| Operation(al) Order(s) | Rebate Order No. 64 Appendix I. | 03/02/1918 | 03/02/1918 |
| Miscellaneous | Amendment To Orders No. 64. | 03/02/1918 | 03/02/1918 |
| Miscellaneous | Daily Working Parties Appendix II. | 03/02/1918 | 03/02/1918 |
| Operation(al) Order(s) | Rebate Orders No.65 App III. | 09/02/1918 | 09/02/1918 |
| Operation(al) Order(s) | Operation Order No. 1 by Lt. Col. E.C. Lieut Comdg 1/9 Manchester Regt. App.4. | | |
| Miscellaneous | Report on a Raid carried out by D Coy 1/9 Manchester Regt on the night 11/12 Feb 1918 Appendix V. | 11/02/1918 | 11/02/1918 |
| Operation(al) Order(s) | Rebate Orders No. 65A Appendix VI. | 12/02/1918 | 12/02/1918 |
| Operation(al) Order(s) | 1/9th. Bn. Manchester Regt. Orders No. 66. Appendix VII. | 13/02/1918 | 13/02/1918 |
| Operation(al) Order(s) | Addendum To 1/9 Manchester Orders No. 66. | 13/02/1918 | 13/02/1918 |
| Miscellaneous | 1/9th Battn. The Manchester Regiment. | | |

| | | | |
|---|---|---|---|
| Miscellaneous | Move Orders. By Lieut-Colonel E.C. Lloyd D.S.O. Commanding 1/9th. Bn. Manchester Regt. Appendix IX. | 18/02/1918 | 18/02/1918 |
| Miscellaneous | Addendum No. 1. To Move Orders. | 18/02/1918 | 18/02/1918 |
| Miscellaneous | 1/9th Battn. The Manchester Regiment. Summary Of Casualties For The Month Of February, 1918. | 28/02/1918 | 28/02/1918 |
| Operation(al) Order(s) | Operation Order No. 97 by Lieut. Col. W.R. Peel. D.S.O. Commanding. | 17/07/1918 | 17/07/1918 |
| Operation(al) Order(s) | Operation Order No. 98. by Lieut. Col. W.R. Peel. D.S.O. Commanding. | 21/07/1918 | 21/07/1918 |
| Operation(al) Order(s) | Operation Order No. 99 by Lieut. Col. W.R. Peel. D.S.O. Commanding. | | |
| Map | 126th Infantry Brigade Dispositions. | | |
| Miscellaneous | Trench Map. La Bassee. | | |

42ND DIVISION
126TH INFY BDE

1-9TH BN MANCHESTER REGT

MAR 1917- FEB 1918

To 66 DIV
199 BDE

WO95/2658 (1)
1/9 Manchester R.
Mar'17 – Feb'18

# 1/9 BATTALION MANCHESTER REGIMENT.

# WAR DIARY. 1916

Title for 1916

| VOLUME | 6 | January | (Mudros & Egypt.) |
| | 7 | February | Suez Canal Defence. |
| | 8 | March | Canal Defence |
| | 9 | April | " |
| | 10 | May | " |
| | 11 | June | " |
| | 12 | July | " |
| | 13 | August | Desert Column |
| | 14 | September | " |
| | 15 | October | " |
| | 16 | November | " |
| | 17 | December | " |

Vol II

SECRET

(4497) W. 4884/M680 250,000 8/16 McA. & W., Ltd. (Est. 279) Forms/W 3091/3.　　Army Form W. 3091.

## Cover for Documents.

### Nature of Enclosures.

WAR DIARY.
1/9th MANCHESTER REGT.
March 1st to 31st
1917

---

Notes, or Letters written.

Army Form C. 2118
Page 1

# WAR DIARY

## ~~INTELLIGENCE SUMMARY~~

of 1/9th Bn MANCHESTER Regt Volume XX

(Erase heading not required.)

| Place | Date | Hour | Summary of Events and Information | Remarks and references to Appendices |
|---|---|---|---|---|
| ALEXANDRIA MOASCAR | 1.3.17 | 2200 | Bn. entrains 2200 departing for ALEXANDRIA 2250. CAPT. D. HOW Comes to rejoin his unit in EGYPT | Appendix 1. Entraining & Embarking Orders. |
| ALEXANDRIA | 2.3.17 | 0600 | Arrive ALEXANDRIA 0600 | Appendix 2. Embarkation Orders. |
|  |  | 0730 | Embark on H.M.T. ARCADIAN with 1/5th East Lancs Regt and details amounting to 106 Officers & 14 WOs 2237 O.R. Col. D.H. WADE afterwards O.C. Troops. |  |
| H.M.T. ARCADIAN | 3.3.17 |  | Remain alongside Quay at ALEXANDRIA |  |
| — " — | 4.3.17 |  | Sail from ALEXANDRIA with escort. |  |
| — " — | 5.3.17 | 1030 | Inspection by Commander and O.C. Troops, and Boat Deck Parade. |  |
| — " — | 6.3.17 | 1030 | Customary Inspection by Commander and O.C. Troops. Test alarm 0930. Medical Inspection. |  |
| — " — | 7.3.17 | 1100 | Arrive MALTA and anchor in ST PAUL'S BAY. Depart with escort of one destroyer & one sloop. |  |
| — " — | 8.3.17 |  | Boat deck parade cancelled on account of rough weather. |  |
| — " — | 9.3.17 | 1300 | Boat deck parade cancelled on account of rough weather. Pass off CORSICA (? PORTO VECCHIO). |  |

Army Form C. 2118

# WAR DIARY
## —or—
## INTELLIGENCE SUMMARY   1/9 MANCHESTER REGT VOL XX Page 2
*(Erase heading not required.)*

Instructions regarding War Diaries and Intelligence Summaries are contained in F. S. Regs., Part II. and the Staff Manual respectively. Title Pages will be prepared in manuscript.

| Place | Date | Hour | Summary of Events and Information | Remarks and references to Appendices |
|---|---|---|---|---|
| HMT ARCADIAN | 10.3.17 | 1450 | Depart PORTO VECCHIO. | Appendix 3 |
| | | 1700 | Practice alarm given by Escort. Stand to dismissed 1745 | Message from |
| | | 2100 | The Escort sloop "CYCLAMEN" moves off to starboard and fires Furnboremies. 14 shots fired to starboard about 2 miles distant. Believes an submarine sunk. | Arrival of Mustapha |
| | | | | O/S |
| — | 11.3.17 | 0930 | H.M.S. CYCLAMEN rejoins. Three cheers given by Troops for HMS CYCLAMEN. | Appendix 4 Disembarkation Orders |
| | | 1400 | Arrive MARSEILLES. Extra blanket issued to each man. | Appendix 5 Entrainment Orders |
| | | 1830 | 19th MANCHESTERS disentrain and entrain | |
| | | 2200 | Depart MARSEILLES. | O/S |
| ORANGE | 12.3.17 | 0400 | Halt Repas 1 hour ORANGE. Rations issued for the day, also hot water for tea. | See App. 6 |
| | | 0930 | Halt Repas 1 hour MACON. Hot water issued at each halt. | Entrainment Orders |
| | | 1830 | Halt Repas 1 hour LES LAUMES. | |
| | | | | O/P |
| MONTEREAU | 13.3.17 | 0400 | Halt Repas 1 hour MONTEREAU. Rations issued for the day. Owing to the Southern Run found to be a sufficient procedure A "Halt is arranged for eating" at the daybreak, and have been most satisfactory. | See App. 6 |
| | | 1100 | Halt Repas JUVISY, near PARIS. Feet orders have not issued here. | |
| | | 1706 | Halt 1706-1815 EPLUCHES. Hot water provided | O/S |

Army Form C. 2118

VOL XX
Page 3

# WAR DIARY
## INTELLIGENCE SUMMARY — 1/9 MANCHESTER REGT.
*(Erase heading not required.)*

Instructions regarding War Diaries and Intelligence Summaries are contained in F.S. Regs., Part II. and the Staff Manual respectively. Title Pages will be prepared in manuscript.

| Place | Date | Hour | Summary of Events and Information | Remarks and references to Appendices |
|---|---|---|---|---|
| | | | Ref. Map. FRANCE 1/100,000 ABBEVILLE 14 | |
| PONT REMY | 14.3.17 | 0730 | Bivve PONT REMY (Sq.K.6) Tea provided to A,B & C Coys by Y.M.C.A. | |
| | | 0730 | Bivve Billeting Area. Roads in muddy condition. March with Left of 15 minutes at the hour, as different from short halts at the hour with Left hour, customary with the DIVISION when in EGYPT. Guides meet the Bn at station to take Coys to their Areas. | |
| | | | A, B, C & HQ billet in DOUDELAINVILLE (Sq. I.6) | |
| | | | D Coy billet in HARCHÉVILLE (Sq. I.6) | |
| | | | Transport at POULTIÈRES. (Sq. I.6) Bde HQ at LIMEUCOURT-VALINS (Sq. I.6) | |
| | | | Men billets in town & outhouses. | G.S |
| | | | Warnes that Inhabitants not over friendly but fairly from obliging. | |
| | | | 2 Lieut G.E.HAYWARD from 3rd Reserve Batt + 2 Lieut DE.JAMES posted to Battalion. | |
| DOUDE-LAIN-VILLE | 15.3.17 | | Bn marches to PONT REMY by Companies to draw rifles. Many men done up after this march @ 18 miles. | G.S |
| | | | 2/Lieut M.I. DUNLOP & NCOs proceed for Course of Instruction in Rifle Grenades | |
| " | 16.3.17 | | Training resumed. Preparation of dummy + live Throwing pits for bombing commenced on Batt. Drawing Ground (Sq. I.6, ½ mile S.E. of S.E. of POULTIÈRES) | G.S |
| | | | Lectures to Officers & N.C.Os. | |
| | | | Steel Helmets issued to Officers + O.R. | |
| | | | 10 O.R. proceed on leave to ENGLAND. | G.S |

Army Form C. 2118

Vol XX
Page 4

# WAR DIARY
# or
# INTELLIGENCE SUMMARY
(Erase heading not required.)

Regt Manchester Regt  1/9 A. MANCHESTER REGT

| Place | Date | Hour | Summary of Events and Information | Remarks and references to Appendices |
|---|---|---|---|---|
| DOUDELAINVILLE | 17.3.17 | | Training continued. C Coy commence digging a "Cruciform" Trench. Rolls of specialists for training prepared for 100% over establishment. 2/Lieut J. CARREY appointed 126 Bde Salvage Officer. 2/Lieut J.R. TOMMIS attached H2 Div Sig Coy for Instruction. LT COL D.H. WADE, CAPT F.W. KERSHAW, C.S.M NEWTON + 2 O.R. attached 1st Div for Instruction in Trench Warfare. MAJOR R.B. NOWELL and remainder of Advance Party who left Battalion at EL ARISH, 31.1.17 rejoin Battalion from 1st Division. | O/S |
| -do- | 18.3.17 | | Divine Service voluntary. Conference of Coy Commanders on New Formation (W.O Pamphlet SS/144) | O/S |
| -do- | 19.3.17 | 1000 | Route march by Coy's. Dress, fighting order. | O/S |
| | | 1400 | Training under Coy arrangements. | |
| -do- | 20.3.17 | | Coys and specialists engaged in Training. Message from MAJOR GEN DOUGLAS received. Forward | APP 7 Message MGEN DOUGLAS. O/S |
| -do- | 21.3.17 | | Lecture to Battn on Bayonet Fighting by Capt BROWN, Superintendent of Gymnasia, III Corps followed by Demonstration of Bayonet Fighting. C + D Coys proceed to test entrainbaths at HUPPY. 2/Lt J. CARREY admitted Hospital. 2Lt G.F. HAYWARD appointed actg 126 Bde Salvage Officer vice 2Lt J. CARREY. | O/S |

Army Form C. 2118.

Vol XX
Page 5

# WAR DIARY
or
# INTELLIGENCE SUMMARY  1/9 MANCHESTER REGT

| Place | Date | Hour | Summary of Events and Information | Remarks and references to Appendices |
|---|---|---|---|---|
| DOUDELAINVILLE | 22.3.17 | | Ref. Map. FRANCE 1/100,000 ABBEVILLE 14<br>LT. COL. D.H. WADE, CAPT. F.W. KERSHAW & 3 O.R.'s return from 1st Division, but another party to proceed but the arrangements cancelled owing to advance orders on III Corps front.<br>A & B Coy proceed to baths at HUPPY.<br>Lectures on gas to Coy training morning. Practice bomb throwing for C & D Coys.<br>Visit of MAJOR GENERAL MITFORD to Battalion.<br>Orders received for reorganization of Battalion in New Formation. | O/8 |
| -"- | 23.3.17 | | Batt<sup>n</sup> engaged in training, and in reorganising Platoons.<br>2nd LT. R.J.M.DALE.  To be Temp Capt<sup>s</sup> LT. T.F.HYDE, 22 Aug.1916, LT. W.H.LILLIE, Dec. 4,<br>LT. O.I. SUTTON, Sec. 4.  (London Gazette, March 1, 1917)<br>LT. COL. WADE & CAPT KERSHAW arrive from 1st Division. | O/8 |
| -"- | 24.3.17 | | Route march through OISEMONT (Ref. FRANCE 1/100,000 16) Inspection by Bde Gen.<br>TUFNELL & Batt<sup>n</sup> in New Formation. | O/8 |
| | | 11 p.m. | Summer Time adopted throughout FRANCE. | O/8 |
| -"- | 25.3.17 | 10 a.m. | Parade Divine Service. | O/8 |
| -"- | 26.3.17 | | Training in Billet Area. | O/8 |

**Army Form C. 2118**

Vol. XX

# WAR DIARY
## or
## INTELLIGENCE SUMMARY 1/9 B. MANCHESTER REGT Page 6

(Erase heading not required.)

| Place | Date | Hour | Summary of Events and Information | Remarks and references to Appendices |
|---|---|---|---|---|
| | | | Ref. Map. FRANCE 1/100,000 ABBEVILLE. 14 | |
| DOUDELAINVILLE | 27.3.17 | | Batt proceeded by bys to HUPPY for looking. A & D Coy practice attack in New formation. Squads of 10 practice rapid wiring. | O.J.S |
| " | 28.3.17 | | 2Lt QUINNEY and 104 O.R. proceed to Musketry School PONT REMY (Sq.K 6) B Coy fill in bombing pits and trenches near ST. MAXENT. Other coys usual training. Billeting parties proceed to BELLEFONTAINE (Sq. ) and BAILLEUL (Sq. ) to arrange billets for Batt for 30th inst. | O.J.S (Sq.K6) |
| " | 29.3.17 | 9 a.m. 10 a.m. 3 p.m. | Lecture to Batt on Gas by Divisional Gas Officer. Fitting of Box Respirators. Bombing Pit and Trenches on Training Ground filled in. | O.J.S |
| " | 30.3.17 | 10 a.m. | Move to new billeting area. A Coy BELLEFONTAINE (Sq.K6) C.D. WHQ at BAILLEUL (K6) B Coy and Transport at Chateau, 1 Kilo S of BAILLEUL. O.R. billets in barns and outhouses. CAPT D.B.STEPHENSON, LT ROBINSON, 2LT B.FREEDMAN rejoin from leave. | O.J.S |
| BAILLEUL | 31.3.17 | 9.15 a.m. | Batt route march through HUPPY (J6). Specialists train under Specialist Officers. CAPT D.B.STEPHENSON takes over command of D Coy vice CAPT N.H.LILLIE reports to A Coy. (See entry 19.2.17) | O.J.S |

R.B. Newsteyour
for
Lieut Colonel
Comm'g 1/9 Manchester Regt.

*0.6*
*1/9th Manchesters*

SECRET.

CMO 2787/6.

**ENTRAINMENT - EMBARKATION ORDERS** (1) Vol xx App. App. I

General Officer Commanding, EASTERN FORCE.
General Officer Commanding, ALEXANDRIA DISTRICT.
----------

1. The embarkation of the 42nd Division will continue at ALEXANDRIA on the 27th instant, when the following will embark :-

| On H.T. "ARCADIAN" - | Off. | O.R. |
|---|---|---|
| 1/5th East Lancs. Regt. | 30 | 999 |
| 1/9th Manchester Regt. | 31 | 1059 |
| 42nd Div. Base Details (Now at ALEXANDRIA) | 4 | 150 |
| TOTAL - | 65 | 2208 |

2. Train arrangements are as follows :-

TRAIN ALLOTMENTS NIGHT OF FEBRUARY 26th/27th -

|  | Off. | O.R. | Horses | Guns or Limbd. | 4-Whrs. | 2-Whrs. | Baggage. |
|---|---|---|---|---|---|---|---|
| Infantry 834/701. |  |  |  |  |  |  |  |
| 1/5th East Lancs. Regt. | 30 | 999 | - | - | - | - | 6 |
| Infantry 834$^A$/701$^A$ |  |  |  |  |  |  |  |
| 1/9th Manchester Regt. | 31 | 1059 | - | - | - | - | 7 |

TRAIN TIMINGS NIGHT OF FEBRUARY 26th/27th.

| Train timing No. | Type of Train | Loading Station | Time to Load | Time Depart. | Destination | Time Arrive |
|---|---|---|---|---|---|---|
| 834/701 | Infantry | (No.1.) MOASCAR | 1930 | 2220 | H.T. "ARCADIAN" | 0540 |
| 834$^A$/701$^A$ | Infantry | (No.2.) MOASCAR | 2000 | 2250 | H.T. "ARCADIAN" | 0610 |

Composition of trains :-

    1 1st Class Coach.
    1 2nd Class Coach.
   21 3rd Class Coaches
   2 30-ton Box Trucks.

P.T.O.

-2-

3.   The orders issued in my CMQ 2787/3 of February 17th will apply to this embarkation.

*R Mainwaring*

G.H.Q., E.E.F.
                                                            Captain,
                                                            D.A.Q.M.G.
23rd February, 1917      ---o---      for  D.Q.M.G.

Copies to :-   A.M.S.;   G.S.(o).;   G.S.(I).;   D.A.G.;   M.G.R.A.;   E.-in-C.;
                D.W.; D.S.T.; D.M.S.; D.O.S.; D.O.S. Base; D.V.S.;
                D.R.; C.P.; D.A.S.; D.A.P.S.; P.N.T.O.; A.A.G. 3rd Echelon.

        H.Q.; 42nd Division.      D.A.D.R.T., Ismailia.
        H.Q., S. Canal Section.   R.T.O., Moascar.
        A.D.R.T., Cairo.          E.S.O., Alexandria.
        D.A.D.R.T., Alexandria.   D.N.T.O., Alexandria.

-----o-----

HV

S E C R E T.                                               CMQ 2787/6.

General Officer Commanding, EASTERN FORCE.
General Officer Commanding, ALEXANDRIA DISTRICT.

----------------------

With reference to my Circulars No. CMQ 2787/6 of the 23rd and 26th instant, and in confirmation of my telegram No. CMQT 3002 of to-day, the programme will be resumed as follows :-

Train arrangements will hold good for night of 1st/2nd March.    Embarkation will take place on 2nd March.

R. Mainwaring.

G.H.Q, E.E.F.                                                           Captain,
                                                                        D.A.Q.M.G.,
28th February, 1917.                                    for             D.Q.M.G.

--o--

Copies to :-   A.M.S.; G.S.(o).; G.S.(I); D.A.G.; M.G.R.A.; E?-in-C.;
               D.W.; D.S.T.; D.M.S.; D.O.S.; D.O.S., Base.; D.V.S.;
               D.R.; C.P.; D.A.S.; D.A.P.S.; P.N.T.O.; A.A.G. 3rd
               Echelon.

               H.Q., 42nd Division          D.A.D.R.T., Ismailia.
               H.Q., S. Canal Section.      R.T.O., Moascar.
               A.D.R.T., Cairo.             E.S.O., Alexandria.
               D.A.D.R.T., Alexandria.      D.N.T.O., Alexandria.

--------o--------

| Train No | Type of Train | Loading Station | Time to load | Time Depart | Destination | Time arrive |
|---|---|---|---|---|---|---|
| 830/741 A | Infantry Special | (No 1) MOASCAR | 1615 | 1845 | H.T. "TRANSYLVANIA" | 0205 |
| 834/701 | Cavalry Special | (No 1) MOASCAR | 1930 | 2120 | H.T. "KINGSTONIAN" | 0540 |
| 834 A/701 A | - do - | (No 4) MOASCAR | 2000 | 2250 | - do - | 0610 |
| 860 A/711 A | Infantry Special | (No 4) MOASCAR | 0140 | 0330 | H.T. "TRANSYLVANIA" | 1115 |

**SECRET**

To:- O.C.1/9th Manchester Regt.

Reference Move Orders from 42nd Division - para 12. dated 24/2/17 O.C.Trains are detailed as under:-

| Train Timing No. | O.C.Train. |
|---|---|
| 834/701. | Officer Commanding 1/5th East Lancs Regt. |
| 834A/701A. | Lieut Colonel D.H.WADE, Comdg 1/9th Man Regt. |

24/2/17
Copies to:-
O.C.1/5th East Lancs Regt
42nd Division.

Captain,
Brigade Major,
127th Brigade

Copy. SC13/785   5   No. A 214/273
G.O.C
126th Brigade   MARCHING OUT STATE   Vol XX App 11

G.H.Q notifies that no addition of officers or other ranks is now to be made to the Marching Out State as amended, up to and including 14th inst.

In consequence, any Officers, W.O's, N.C.O's and men rejoining the division making additions to the total number already submitted by each formation will have to be sent to the 42nd Divisional Base Depot at Alexandria, and will embark with the details from there.

These surplus officers, and other ranks need not however be sent to Alexandria until the orders for the flight to move are received.

Units will continue to render the usual daily amendments to the Marching Out States.

15/2/17
(Sd) Reginald J Slaughter. Lt Colonel
A&QMG
42nd Division

SC13
785

② 

Please pass in above order & last named return to this office.

16/2/17
(Sgd) C.G.H Bolton Lieut
for Staff Captain
126th Inf Bde

MOVE ORDERS.  SECRET.

Vol xx App. 1

9th Man.

2. Camp Equipment, and Tentage. Camp equipment,(including latrine buckets), and blankets surplus to the 1 per man taken, will be handed into a dump in MOASCAR CAMP close to where the RIFLES were handed in. Tentage will be left standing, a party from troops not yet embarking being left in charge. The Charge of Standing Camps will eventully be taken over by units not belonging to this Division.

3. Supplies. Units will entrain with the unexpended portions of their ration for the 26th inst, and will take with them one days preserved rations for the 27th inst,(This latter ration is already in possession of units, being the reserve ration held on charge by all units of Mobile Column.)

4. Sacks. There are a large number outstanding. These must be returned to Supply Depot before entrainment or they will be charged for.

5. Imprest Accounts and Officers Allowances. Attention of all units is directed to Circular Letter issued under this office No A.212/48 dated 3rd inst.

6. Exchange of Egyptian Money. Attention is directed to the last para of Circular Letter A.214/253 dated 8th inst.
Changing Money. - A representative from the Field Cashier's Office will attend for the purpose of exchanging Egyptian currency at full value. Troops should avoid dealing with professional money exchangers on the quays.

7. Transport to Moascar Station. Units will submit indents to the D.T.O. by 0800 on the 25th inst., for transport required. Sites for units will be allotted at the station by the R.T.O. on the 25th inst, on application.

8. Baggage and Stores. No baggage or stores are to be left at Moascar Camp, Alexandria Quay, or elsewhere, witout a proper guard.

9. Marking of Vehicles, Baggage, Cases etc. All vehicles are to be legibly marked before entrainment, with the name of the unit to which they belong. Care should be taken that both portions of the limber vehicles are so marked. In addition, all baggage, cases etc., will be clearly marked with the names of the units to which they belong.

10. Moascar Camp Standing Orders. Copies in possession of units entraining will be returned to D.H.Q. on the 25th inst.

11. Vacation of Camp Sites. Camp sites are to be thoroughly claened up before troops vacate. Arrangements will be made for other units of the same formation, not yet entraining, xxxxxxxxxxxxxxxxxxxxx to finally clea up, cleanse incinerators, horse lines etc. Any surplus stores, equipment, etc., excluding camp equipment and blankets already provided for, not accompaning the units when it entrains, are to be returned to the Supply or Ordnance Depot not later than the 25th inst.

12. Entrainment. Care is to be taken that the approaches to the Station are not blocked by vehicles awaiting entrainment, or baggage and stores. All vehicles and animals are to be actually in the train 20 minutes prior to the schedule time of departure of the train.
G.O.C. 127th Brigade will detail an O.C. Train and O.C. Ship by name, subject to the approval of Embarkation Staff, Alexandria.
O.C. Train, in conjunction with the R.T.O. will be responsible for allotting the train to units, immediately it is drawn up for loading.

Continued.

Continued.

Vol XX/App. 1

13. **Embarkation orders.** Special attention is directed to those issued under this office A.214/252 of the 8th inst. The returns referred to in para 6 are to be prepared prior to entrainment, ready to hand in on arrival at Alexandria.

14. **Number entraining.** Number of Officers, other ranks, horses and vehicles entraining must conform strictly to those laid down in the Embarkation orders C.H. Q. 2787/4 of the 19th inst. If necessary, officers and men from other units of the same arm will be detailed to complete the numbers required.
A report will be sent to D.H.Qrs, showing the number of officers and other ranks, horses and vehicles so detailed.

---

Tea will be the first meal issued on board ship.
No leave will be granted, or passes issued after troops have been paraded for entrainment.
Rifles for 10% of the troops embarking and 100 rounds of Ammunition, per rifle, will be placed on board by the Director of Ordnance Services, Base.

Attached is a Secret letter to be handed to O.C. Ship and not to be opened until after sailing.

Captain.
D.A.C.M.G.
42nd Division

24/8/17.

Copies to:-

127th Bde. (3)
S.S.O.
D.A.D.O.S.
D.Y.O.
D.A.Q.M.G.
File.

78 SE/H 639
Vol XX App 1

O.C., 9th Manchester Regt

Reference move orders issued today.
Special attention is directed to the following points:-

1. <u>Reference para 2.</u>   When the Brigade moves tents will be left standing, and handed over to the Australians.

2. The first units to move will arrange with the last units ordered to move to provide men to stay in the tents until handed over.   The latter units will inform Staff Captain 127th Infantry Brigade, who will, when they are leaving provide men to occupy the tents.
   1 Sergt and 20 men will be put in charge of each camp. 5th Bn. East Lancs Regt will provide this party for 4th Bn. E. Lan. Regt and 126th Machine Gun Coy. the party for Brigade Headquarters ( 1 N.C.O. and 10 men).

3. <u>Reference para 10.</u>   Moascar Camp Standing Orders will be returned to Brigade Headquarters by 1500 on 21st inst.

4. <u>Reference para 11. "Cleaning".</u>   5th Bn. E. Lancs Regt will perform these duties for 4th Bn. E. Lancs Regt, and 126th Machine Gun Coy. for Brigade Headquarters.   Remaining Units will arrange with the unit nearest them to perform the duties.

5. <u>Reference para 14.</u>   Units will report if they are unable to provide the numbers laid down so that steps can be taken to make them up.

20/2/17.

Captain.
Staff Captain.
126th Infantry Bde.

SECRET.

MOVE ORDERS.

*9 [illegible] Regt*

1. In continuation of my A.214/278 dated 19th. inst. I forward herewith Embarkation and Entrainment orders for the units specified therein under your command.

2. Camp Equipment and Tentage. Camp equipment and blankets, surplus to the 1 per man taken, will be handed in to a dump in MOASCAR Camp close to where the rifles were handed in. Ablution benches and latrine seats (except a small proportion for final use) Forms and tables (other than Ordnance folding tables) to works office.
Tentage will be left standing, a party from troops not yet embarking being left in charge. The charge of Standing Camps will eventually be taken over by units not belonging to this Division.

3. Supplies. Units will entrain with the unexpended portion of their ration for the 22nd. inst., and will take with them one day's preserved rations for the 23rd. (This latter ration is already in possession of units, being the reserve ration held on charge by all units of Mobile Column.)

4. Sacks. There are a large number outstanding. These must be returned to Supply Depot before entrainment or they will be charged for.

5. Imprest Accounts and Officers' Allowances. Attention of all units is directed to circular letter issued under this office No. A.212/48 dated 3rd. inst.

6. Exchange of Egyptian Money. Attention is directed to the last para of Circular Letter A.214/253 dated the 8th. inst Changing Money - A representative from the Field Cashier's Office will attend for the purpose of exchanging Egyptian currency at full value.
Troops should avoid dealing with professional money changers on the Quays.

7. Transport to Moascar Station. Units will submit indents to D.T.O. by 1600 on the 20th inst. for transport required. Owing to shortage of transport as much baggage and stores as possibe will be stored at Moascar Station on the 21st. inst. Sites for units will be allotted at the station by D.A.Q.M.G. at 0700 on 21st.

8. Baggage and Stores. No baggage or stores are to be left at Moascar Camp, Alexandria Quay, or elsewhere, without a proper Guard.

9. Marking of Vehicles, Baggage, Cases, etc. All vehicles are to be legibly marked before entrainment with the name of the unit to which they belong. Care should be taken that both portions of the limber vehicles are so marked. In addtion, all baggage, cases, etc. will be clearly marked with the name of the unit to which they belong.

10. Moascar Camp Standing Orders. Copies in possession of units entraining will be returned to D.H.Q. on the 21st. inst.

/CONTINUED.

- 2 -

11. **Vacation of Camp Sites.** Camp sites are to be thoroughly cleaned up before troops vacate. Arrangements will be made for other units of the same formation, not yet entraining, to finally clear up, cleanse incinerators, horse lines, etc.

   Any surplus stores, equipment, etc., excluding camp equipment and blankets already provided for, not accompanying the unit when it entrains, are to be returned to the Supply or Ordnance Depot not later than the 21st inst.

**Entrainment.**

12. **Entrainment.** Care is to be taken that the approaches to the Station are not blocked by vehicles awaiting entrainment, or baggage and stores. All vehicles and animals are to be actually in the train 20 minutes prior to the scheduled time of departure of the train.

   G.O.C., 126th Inf. Brigade will detail an O.C. Train for 1st, 2nd and 8th Trains. C.R.A. will detail an O.C. Train for all other trains. O.C. Trains will be responsible for allotting the train to units, immediately it is drawn up for loading.

   Horses are to be watered and fed prior to entrainment. Two feeds will be taken on the train for all horses. Saddlery and harness will be removed. Harness and saddlery will be packed in sacks, clearly marked, with the name of the unit to which it belongs.

## Alexandria District.

13. **Embarkation Orders.** Special attention is directed to those issued under this Office No. A.214/252, of 8th inst. The returns referred to in para 6, are to be prepared prior to entrainment, ready to hand in on arrival at Alexandria.

14. **Numbers Entraining.** Numbers of officers, Other Ranks, Horses, vehicles entraining must conform strictly to those laid down in the Embarkation Orders G.M.Q.2727/4, of the 19th inst.

   If necessary, officers and men from other units of the same arm will be detailed to complete the numbers required.

   A report will be sent to D.H.Q. shewing the number of Officers, other ranks, horses and vehicles so detailed.

   The One Officer detailed to go on "KINGSTONIAN" in charge of D.H.Qrs. horses will be provided by C.R.A. thus giving R.A., 1 additional Officer to embark on 23rd.

   This officer will entrain on Cavalry Train 834/701, and will take charge of D.H.Q. horses and personnel from thence onwards.

15. **Attachment.** All units of the 126th Brigade not entraining on 22nd/23rd inst. will be attached to 127th Brigade.

   G.O.C., 127th Brigade will detail a party to take over charge of the camp left standing by 125th Brigade from 1700 on 22nd inst. C.R.A. and A.D.M.S. will arrange for attachment of details left behind to other R.A and R.A.M.C units and will arrange for necessary parties to take charge of vacated camps.

-----

Tea will be the first meal issued on board ship.

No leave will be granted, or passes issued, after troops have been paraded for entrainment. Rifles for 10 per cent of the troops embarking and 100 rounds of ammunition per rifle will be placed on board by the Director of Ordnance Services, Base.

Sgd. Reginald J. Slaughter, Lt. Col.
A.A.& Q.M.G. 42nd Division.

20/2/17.

Vol XX App 2

# EMBARKATION ORDERS

Secret.    Extracts from Embarkation Instructions.

1. The Embarkation of the 42nd Division will continue at Alexandria on the 23rd instant, when the following will embark:-

| On H.T. "TRANSYLVANIA" | Off. | O.R. | Horses. |
|---|---|---|---|
| 1/7th Bn. Lancs Fusiliers. | 28 | 849. | - |
| 1/8th Bn. Lancs Fusiliers. | 30. | 776. | - |
| 126th Infantry Bde. H.Qrs. | 4. | 42. | |
| 1/4th Bn. E. Lancs Regt. | 26. | 769. | |

| On H.M.T. "KINGSTONIAN". | Off. | O.R. | Horses. |
|---|---|---|---|
| 126th Inf. Bde. Headquarters. | - | 3 | 6. |
| 1/4th Bn. E. Lancs Regt. | 2 | 163. | 11. |
| 1/5th Bn. E. Lancs Regt. | - | 4. | 11. |
| 1/9th Bn. Manchester Regt. | - | 4 | 11. |
| 1/10th Bn. Manchester Regt. | - | 4. | 11. |
| 126th Machine Gun. Co. | 1. | 4. | 10. |
| 428th Field Co. R.E. (Now at Alexandria). | 1. | 89. | 8. |

All vehicles for this unit will be embarked in this ship.

2. Train arrangements are as follows:-

### TRAIN ALLOTMENTS OF FEBRUARY 22nd/23rd.

| UNIT. | Off. | O.R. | Horses. | Limb. | 4 Wheers. | Baggage. |
|---|---|---|---|---|---|---|
| **Infantry Train. No.830/741a.** | | | | | | |
| 126th Inf. Bde. H.Qrs. | 4. | 42. | - | -- | - | 2. |
| **Cavalry Train 834/701a.** | | | | | | |
| 126th Bde. H.Qrs. | | 3. | 8. | 1. | | ½. |
| 1/4th Bn. E. Lan. R. | 1. | 30. | - | - | - | |
| **Cavalry 834A/701A.** | | | | | | |
| 1/4th Bn. E. Lancs. R. | 1. | 133. | 11. | | | 1. |
| 1/5th Bn. E. Lancs. R. | - | 4. | 11. | | | - |
| 1/9th Bn. Manch. R. | - | 4. | 11. | | | -- |
| 1/10th Manch. R. | -. | 4. | 11. | | | --- |
| 126th M. Gun. Co. | 1. | 4. | 10. | | | -- |
| **Infantry Train. 800A/711A.** | | | | | | |
| 1/4th Bn. E. Lan. R. | 26. | 769. | | | | 9. |

**SECRET**

To:— Lieut Colonel D.H. WADE,
Commanding 1/9th Manchester Regt.

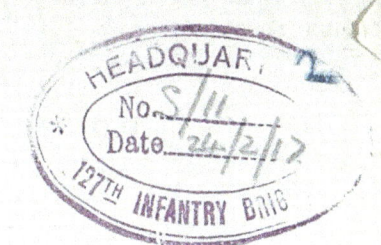

I forward herewith CMQ 2787/6 dated 23/2/17, and Move Orders by the 42nd Division dated 24/2/17.

Reference para 12 of the latter, you will command the troops on board the H.T. "ARCADIAN".

I enclose a secret envelope to be opened after the ship is clear of harbour.

Please acknowledge receipt.

Captain,
Brigade Major,
127th Brigade.

Copies to:—
O.C. 1/5th East Lancs Rgt.
42nd Division.

Vol XX App 2     App 3

S.C.B. 760.

O.C. *9th Manchester Regt*

     Herewith 1 Copy of EMBARKATION ORDERS and 8 copies of White Embarkation Forms to be handed, completed, to Embarkation Staff Officer, by O.C. Troops embarking.
     Also 1 copy of Instructions re entrainment & Embarkation.
     Attention is directed to G.R.O. No. 252 dated 27/12/16, para. 2084 "Government Property in Kits for Overseas

10/2/17.
                                      Lieutenant,
                                for Staff Captain,
                                126th Infantry Bde.

EMBARKATION ORDERS
BY
BRIGADIER GENERAL R.C. BOYLE, C.B.
COMMANDING ALEXANDRIA DISTRICT.

1. EMBARKATION STAFF.
   A Military Landing Officer will be detailed to superintend the Embarkation of each Transport. He will hand to the O.C. Troops copies of Local Orders for embarkation.

2. (A) On arrival of Troops for embarkation officers commanding units will report to the Military Landing Officer on the ship and hand over their order to embark along with the returns vide para 6.

   (B) Individual Officers and other ranks will report to the E.S.O., at Customs House Buildings, Gate 14, before joining the ship, and produce their orders to embark which will be exchanged for a passage permit. This permit will be shown to the N.C.O., or Sentry on the gangway who will detach the right counterfoil, and pass the holder with his permit on to the M.L.O., on the ship. The M.L.O., will take the permit, leaving the counterfoil in possession of the person embarking who must be prepared to produce it at any time during the voyage.

   (C) A guard of 1 N.C.O. and 6 men will be detailed and posted in consultation with the M.L.O., on the quays, on which the ship is berthed to prevent troops leaving the quays without orders and keep unauthorised persons off the quays. They will prevent any communication between the troops and private individuals. The O.C., Troops will increase this guard or post picquets as may be necessary, to meet special cases.

   (D) Troops must be prevented from fouling the ground, the ships latrines alone being used.

   (E) QUARTERS - Each unit on arrival will take over the quarters allotted to it in the ship. N.C.Os and men must not be permitted to leave the ship unless they belong to a shore working party, in charge of an officer, or have a permit signed by O.C. Troops.

   (F) The O.C. Troops is responsible that no officer, soldier or civilian boards or leaves the ship without due authority. He will have sentries at each gangway and elsewhere as may be necessary.

   (G) When it is necessary to tie up animals on the quays, temporary lines should be tied to vehicles or to posts and lines provided for the purpose. It is forbidden to tie animals to trees, standards, fences or fittings of any description which are not provided for the purpose.

   (H) In future while at sea lifebelts are to be constantly worn by officers and troops, except when the men are turned in, when lifebelts are to be hung up on their hammocks.

   (I) Army Order VII of 25th. November 1915, 1596A. Rifles or other articles of steel or iron are not to be brought within 20 feet in any direction from the ships compasses.

   (K) When Transports carry mails, supplies, stores or similar cargo, steps must be taken to secure the packages against pillage at sea. Guards must be mounted and the stores signed for by each relief as all correct.

   (L) O.C. Troops will report to Embarking Staff Officer, Customs Hse, Buildings before midday on day of embarkation for final and confidential orders.

(M) O.C. Troops of Transports in Harbour awaiting orders to proceed, will under no circumstances permit officers or men to quit the ship, except under the authority of the E.S.O.

3. RATIONS- *embark*
Troops should arrange with the unexpended portion of the rations issued before leaving camp, tea on the day of embarkation is the first meal provided by the ship.
Animals should be watered before embarkation.

4. EMBARKATION MEDICAL OFFICER.
The Embarkation Medical Officer is responsible that complete supplies of Medical Stores are placed on board all Transports before sailing He will arrange for removal to Hospital of any cases of sickness unfit to travel.

5. EMBARKATION VETERINARY OFFICER.
The Embarkation Veterinary Officer will superintend the loading of animals, and will take over all animals not considered fit to embark. He is responsible that sufficient Veterinary Medicines and supplies for the voyage are placed on board. No animals are to be embarked until passed fit by the E.V.O.

6. RETURNS.
The following returns will be prepared and handed over to the Embarkation Staff Officer or his representative.
Transports proceeding to Salonika, Sollum, Matruh, & Marseilles -
    White Embarkation Forms.    4 copies.
        Includes one copy for O.C. Troops.
    Complete Nominal Rolls.    4 copies.
        Includes one copy for O.C. Tropps and
        one copy for O.C., Draft.

Transports proceeding to U.K., Malta and Cyprus -
    A.F., B 141 for Complete Units    )
    A.F., B 126 for Detachments      )  5 copies.
        Includes one copy for O.C. Troops.
    Complete Nominal Rolls         4 copies.
        Includes one copy for O.C. Troops.

Alexandria.
8/8/16
TJS.

(Sgd) J. NEWTON BROWN.
Lt. Colonel.
Embarkation Staff Officer.

## "A" Form.
## MESSAGES AND SIGNALS.

Army Form C.2121
(in pads of 100).

TO: 9 MAN

Sender's Number: SL 400　　Day of Month: 20

Special orders received to ensure that all 1st line transport accompanies unit already under orders to embark strength should be 1 offr 1 sergt 29 OR per battn. and 1 offr 1 sergt 20 R per m.g. coy. and drivers of 1/5th East Lancs 9th and 10th Manchesters and 126 m.g. Coy. will be sent by ship of ----- Scout ------

From: 126 Bde
Time: 2105

Vol XX App 2   App. 6

42nd DIVISION.
A.214/253.

INSTRUCTIONS RELATING TO ENTRAINMENT AND EMBARKATION.

1.   The Major General desires that all G.O's.C. and O's.C. formations will take every opportunity to instruct officers in their duties whilst entraining, embarking and disembarking troops, and their duties whilst on board the troop ship. The instructions on these subjects are laid down in King's Regulations Paras. 1488 to 1682 inclusive.

2.   The Paras. require some modification on "Active Service" but are generally applicable.

3.   The Paras. applicable to the duties of officer in command of a Transport, a Ship's Adjutant and Quartermaster, are given in the following sub-Para. (a); those with which all officers should be acquainted are given in sub-Para (b).

Important Paras. are singly underlined; those of special importance are doubly underlined:-

(a). Para. 1494, 1498, 1499, 1500, 1503, 1506, 1521, 1554, 1556, 1557, 1562, 1563, 1564, 1566, 1568, 1570, 1571, 1572, 1573, 1575, 1576, 1577, 1578, 1579, 1580, 1581, 1586, 1587, 1588, 1589, 1590, 1591, 1592, 1593, 1594, 1595, 1597, 1598, 1600, 1601, 1602, 1603, 1604, 1605, 1607, 1608, 1613, 1614, 1615, 1616, 1617, 1618, 1619, 1620, 1621, 1622, 1624, 1625, 1626, 1627, 1630, 1631, 1634, 1635, 1640, 1641, 1642, 1643, 1645, 1646, 1647, 1648, 1652, 1654, 1659, 1660, Arrivals:- 1662, 1663, 1664, 1665, 1666, 1667, 1668, 1669, 1671, 1672, 1673, 1674, 1675, 1676, 1677, 1678, 1679, 1680, 1681,

(b). Para. 1554, 1557, 1561, 1562, 1563, 1564, 1566, 1568, 1569, 1580, 1587, 1588, 1592, 1593, 1594, 1595, 1596, 1597, 1600, 1601, 1602, 1603, 1604, 1605, 1608, 1615, 1616, 1619, 1631, 1634, 1641, Animals:- 1662, 1663, 1664, 1665, 1666, 1667, 1668, 1669, 1671, 1672, 1673, 1674, 1675, 1676, 1677, 1678, 1679, 1680, 1681.

4. Marching-Out States, in duplicate, are to be rendered to D.H.Q. as soon as possible after receipt of orders to be ready to move by rail or ship; any amendments thereto being sent by 1200 daily.

Much trouble would be saved if on receipt of these orders, unit commanders would make inspections of their lines and get rid of the superfluous and useless articles soldiers accumulate and which cannot be taken.

5. When the date of the move is finally fixed, pits should be prepared along side incinerators ready to finally dispose of incinerated material; horse lines should be thoroughly cleaned, and manure got rid of by incineration. Men's huts should be cleared of all old paper and other refuse before tents are struck. Any surplus fuel, wood, forage, etc., should be returned to the Supply Depot.

Prior to marching off, an officer's party will be detailed to inspect huts, kitchens, camp ground, etc., to ensure that no rifles, kits, vehicles, tents or other articles are being left behind.

The main body will usually be clear of its camp ground in sufficient time to admit of a small rear party in charge of an officer staying behind to finish clearing up the camp. Rear Parties are not, however, intended to do the whole work of the unit as regards clearing up. They are only meant to put the finishing touches to work already done.

6. If units have complete trains allotted to them, the O.C. Train should be detailed before the unit arrives at the station and the actual entrainment of troops should be carried out under his orders. He should ensure that separate parties are told off:-

    (a). To load baggage.
    (b). To load vehicles.
    (c). To load animals.

All these duties should be carried out simultaneously.

Much labour is wasted in entraining through lack of organization. Subaltern officers in charge of parties must make up their minds how best to employ the labour at their disposal. They should fall the party in opposite the train, and tell off their men, for their duties, so that each man knows exactly what he has to do.

Officers baggage in the field is limited to 70 lbs. for Commanding, and 55 lbs. for other officers.

Each officer is allowed in addition 100 lbs. as Base Kit. Such kit will be clearly marked with the rank, name and regiment of the officer to whom it belongs and will have on it a label marked "Base Kit."

Kit for W.O's., N.C.O's., and men will be taken in accordance with the allotted scale.

7. If it is intended to send on baggage etc., prior to the hour of entrainment, an officer should be sent to ascertain from the R.T.O. where the baggage trucks will be halted for loading and where the baggage etc. can be dumped so as not to interfere with station work.

8. All ranks must be warned that SILENCE is absolutely necessary if rapid entrainment is to be effected. The practice of shouting at unruly animals cannot be too strongly deprecated; animals already frightened are not soothed and rendered more tractable by noise. All men must be warned to lead animals straight into the railway trucks; on no account should they face their animals or look at them whilst trying to lead into trucks.

9. Vehicles are usually taken loaded; care must be taken that loads are thoroughly secured, that nothing projects beyond the tail board or front board of the vehicle. Pole pins must be cased and greased so that they can be readily removed if necessary.

- 4 -

10. If the journey is to be one of over six hours and harness has to be removed, harness in double sets should be placed in sacks (if available), properly secured, and the sack bearing a label with the numbers of the horses and the driver's name clearly marked thereon.

Animals will invariably be watered just prior to entrainment and feeds will be taken.

11. On arrival at destination, on the signal being given to detrain, the same parties that loaded the train will at once fall in under their N.C.O's. and be marched off by the officer in charge of the party to the vans, etc., they are detailed to off-load. No fresh telling-off of the parties should be necessary.

12. Troop Ships.-Embarking. The following points require special attention.

(a) Returns required:- White Embarkation Forms issued with A.214/252 dated 7th inst., in quadruplicate, (includes one copy for O.C. Troops), to be handed in to Embarkation Staff Officer.

(b). Seniority list, in duplicate, of officers to embark to O.C. Ship.

(c). Nominal Roll of W.O!s, in duplicate, to Embarkation Staff Officer.

(d). Complete Nominal Roll of Officers, W.O's., N.C.O.s. and men, in quadruplicate, to Embarkation Staff Officer; (includes one copy for O.C. Troops, and one copy for O.C. Unit.)

(a) and (d) are referred to in Para 6, Embarkation Orders issued under A.214/252 dated 7th inst.

Officers parties should be detailed to supervise the loading into slings, etc. on shore and stowing in the holds. When two or more units embark in the same ship there should be a representative officer from each unit on shore and on the ship supervising the loading of the baggage.

- 5 -

No baggage, stores, ammunition, etc., are ever to be left on platforms, quays, etc. except under the charge of a guard, and a baggage guard will invariably accompany baggage proceeding by rail.

The kit inspection provided for in para. 1694 K.R.s. will always be carried out. *Parade in Marching Order once a week for inspection. See that clothing & necessaries are complete & arms & appointments in serviceable order.*

*allotment is kept & men own equipment properly disposed of. Hammocks & bedding also out. I marked. Sentries in rolling bedding & slinging hammocks*

Company Commanders will, as soon as possible after embarkation, satisfy themselves that the men, their kits, etc., are disposed of in accordance with para. 1566 K.R.s.

Alarm Stations. As soon as these have been told off, all Company Commanders should satisfy themselves that the N.C.O.s and men know exactly what is required of them on the Alarm sounding.

If there is only one hold for the storage of kits of men belonging to separate units, the key will be kept by O.C. Ship. The room will not be entered by anyone belonging to one unit unless representatives of the other units are present.

Men should be cautioned against making any reference to the move in their letters.

Cash. No Egyptian notes or money to be taken out of Egypt. On arrival at the place of embarkation, O.C. units will make direct arrangements with the local cashier for the exchange of all Egyptian for English money in possession of officers and other ranks.

Reginald J. Slaughter
Lt. Colonel,
A.A. & Q.M.G.,
42nd Division.

8/2/17.

SCB/761

O.C. 1/9th Bn. Manch R

A. 214/262.

Army Council Instruction No. 91 of 10th January 1917 is circulated for information and future guidance.

**91. LOSSES, &c., OF STORES ON BOARD SHIP.**

1. Difficulty having frequently been reported in regard to the carrying out of the procedure prescribed for the recovery from troops of sums due for losses, &c., on board ship, it has been decided to modify the arrangements with a view to the duties of the O.C. Troops in this respect being completed before the commencement of the actual disembarkation.

2. The O.C. Troops will be responsible for seeing that the two lists (one for Government stores and one for Owner's stores) of losses and damages referred to in paras. 1646 and 1647, King's Regulations, are kept up as the voyage proceeds, and are completed as soon as the final check of stores in the custody of troops has been made. These lists should give, by units, full particulars of the charge against each individual, the O.C. Troops obtaining from the master the appropriate prices to be charged, e.g.:-

2/4th Hampshire Regiment –
                s. d.
9999 Pte A.B. Castle, 1 hammock    ...  ...  9 4½
3/5th Inniskilling Fusiliers – s. d.
8888 Cpl D.E Fagan, 2 blankets at  7 6  ...  15 0

If the troops are being paid on the active service system (acquittance roll and pay book) the charge against each man will be recorded, with an explanatory note, in the cash payment columns of his Pay Book (A.B.64).

3. The lists will be handed to the master as soon as completed, and any discrepancy between them and the master's record of losses, &c., will be at once investigated and adjusted. A separate explanatory statement of any losses, &c., of Government stores, not chargeable to troops, will be made out by the master and signed by the C.O. No further action by the O.C. Troops will then be required.

4. The master is responsible for the preparation of lists in duplicate as prescribed in Regulations, but will in future submit them (with the O.C. Troops' lists) to the Embarkation Staff Officer instead of to the O.C. Troops. The Embarkation Staff Officer will see in all cases that the form is received from the master, and will forward one copy with the O.C. Troops' lists to the Base or other Command Paymaster (securing an acknowledgment). He will return the other copy to the master, endorsed "Certified that a copy of this list, with particulars of individual liability, has been forwarded for recovery to the C.P........."

No recoveries in cash from troops will be made at the time either for Government or Owners' stores, and no payment will be made to the ship's representatives.

On receipt of the list of charges, the Command Paymaster will credit the amount to Vote 6 H.; and will at once take the necessary steps to adjust with the paymasters dealing with the men's accounts.

(120/Gen. No./8019 (Q.M.G. 2).

Reginald J. Slaughter
Lt. Colonel,
A.A. & Q.M.G.
42nd Division.

10/2/17.
Copies to all units.

SECRET.
D. 8861.

H.Q. 2nd A. & N.& Z Army Corps.
H.Q. Tel-el-Kebir.
-------------------

   Information has been received from the British Expeditionary Force that explosives have been found in the base kits of the 1st A. & N.Z. Army Corps on their arrival. These explosives are presumed to have been placed in the kits in this country.

   There is as yet no further information to hand, but it appears to be probable that this was done at the port of embarkation in EGYPT.

   It is important, therefore, that when orders are received to move overseas, most stringent instructions should be issued by you to the effect that all baggage of whatever description should be adequately guarded while in transit to the port of embarkation, and while in the dock before being loaded into a transport. From the time when baggage is stacked before entraining, to the time when it is finally stowed on a transport, it should be continually under observation to ensure that no unauthorised person has access to it.

G.H.Q.           (Sgd). D.MacLeod, Capt.
23/5/16.            for D.A.G.


          (2).

-------------------

   The above secret minute is the one referred to in orders that have been or will be issued by G.H.Q. for embarkation.

              Lt. Colonel,
              A.A. & Q.M.G.
19/2/17.            42ND DIVISION.
Copies to all units.

C O P Y.
(1)

Vol. XX Appendix. 3
SUBMARINES

From Commander
To O. C. Troops.

The Admiral instructs me to tell you that "all possible steps are to be taken to prevent last night's action being spoken about on arrival by the troops. Troops should be paraded and instructed.

(SG.) W. W. A.

(2)
To O. C. D Coy 19th Manchester Regt

For information and necessary action. Please arrange to read via. 1 to your (Coy.) details on parade and render certificate to the orderly Room before disembarking that this has been carried out.

(SG.) C. W. H. Bolton
Lieut & Adjutant.

I certify that min, has been read on parade to all Ranks of D Coy.
W H Lillie Lt
OC D Coy. 11.3.17

Bexx Appendix 4

## DISEMBARKATION ORDERS BY COLONEL A. FN. TINLEY. C.B.
### BASE COMMANDANT, MARSEILLES.

1. **GENERAL.** No Officer or man will leave the ship until authorised by the A.M.L.O. who will board each ship immediately she is birthed.
The poop and forecastle will be kept clear of men and all noise forbidden.
The Officer Commanding Troops will assemble Officers Commanding Units on board to have the general arrangements on the quays explained by the A.M.L.O.

2. **RETURNS.** On arrival, O's.C. Troops will hand the following returns to the A.M.L.O.:-
    1. "Landing Return".
    2. "Voyage Report" (induplicate)
    3. "Nominal Roll of Officers".
    4. Return of passengers for United Kingdom. These should not be included in the "Landing Return" but shown separately on Form "B".

3. **ORDER OF DISEMBARKATION.** The following is the general system of disembarkation:- (a) Cavalry. Before coming alongside saddles will be brought on deck and got ready for saddling up.
The men will file off the ship carrying their saddles rifles, leave these on the forming up place, return to the ship, and bring off lances, swords and kits.
(b) Artillery. Before coming alongside, harness and saddlery will be brought on deck. The men will file off carrying kits and rifles and deposit in the forming up place, return to the ship and bring off saddlery and harness.
(c) Infantry. The men, carrying their rifles and kit, will file off the ship and fall in on their forming up spaces.
(d) Animals. The O's. C. Troops will detail one Officer to supervise the leading of horses etc., to the place on the ship where they are to be slung or enter the horse brow and another Officer to supervise their landing on the quay.

4. **VEHICLES.** No motor or horse drawn vehicle in excess of establishment may proceed beyond the Port of Disembarkation.

5. **AMMUNITION.** O's. C. Units are responsible that any pistol ammunition (Mark IV) and any ammunition of Indian manufacture is exchanged.

6. **RATIONS.** Troops will land with one day's cooked rations on the person and grain for animals for day of disembarkation. Train rations and forage for three days will be drawn at entraining point and poaded on the train in bulk.
The O.C. of each train will give the receipted indent (Army Book 55 France) for rations and forage required to the S.&T. Warrant Officer at entraining point.
The indent should show the number of men and animals of each unit separately. Iron Rations will be loaded in the train in bulk.

7. **WATER.** Drinking water is provided in barrels in each shed. All other water is unfit for drinking.

8. **LATRINES.** Latrines are situated at the outer and inner end of each Wharf.

9. **SMOKING.** Smoking is forbidden on the quays and in the Hangars.

A.214/285.
C.M.55.

To:-
The Disembarkation Staff Officer.
42nd. Division.

- - - - - - - - - - - - - - - - - - - -

Herewith Map of the Town and copies of Standing Disembarkation and Entrainment Orders to-gether with train regulations ( discipline etc.)

The following arrangements are proposed as having been found most satisfactory for ensuring expeditious and smooth working of disembarkation and entrainment:-

Disembarkation Staff Officer keeps in touch with the D.A.Q.M.G. ( movements) at Base Headquarters.

6 Divisional A.M.L.O's. work in liaison with Base A.M.L.O's ( M.L.O's. Office, Chambre de Commerce, Docks)

3 Divisional R.T.O's. work in liaison with Base R.T.O's. ( D.A.D. R.T's. Office6, Rue Muguet, near Main Station).

Preliminary arrangements for entrainment of troops, based on cabled advices from Egypt, are made with the D.A.D.R.T. by the D.A.Q.M.G. and Divisional Disembarkation Staff Officer.

The Base A.M.L.O's. report immediately troops have been passed free of infection by the Medical Authorities and train timings are arranged accordingly to be communicated forthwith to O's.C. Troops by the Divisional A.M.L.O's together with any necessary instructions from Divisional Disembarkation Staff Officer. The Divisional R.T.O's. appointed to load the trains with the Base R.T.O's. should be arrangement with the latter, see the O's. C. Troops before troops march off, with a view to communicating in advance any special entrainment require--ments. The Divisional A.M.L.O's. in concert with the Base A.M.L.O-'s. are responsible for ensuring that troops arrive at the entraining point at the proper time.

With reference to paras. 1 and 2, Entrainment.Orders, the Movements Orders will be in all cases sent to the D.A.D.R.T.'s Office by the D.A.Q.M.G., the copy for O's. C. Trains being handed to them at the entraining point by the R.T.O's. Officers.

Transport will be arranged by the Base A.M.L.O's. on the written demand of the O's. C. Troops on the prescribed Form.

Rations ( except for small parties entraining at Gare St Charles ) will be drawn at the points of entrainment.

Troops will in all cases proceed direct from the ship tp point of entrainment unless prevented by unforeseen circumstances such as the existence of disease necessitating segregation. It is imperative that vessels should be cleared with the utmost expedition.

Marseilles.
8th Febuary 1917.

(Sd) A.S. BUCKLAND COCKELL, Capt.
D.A.&Q.M.G.

Copies to:- Disembarkation Staff Officer, 42nd. Division, P.N.T.O., A.D.M.S. A.M.L.O. (12) D.A.D.R.T. B.S.O. B.T.O. S.M.T.O.

(3)

Latrine　　　　　　　　　　　　　Latrine

13　　　　　　　　　　　　　　　　　　　　　　　　14

　　　　　　　　　　Phone 39
　　　　　　　　　　R F C

　　Clothing
　　To M F O

　　Saddlery &
　　Equipment　　Road

Fresh
Water

　　Passage

Fresh
Water
　　　　　　　　　　　　　　　　Phone 36
　　Armoury　　　YMCA Hut　Base Supply Officer
　　　　　　　　　　　　　　　　　Phone 35

　　　　　　　　　　　　　　　　　　　　　　　　15

　　　　　　　　　　Road　　　　　　　Water

　　Camp Equipment
　　　　　　　　　　　　　　　　Army Post
　　　　　　　　　　　　　　　　Office

12
　　　　　　　　　　T.182.
　　　　　　　　　　　　　　O C Labour Coy.
　　C.C.O Office
　　Phone 39　　　　Retail
　　　　　　　　　　System

No 7 Hangar (Ordnance)　　　　　No 8 Hangar (Supply)

　　　　　　　　　Horse Troughs

To Medical First Aid Post,
Military Landing Office
　　(150 Yards)　　　　　　To Camp Carcassone
Base H Quarters (3 Miles)　　　(2 Miles)
La Valentine (8 Miles)
Mussot (4 Miles)
Point 2 (300 Yards)
Gare St Charles - 2 Miles
Camp Fournier - 1 Mile
　　　　　　　　　To Point 1
　　　　　　　　　(150 Yards)

Vol. xx Appendix 5

ENTRAINMENT ORDERS BY COLONEL G.F.H.TINLEY. BASE COMMANDANT. MARSEILLES

1. **Movement orders.** Applications for movement orders stating numbers (and in the case of Officers, names) and authority for journey, will be addressed to the D.A.Q.M.G. (Movements)., Base H.Qrs., who will issue instructions as to entraining arrangements.
   The O.C.Train will in all cases arrive at the entraining point with the main body in such time as is necessary to entrain the unit.  One Officer to meet the R.T.O., at the entraining point 3 hours before the time of departure to furnish exact particulars of troops to entrain.
   This Officer will receive from the R.T.O. instructions as to the loading of baggage etc.,.
   O.C's Trains must strictly adhere to directions communicated to them by the R.T.O.

2. **Returns.** Officers Commanding all travelling, will produce on arrival at the entraining point the following:-
   (1). A Movement Order in duplicate issued by the D.A.Q.M.G
   (2). Nominal roll of all Officers in duplicate.
   (3). Certificate shewing date to which party is rationed, in duplicate.
   Reinforcements will also have a return if triplicate, shewing Corps, Division, Unit, number of Officers and men Rank, Initials, and names of Officers: remarks and name of O.C.Party. (Routine Order I.G.C.No.77 dated 5/3/1915).
   Above will be disposed of as follows:-
   Entraining R.T.O., will take one copy of each of (1), (2), (3), and one copy of reinforcements return.  The Other copies will be delivered by O.C.,Train to the detraining R.T.O., at Destination.
   The Entraining R.T.O, will furnish O.C.Train with a French Railway form for delivery to the detraining R.T.O.

3. **Rations.** Reinforcements entraining for the front will take with them:-
   (1) The current day's rations and forage.
   (2). Three day's rations and forage (3). the iron ration.
   The iron ration will be placed in bulk on the train and issued after detrainment.

4. **Accommodation.** Men are conveyed either in third class carriages accomodating 8 men per compartment, or in fitted wagons accomodating thirty two, 36 or 40 men; , a space is left at both ends of these wagons for rifles and accoutrements.
   Horses and mules are conveyed in covered wagons accommodating 8 horses in two rows of four., or ten mules in two rows of five, facing each other. Ropes for securing the animals to be improvised from picketing ropes. Animals travel unharnessed, saddles, harness, forage, etc., being stacked in the cetral place. Two men will travel with the animals with each wagon and are not permitted to smoke in the wagons.

5. **Timing.** On French Railways hours of the day are numbered from 0 heures (midnight) to 24 heures ( also midnight): thus 6-0 p.-M/ is 18 heures.

6. **Halts.** For Troop trains, Halts for refreshments, ( halte-repas) will be arranged so as to allow one halt of three hours during every 24 hours during which the men can cook.
   At these points wood and water will be provided. A second halt of about half an hour's duration will also be made during the day.
   Arrangements will also be made for Halts for the purpose of watering horses.

ENTRAINMENT ORDERS BY COL. G.F.N. TINLEY. BASE COMMANDANT,
MARSEILLES.
(continued)

7. **Water.** Officers commanding Units will arrange to take with them from their camp to the point of entrainment sufficient water to last the troops for 12 hours beyond the fixed time for departure of their train, also to have buckets for watering animals ready for use at the entraining point and during the journey. Water for animals is available at the entraining point but no supply of water for troops is available.

8. **Refreshments.** Arrangements have been made with the French Red Cross at Gare St. Charles to supply (1) Tea (2) coffee (3) hot water and to cook any rations that may be required for small parties of British details travelling (1) and (2) on payment.

9. **Destination.** The information as to the detraining station and the final destination of the unit is for the personal information of the Officer Commanding only, and must be kept absolutely secret throughout the journey.

10. **Discipline.** Officers and N.C.O's. in command of parties may not leave their detachments while passing through Paris.
O's. C. Troops Trains are reminded that they are responsible for the detailing of the necessary guards at all stopping places to prevent pilfering and straggling. Special precautions should be taken in the vicinity of Paris.
O's. C. Trains will take over any stragglers brought in by the French Railway Authorites.

Marseilles.                (Sd) A.S. BUCKLAND COCKELL, Capt.
16th May. 1916.                        D.A.Q.M.G.

## TRAINS MOVING WITH TROOPS.

### STANDING ORDERS FOR THE OFFICER 1/C TRAIN.

1. THE SENIOR OFFICER on the train is held personally responsible ffor the discipline of all in the train and that all ranks, before departure, are made acquainted with the following orders:-
   (1). No man is to travel on the top of, or on the steps of, a vehicle.
   (2). No Officer or man is to be allowed to travel on the engine or in the compartment or brake van set apart for the French Railway Staffs.
   (3). No man is allowed to leave the train at any but authorised stopping places.
   (4). No beer, wine or spirits, will be allowed on the train.
   (5). Any man left behind at a Station will report at once to the R.T.O.
   (6). When the train is moving all carriage doors must be kept closed.
   (7). The iron ration is on no account to be touched.
   (8). Under no circumstances are rations (drawn by troops for subsistence during the journey) to be destroyed, thrown away or given away.
   (9). All station refreshment rooms and buffets are out of bounds.
   (10). Bottles and other articles are not to be thrown out of the windows; any rubbish should be put under the seats.
   (11). No braziers or fires whatever are allowed in, or hanging from vehicles occupied by troops.
   (12). No British Officer, Soldier or Civilian, is allowed to join the train without the authority in writing of the R.T.O.
   (13). In trucks carrying horses, the door on the right, when facing in the direction the train is moving, must always be kept closed.

2. He will ascertain before starting that there are on the train the proper rations of the journey, and will ensure that the rations provided on the trains, in addition to the un-expended portion of the day's rations, are only consumed at the proper rate, viz, One day's ration for each day of the journey.

3. He will see that his compartment is indicated by a label attached to the door.

4. He will tell off a guard (strength at discretion) which will be located in a separate vehicle or vehicles from the rest of the men
   One or more Officers will be detailed to the Guard.
   The duties of the Guard are as follows:-
   On arrival at an authorised stopping place, it will detrain before any other men leave the carriages. Sentries will be posted at once on all exits, refreshment rooms, latrines, washing places, and any points indicated by the R.T.O. To warn men when time for departure is drawing near. It will see that men do not straggle, and that no man leave the Station premises on any pretext.
   If the journey is a long one, arrangements will be made to relieve the guard en route. It will remain armed and equipped throughout its period of duty.

5. He will see that a N.C.O. or Senior Soldier is placed in charge of each vehicle: this N.C.O. (or senior Soldier) should at once make a list of all men in his carriage and detail 2 men, one to each side of the truck or carriage, to assist him in carrying out the train orders, and see that no unauthorised persons enter the compartment.

6. He will receive from the R.T.O. a form shewing the times his train is due to arrive at and depart from each halting place.

7. He will see that, at the halting places all men are warned of the length of the halt, and ordered to parade outside their carriages five minutes before the train is due to start.

8. In the event of any man being missing he will report the name and number and the Regiment of the man to the R.T.O., at the next stopping Station, stating when the man left the train.
    The arms and accoutrements of missing men will be handed over to the R.T.O.

9. If he finds it necessary to issue rations, or to perform any other service which may cause delay at any but the authorised stopping places, he will at once inform the R.T.O.

10. He will arrange with the R.T.O. to place all the men belonging to each formation in the same part of the train.

11. He will issue the necessary orders to the Senior Officer or N.C.O. of each formation.

12. He should note that the train conducting Officer is the representative of the Railway Service, and as such is entirely responsible for all details in connection with the control of the train as regards halts, and arrangements necessary during halts. This T.C.O. will act as Staff Officer to the Officer I/c Train, but if he the (T.C.O.) is the Senior Officer in the Train, he will perform the duties of both "O.C. Train" and "Staff Officer".

13. He (or the T.C.O. if there is one) will carry the yellow feuilles for all parties travelling in his train, and will deliver these to the D.A.D.R.T. at the detrainment Regulating Station, where he will receive the reconsigned (or new feuilles) for the Stations beyond.

15. At halting places, he should warn the Officer or N.C.O., in charge of each party to assure himself that all his men are on board, and to report to the O.C. Train Guard before the train leaves.

16. He will report to the D.A.D.R.T., at the Regulating Station, where the train is split up, the number of missing men, if any.

17. He should note that movement orders should always be carried separately for Divisions, or for Corps Troops by the Officer or N.C.O., I/C of each party, and should be delivered by him to the R.T.O. at the Station at which each party detrains.

18. He should warn the Officer or N.C.O. in command of each party that he is responsible that all surplus rations, whether iron or ordinary, are collected and handed over by him to the Railhead Supply Officer, on arrival at destination, otherwise to the R.T.O.
    To ensure compliance with this order, no more tins of meat, loaves of bread, or biscuits, should be distributed at one time than are required for a single meal.
    The Draft Conducting Officers will hand over to the Officer taking over the Draft at Railhead, a statement shewing the number of Iron Rations issued to the men, and certifying that the men of the Draft have been warned collectively of the consequences to which they render themselves liable by disposing of the Iron Ration.

CHARLES WOOD
LIEUT. COLONEL.
A.A.G.

HEADQUARTERS. I.G.C.
27th September, 1916.

4  Vol xx App.6.
Entrainment Orders.

## IMPORTANT NOTICE.

At all the Haltes Repas you will be supplied with HOT WATER ONLY, free, to make Tea. This is useless unless you arrange with your ration party in your ration wagon to take their "DIXIES" with them and have them ready, before arrival at Halte Repas stations, with tea etc. in them, to receive the hot water and make the Tea. The orderlies can then come to the ration wagon and take the dixies of tea away, ready made, to their companies.

The dixies must be kept in the ration wagon for this purpose. The ration party should also open out and have ready for distribution at Haltes Repas, the mens' rations.

Marseilles.  
23rd. May, 1916.

A. POPE. Lt. Col.  
D.A.D.R.T.,

Vol XX.  App 6

## ENTRAINMENT ORDERS.
### BY
A. Pope, Lieut - Colonel,
D.A.D.R.T.

**MARSEILLES.**

### 1/9th. Bn. Manchester Regiment.

| | | | | |
|---|---|---|---|---|
| March 11th, 1917. | 2200. | | Depart MARSEILLES. | |
| "   12th   " | 0400 - 0500. | Halte Repas. | | ORANGE. |
| " | 0930 - 1035 | "      " | | MACON. |
| | 1830 - 1925 | "      " | | LES LAUMES. |
| "   13th   " | 0400 - 0505 | "      " | | MONTEREAU. |
| | 1055 - 1200 | "      " | | JUVISY. |

Further order will be issued at JUVISY.

## SPECIAL ORDER OF THE DAY.

**FAREWELL MESSAGE FROM MAJOR GENERAL SIR WILLIAM DOUGLAS, K.C.M.G., C.B., D.S.O.**

"In bidding the 42nd Division goodbye I wish to express my heartfelt thanks to my Staff Officers, the Commanders and Regimental Officers, for their loyal and whole-hearted support and superb work during the period of my command.

My admiration for the conduct, fighting qualities, grit and endurance of all ranks is profound. Never have I met a more responsive, willing, and lovable lot of men than these Lancashire lads, and, to my last days, I shall remember with affection and pride the 3¾ years that I have had the honour to command them.

I know how well you, officers and men, will add to the great name that you have already earned for the Division. I wish you the best of good fortune and a rich reward."

(4497) W. 4884/M680 250,000 8/16 McA. & W., Ltd. (Est. 279) Forms/W 3091/3.    Army Form W. 3091.

## Cover for Documents.

Nature of Enclosures.

SECRET

WAR DIARY
1/9TH MANCHESTER REGT
April 1917
Vol. XXI

Notes, or Letters written.

Army Form C. 2118.

WC XXI
Page 1

# WAR DIARY
## or
## INTELLIGENCE SUMMARY.
(Erase heading not required.)

1/9 Manchester Regt.

| Place | Date | Hour | Summary of Events and Information | Remarks and references to Appendices |
|---|---|---|---|---|
| BAILLEUL (K6) | Apl 1 1917 | | Ref. Map. FRANCE 1/100000 ABBEVILLE 14 Divine Service voluntary. MAJOR T.E. HOWORTH proceeds to course of instruction for Coy Commanders at MONTIGNY. | @A |
| " | Apl 2 | 7.30am | C & D Coys proceed to musketry range at PONT REMY (K6) for musketry practice. Orders taken on range. A Coy proceed for musketry owing to leave not found back on account of heavy rains. | @K6 |
| | 9.30am | A & B Coys engaged in training & lectures. | @K |
| " | Apl 3 | | All Coys proceed to Range for musketry practice. S.A.A. drawn on Range. Lieut Col WADE & 7 O.R.s proceed on leave to U.K. Major R. B. STONELL takes over command of Battalion in absence of Lt.Col. WADE. | @B |
| " | Apl 4 | | All Coys proceed to Range for musketry practice. Orders received to proceed to new area by march route, 4.2 to 5 miles. Show men cancelled & orders received for Battn. to proceed by rail in lieu of mst. Transport to proceed by road. | @B |

Army Form C. 2118.

Vol XXI Page 2

# WAR DIARY
## or
## INTELLIGENCE SUMMARY.

(Erase heading not required.)

Reg Mp (ABBEVILLE) FRANCE 1/9 gno 14 Summary of Events and Information

Reg Mp 1/9 MANCHESTER REGT.

| Place | Date | Hour | Summary of Events and Information | Remarks and references to Appendices |
|---|---|---|---|---|
| BAILLEUL | Ap.5 | 9 p.m. | Coys engaged in training. 5 OR's proceed on leave to U.K. Sgt QUINNEY & 102 OR's return from Musketry Camp PONT RÉMY (Sh 22.3.17) | C.S. |
| " | Ap.6 | | Battalion engaged in training. CAPT F.N.KERSHAW proceed to London on instruction for Coy Commandant at MONTIGNY. Major T.E.HOWORTH returns from course & is attached in PONT RÉMY & joins battalion at Station on the 7th inst. (See Ap.15) Lt R.J.N.DALE & 2 NCOs proceed in advance of Battalion on billeting party. 5 ORs proceed on leave to U.K. | C.S. |
| " | | 6.30 am | Transport proceed by road to MORCOURT (Map FRANCE 1/80000 AMIENS 2,H.2) Report BAILLEUL 6.30 am. Officers LONGPRÉ (Map AMIENS 5, G.2, C1) 7th inst to HAMEL (Map AMIENS 5, G.2) proceed great day to SAINT SAUVIER (Map AMIENS 5, C1) 7th inst to MORCOURT (Map AMIENS 5, H.2) AMIENS (Map AMIENS 5, D2) 8th inst to MORCOURT | C.P. |
| " | Ap.7 | 6.30am | Lieut N.G.GREENWOOD departs in charge of 106 B9L MOTR Convoy to MORCOURT. MAJOR T.E.HOWORTH rejoins battalion. | |
| | | 10 am | Battn entrains at PONT RÉMY Station & proceed to LA FLAQUET (Map FRANCE 1/80000 AMIENS 57, J.2) for MORCOURT. | |
| | | 5.30 pm | Battn billets at in "France". Rats. Orderly room in house at MORCOURT. Allotment of leave to U.K. 7th inst to 12th inst 2 Officers & 42 O.R. (7 per diem) | C.P. |

Army Form C. 2118.

Vol xxp
Page 3

# WAR DIARY
# INTELLIGENCE SUMMARY. 1/9 MANCHESTER REGT
(Erase heading not required.)

Instructions regarding War Diaries and Intelligence Summaries are contained in F. S. Regs., Part II. and the Staff Manual respectively. Title pages will be prepared in manuscript.

| Place | Date | Hour | Summary of Events and Information | Remarks and references to Appendices |
|---|---|---|---|---|
| MORCOURT | Ap.8 | | Ref Map. FRANCE 1:100,000 AMIENS 17 | |
| | | | 2Lieut R.J.N.DALE and Sgt CHORLTON (Sgn in Cusp of Scouts attd gun) proceed to Course of Instruction at ARMY TELESCOPE SIGHTS SCHOOL. | |
| | | 3 pm | Divine Service (EASTER SUNDAY) | |
| | | | Orderly Room moves from village to small wooden hut near to Bath tents. | G/3 |
| | | 11 pm | Transport arrives. | |
| " | Ap.9 | 10 am | All Officers & NCOs & 1 Watson per Coy to initial demonstration by a platoon of the 1/1 EAST LANCS REGT of the Normal Formation. Remainder of Battn pass over manner. During morning & proceed to Baths at MORCOURT during afternoon. SAA a/c issued 120 rds per man. | G/8 |
| | Ap.10 | 9.30 | 2Lt. E.K.P. FUGE proceeds on leave to U.K. Battn practises attack in Normal Formation by Coys and Half Battalion. Orders received to move on 11th inst. Party proceeds to draw establishment of MILLS grenades for Battn & to wait at ECLUSIER (Reference 1/9 Staff Brigade arrives). | |

Army Form C. 2118.

# WAR DIARY
## or
## INTELLIGENCE SUMMARY.
(Erase heading not required.)

Vol XXI Page 4

1/9 MANCHESTER REGT.

| Place | Date | Hour | Summary of Events and Information | Remarks and references to Appendices |
|---|---|---|---|---|

Ref Map FRANCE 1/100,000 AMIENS 17.

**MORCOURT** Ap.11

Move to FEUILLÈRES (5.H.1) by march route in open formation - 100 yards between platoons - via CAPPY and ÉCLUSIER (F.J.1).
2nd Lieut L.W. PICKFORD joins Battn at CAPPY from 3rd/8th Reserve Bn MANCHESTER REGT.
Battn billets in village in cellars and dugouts - billets poor owing to battered condition of village. Many billets not fit for use on account of damp floors and rain.
Blankets arrive by Motor transport 2 a.m. 125 m.t. owing to bad roads. C/S

**FEUILLÈRES** Ap.12
(Ref map 59. J.1.)

Bn engaged in training.
Capt E.N. KERSHAW rejoins (see Ap.6.) 2 Lt B.T. ROBINSON rejoins from Div Scout School which is broken up & whence he has been attending as instructor (1 Mar - 2 31st).
2 Lt T. AINSWORTH proceeds to Divnl Mortar School. Capt G.H. HANDFORTH proceeds to course of Instruction for Coy Commanders at MONTIGNY.
Fall of snow during afternoon. many dugouts unfit for use on account of water leaking in. C/S

" " Ap.13

Coys engaged in training, rapid loading, attack by platoon from trenches, specialist training including line training for bombers.
Orders received to be ready to move forward from CARTIGNY (1/100,000 Sht 18 S, A 2) 17th M.C. in trenches, 185 m.t.
2 Lt J.H.CLARKE proceeds on course to U.K.

Army Form C. 2118.

# WAR DIARY
## INTELLIGENCE SUMMARY. 1/9 Manchester Regt

(Erase heading not required.)

Instructions regarding War Diaries and Intelligence Summaries are contained in F. S. Regs., Part II. and the Staff Manual respectively. Title pages will be prepared in manuscript.

Vol XX I
Page 5

| Place | Date | Hour | Summary of Events and Information | Remarks and references to Appendices |
|---|---|---|---|---|
| FEUILLÈRES | Ap 14 | | Coys engaged in training & practice in Manoeuvre formation. Borders practice line shooting. Stores overhauled in view K issue amount of baggage. | Ops |
| | | 11 am | Transport inspected by Div. Train at HERBÉCOURT. (Ref Map Sq K1) | |
| -"- | Ap 15 | 9.30 am | Lieut Col WADE rejoins from leave to U.K. Coys engaged in training during morning. Divine Service cancelled on account of inclement weather. | Ops |
| -"- | Ap 16 | | Training during morning. Preparation made for early move following morning. Baggage kits taken by Motor Transport dumped at HERBÉCOURT (Sq K1) | Ops |
| -"- | Ap 17 | | Battn moves to CARTIGNY (1/100,000 Sheet 78 Sq A2) Rendezvous 7.30 am. Cross Roads HERBÉCOURT. Order of March 9th MANCH R., BDE HQ, M.G Coy, T.M.B, 5th E Lancs Col. WADE commanded column on the march owing to absence of Brigadier in the line. Route HERBÉCOURT, BIACHES, crossing the SOMME by the FAUBERG de PARIS Bridge to PÉRONNE. After leaving PÉRONNE the Battn marched independently to CARTIGNY via DOINGT. Every village devastated & accommodation very poor accordingly. Billets at CARTIGNY where Battalion stayed the night fairly good compared with billets of previous nights | O.S |

A 5834 Wt. W4973/M637 750,000 8/16 D. D. & L. Ltd. Forms/C.2118/13.

Army Form C. 2118.

# WAR DIARY / INTELLIGENCE SUMMARY.

(Erase heading not required.)

1/9 MANCHESTER REGT

Vol XX/1 page 6

| Place | Date | Hour | Summary of Events and Information | Remarks and references to Appendices |
|---|---|---|---|---|
| Ent. | | | Ref Map 1/100,000 Sheet 7/8 2/Lt RUTTSMAN proceeds on leave to U.K. 2/Lt DALE returns from leave. Capt. STEPHENSON proceeds to arrange for instruction for Coy Commanders in MORTARS. D Coy supply working party of 130 O.R. to work at CATELET (Sq A2) | O/R |
| CARTIGNY Sq A2 | Ap 18 | 9.30 a.m. | Batt. less D Coy move to MARQUAIX (Sq A1) + 9 O.R. billets. Accommodation very poor. All ranks & their trans. & bagage from Tilsit Rail to billets, serious accident being occurred when the lorry fell over in reinforcing & villages with bombs and trench explosives. D Coy remains in billets at CARTIGNY to provide working parties for CATELET. Only force being only 2 officers in D Coy, 2/Lt QUINNEY and 2/Lt KNIGHT are attached. | C/R/B |
| MARQUAIX Sq A1 | Ap 19 | | A + B Coys provide 110 O.R. each Coy to work under 5th ROYAL SUSSEX REGT. at TILLERS-FAUCONT (Sq B1) reporting 8 a.m. C Coy provide 130 O.R. for work on no. 29/1 rails 5th ROYAL SUSSEX REGT at ROISEL (Sq B1) Orders received for working parties in cases for 20th inst. | O/R |

# WAR DIARY
## INTELLIGENCE SUMMARY. 1/9 MANCHESTER REGT.

Page 7

Army Form C. 2118.

| Place | Date | Hour | Summary of Events and Information | Remarks and references to Appendices |
|---|---|---|---|---|
| MARQUAIX | Feb 20 1917 | | Ref. Map FRANCE 1/40,000 62 C | |
| | | 10.30 am | Orders for marching parties cancelled & orders for move received. A + B Coys (MAJOR HOWORTH & CAPT KINSHAW) proceed to EPÉHY (Sheet 62c F.I.) C Coys (COLSGT HANDFORTH) acting OC proceeds to VILLERS-FAUCON (E 22 & 28) BROWN A Coy occupy reserve line along railway embankment (F 1 d) B Coy in billets v Huts in village (F 1 c) under 143rd Bde | |
| | 1 am | | (Capt STEPHENSON arrives at CARTIGNY (see App 7) | |
| VILLERS-FAUCON | 21.2.1 | | D Coy proceed from CARTIGNY to VILLERS-FAUCON. A Coy man reserve line at dawn, B Coy in support to the working parties provided from all Coys. C Coy in afternoon repairing Cem Road (F 8 a) their ruts 3.5 p.m. D Coy at night repairing level crossing at (F 1 c) Party under Major NOWELL marking out tasks at F 1 f sheets 3 p.m. All officers warned not to occupy houses or cellars on account of danger from mines. Search made for traces of mines or traps. Bn remains under orders of G.O.C. 143rd Bde until relief completed on 22nd inst. C.O. ordered to prepare scheme for capture of spur on X 29 d + X 30 c by our Battalion at dawn in near future. The question to be decided by operation further South. | |

Army Form C. 2118.

**WAR DIARY**
or
**INTELLIGENCE SUMMARY.** 1/9th Manchester Regt.

(Erase heading not required.)

Ref. Maps: FRANCE 1/40,000
57c S.E.
62c N.E.
62a N.W.

| Place | Date | Hour | Summary of Events and Information | Remarks and references to Appendices |
|---|---|---|---|---|
| EPEHY F.1. | Ap. 22 Night 22/23 | | Bn. takes over line from 4th E.L. during night 22/23.<br>Bn. Boundaries. Right: E.28 b.57 to E.8 c.83 — MAYE COPSE (incl. & Are. on right) — about 200y. NW of TOMBOIS FARM — canal at 6.A.3.a.08.<br>Left: East crown at F.16.53 along the track to X.27.6.99. Thence in a straight line through X.24 central. Boundary 23/25 — 25th in 10pm - Junction of dotted lines at F.4.9.9 — Picquet Line runs from TOMBOIS FARM (F.11) — "LITTLE PRIEL FARM. CATELET COPSE. Thence along the old German wire, following approximately the dotted line through "O" of TANGELLO RAVINE (X.15.d). Thun line to be held as a line of resistance.<br>Support Line 9through SART FARM (F.9.c) — No.13 COPSE (X.26.F.4.a.26) — X.27 central. This becomes the principle line of RESERVE LINE, runs through LEMPIRE (X.15.d) - MAY COPSE (F.9.c) in front of MALASSISE FARM (F.8.b) continuing just in front of railway line to X.25 central.<br>Advanced posts QUARRY (X.29.a) — X.28.b — X.22.c — X.17.c.<br>Posts taken over from 4th E. LANCS as follows:-<br>F.4 & 8.7 & 2. LITTLE PRIEL FARM No.2 A Coy. H.Q. + 2 Platoons MAJOR HOWORTH<br>5.c.86.<br>5.c.91. SUNKEN ROAD TRENCH 3 Sections Lt KNIGHT<br>X.29.d.24. QUARRY " " 3 " 1 Section<br>X.28.c.96. CATELET COPSE " " 3 " 1 Platoon Lt COOKE<br>X.28.a.14. " " 6 " B Coy. HQ. CAPT KERSHAW<br>X.29.b.33 OSSUS WOOD POST " " 2 " 1 Pl. CAPT MAKIN<br>X.23.c.97 GRAYS POST " " 7 " 1 Pl. Lt. QUINNEY<br>" " 1 Pl. Lt GRAY | APPENDIX I.<br>MAP.<br><br>Vol XXI<br>Page 8 |

Army Form C. 2118.

# WAR DIARY or INTELLIGENCE SUMMARY

1/9 MANCHESTER REGT

Ref Map FRANCE 1/20000
57 c S.E.
62 c N.E.

Page 9

| Place | Date | Hour | Summary of Events and Information | Remarks and references to Appendices |
|---|---|---|---|---|
| EPÉHY | | | Support line.  F3 & 72  12 COPSE  C Coy  1 Platoon  2/LT BURY | S2 |
| | | | F4 a 28  13 COPSE  C Coy  " | |
| | | | X 27 c 66  1H COPSE (Sect. of) C Coy  2/LT 27 d 41 2/LT BUTTERWORTH | S3 |
| | | | X 27 a 28  REDRUIN  C Coy  ? | S5 |
| | | | | |
| | | | BROWN LINE. HQ. F7 & 79  D Coy  2/LT RODMELL | |
| | | | Post at F 8 d 18, F 82 86, F 2 c 45. | |
| | | | 1 Platoon solute at MALASSISE FARM (F 8 & 19) 3 platoons in Railway Embankment. CAPT STEPHENSON. | |
| | | | Bn HQ. at EPÉHY ('F1 c 55'). MAJOR R.B. NOWELL'S HQ at 13 COPSE F3 a 99 | |
| | | | All reliefs carried out during early part of night without incident except relief of | |
| | | | GRAYS TRENCH POST (X 25 c 97) which was not found till 3.30 am—2/3rd while heading | |
| | | | for trench party was observed by enemy machine gun fires a wounding 3 casualties. | |
| | | | the los of a Lewis Gun. | |
| | | | 1/10th MANCH R. on left. A GLOUCESTER RGT on Right. | |
| | | | Patrols enter OLIOT WOOD. | |
| | | | Wiring one in BROWN LINE. | |

Army Form C. 2118.

# WAR DIARY
## or
## INTELLIGENCE SUMMARY.

(Erase heading not required.)

Army Form / 1/9 MANCHESTER REGT

YOC XX/
Page 10

| Place | Date | Hour | Summary of Events and Information | Remarks and references to Appendices |
|---|---|---|---|---|
| EPÉHY | Night 23/24 | | At Dawn the 4th Batt LANCS REGT attacked the line at X 29 d + X 30 c + gained their objectives, capturing twelve of their portion. Operation was assisted by attacks on KNOLL, GILLEMONT FARM, by troops on our right. Bde Cavalry reported SS with our troops, advancing between LITTLE PRIEL FARM & CATELET COPSE. | OP |
| | 24/2 | 9.50am | HOIDICE, CAMUS, EPÉHY F10 65 blown up & probably by enemy delayed mines. L'EXP FUGE returns from lines to U.K. | |
| | | | Operation of the morning to be continued, the 15th EAST LANCS to attack the KNOLL from the N.W. and W. | OP |
| | Night 24/25 | 8.45pm | 4 K BATT LABEL given out by Brig Gen Fbs by German counter attack, is active in LITTLE PRIEL FARM. The 4th EAST LANCS ordered to reoccupy the 13 COPSE. The attack of the 5th E. LANCES tunes for 11 A.m. delays the situation clears up. 5th E. Lance attack about 2 a.m. but was not successful. Reported that KNOLL was taken by the enemy. C Coy provided artillery escort to 2 sections at F. 3. d. 88 until supported in enemy front to renew. Patrols penetrated DEGUS WOOD to about 200 yards & fighting pot artillery West end of WOOD by our bombers but the enemy spent grenades. Enemy Machine WOOD but not located. Guns known to be in OTEVT | OP |

Reg.No. 1/20000  1/9 MANCHESTER REGT.
BK XXI
Page 11

# WAR DIARY or INTELLIGENCE SUMMARY

| Place | Date | Hour | Summary of Events and Information | Remarks and references to Appendices |
|---|---|---|---|---|
| EPEHY | April 25/26 | | 186 Bde Operation Order No. 8 recd. Enter 12hr Bombard 12 mts 4 posts 21×28 & 74 22 & 75 Feb over by 1/10 MANCH R. Attempt to relieve 27½ GRAY at GRAYS POT (X.23.8.97) unsuccessful owing to sniping & rifle gr. fire post. REDRUIN and 14 COPSE CAPT STEPHENSON & 1/8 Native 2/G & 2 Plations relieve 4/6 E. LANCS in SPUR POST Coy by H.Q. E. LANCS on morning of 24th inst. and Relf by 3 Officer & 60 O.R. 1/6 E. LANCS fell back on evening of 24th. Relief then place without incident. LT SHATWELL & 2 platoons of G Coy attack OUTGERMAN TRENCH & Posts F, 6 & 5C for 1st time strongly manned by enemy & this forced to withdraw. Heavy bombs & M.G. fire caused casualties including 2Lt E.K.P FUGE wounded. R.E. assist in wiring and consolidating trenches. Hostile shelling continuous intermittently during night. Shelling Day on LITTLE PRIEL FARM, and CATALET COPSE and No.12 COPSE. CAPT KEESHAW moves HQ to Sunken road just N. of CATALET COPSE because of heavy shelling. Support trench S.1 established at F.4 a 88 on Sunken road. New Batt boundary to the N. is as follows. Level crossing in F.1.6.63 - through X central - and X.24.c central. 2Lt B.F.ROBINSON attached to CORPS SCHOOL as Instructor. | APPENDIX 2. OPERATION ORDER.2 APPENDIX 3. Reports attack on OUT GERMAN TRENCH. |
| | 26th | 3 p.m. | QUINNEY'S POST (OSSUS WOOD POST X.29.R.33) shelled | |
| | | 4 p.m. | House in EPEHY (F.1.a.65) near site of explosion of 24th inst blown up probably by enemy delayed mine. This found very important & one Lt & 6 men mussing & kept army from it. Lt GREENWOOD proceeds on leave to U.K. | |

# WAR DIARY or INTELLIGENCE SUMMARY

Army Form C. 2118.

1/9 MANCHESTER RGT. Vol 1 Page 12

Ref. Maps 1/20,000 57c S.E. 62 S A.W.

| Place | Date | Hour | Summary of Events and Information | Remarks and references to Appendices |
|---|---|---|---|---|
| EPEHY | Ap 26/27 night | | Bn relieves in front line and supports by 1/4th EAST LANCS RGT & 1/5th EAST LANCS RGT. Relief complete about midnight. GRAYS POST (X 28 c 97) relieved at 3 am by 1/5th EAST LANCS R.G.T. after preparation for relief had been made by CAPT KERSHAW, a tape being laid from the Point to sunken road at X 22 c central. A & D Coys occupy BROWN LINE men MAJOR HOWORTH. B & C Coys occupy Billets in EPEHY | APPENDIX 4 OPERATION ORDER 3. O/O |
| | Ap 27th | | Lt. Col. D.H. WADE to hospital sick. Major R.B. NOWELL takes over command of Battalion. | O/O |
| | Ap 28th | | Bn relieves by 1/5th MANCHESTER RGT. and proceeds to Camp at BUIRE (a/J 27) | O/O |
| | Ap 29th | | Bn moves to MARQUAIX and occupies Billets vacated on Apl 20/21 As cellars in Billets on still being used as many first billets too to be improvised. Billets inspected by BDE. GEN. TUFNELL. Bn resting + constructing to-Mess | O/O |
| | Ap 30th 10 a.m. | | Major Comm 19 1/9. Manchester Rgt | APPENDIX 5 CASUALTY RETURNS |

R.B. Nowell
Major Comm.g 1/9 Manchester Rgt.

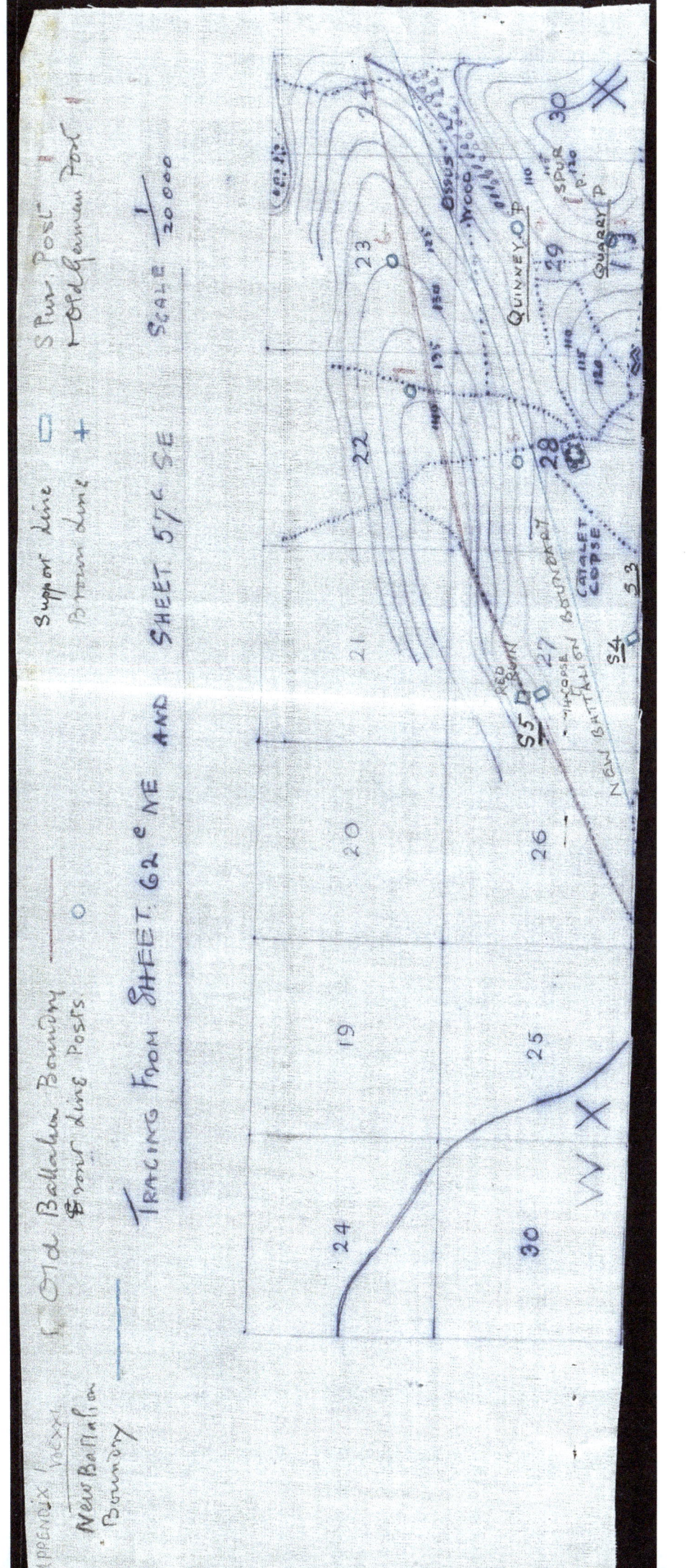

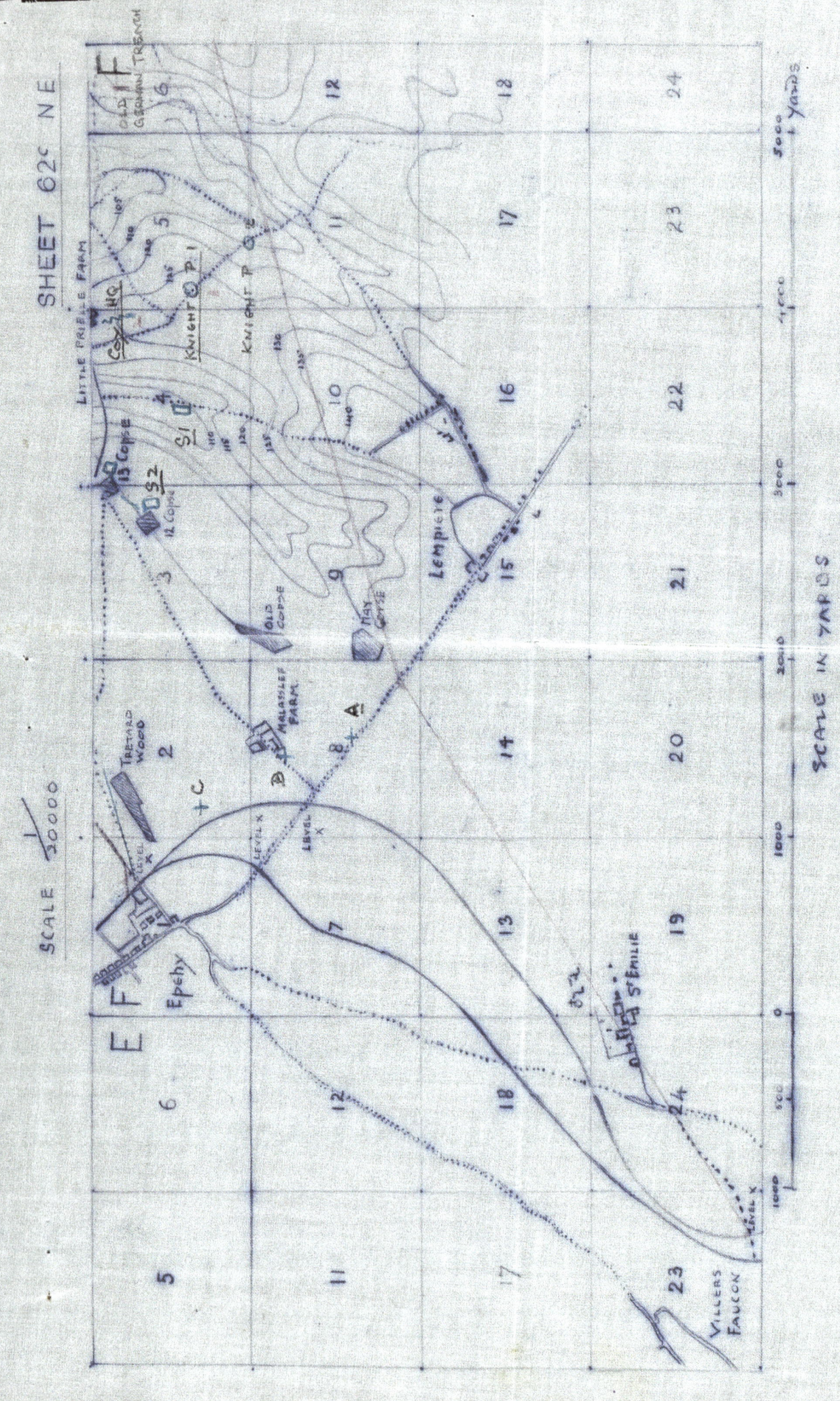

SECRET.  1/9th. Bn. Manchester Regt.  Copy No. 7

Vol XXI APPENDIX 2

## ORDER No. 2.

Map Ref. 1/20,000.  57. S.E. & 62. N.E.

1. A party of 3 Officers and 60 men 1/4th. E. Lancs. is still holding the Spur in X.29.d. which they captured yesterday morning. This party will be relieved immediately after dusk this evening by 2 Platoons "D" Coy. 1/9th Manchester R. under Capt. STEPHENSON. 2 Lewis Guns will be taken. The party at present holding the trench has been ordered to send 2 guides to meet the relief at Quarry X.29.d.32. at 8-30 p.m. O.C. "A" Coy. will send guides to meet party on road between MALASSES FARM and No. 13 COPSE at 8-0 p.m. ( about half way between these places ) to guide party to QUARRY.

2. At the same time 2 platoons, "D" Coy. 1/9th Manchester R. with 1 Lewis Gun under Lieut. SHATWELL and accompanied by half section R.E. will establish and consolidate a post in the Old German Trench about F.6.a.3.5. The O.C., 1/4th E. Lancs. will furnish an Officer as guide. O.C. "A" Coy. 1/9th. Manchester R. will send guide to meet Lieut. SHATWELL's party on a point mid-way between MALASSES FARM and 13 COPSE. This post should be occupied in silence in order to avoid fighting if possible.

3. Each of the above parties will be accompied by half section FIELD COY. R.E. and plenty of wire will be taken. The R.E. personnel will be withdrawn before daylight on the 26th.

4. Any men still remaining mixed with other units as result of last two days operations will be returned to their own units under arrangements to be made by C.O's of the units with which they are at present.

5. The inter-battalion boundary will be adjusted tonight to run from the level crossing F.1.b.6.3. through X.28 Central and X.24. C. Central. The additional post Southwards will be taken over from the 1/9th Manchester R. by the 1/10th Manchester R. commencing at 10-0 p.m. to-night provided the situation is normal. "B" Coy. less 1 platoon will be relieved as per special orders issued. The 2 Left Platoons of "C" Coy. which are North of the new inter-battalion boundary and situated at Red Ruin and No. 14 COPSE will be relieved by a party from 1/10th. Manchester R. A guide from 1/10th Manchester R. will report during the day at RED RUIN. The 2 platoons of "C" Coy. when relieved will move into BROWN LINE at MALASSES FARM. This relief will not take place till after 10-0 pm and then only if situation is normal.

6. The 1/5th Bn. E. Lancs. R. will be prepared to take over the Left Sector ( as extended by para. 5. ) from the 1/10th Manchester R. commencing at midnight 25/26th. This relief can only be carried out if situation is normal.

7. Advanced Brigade Headquarters will open at 8-30 p.m. at F.1.b.3.5. and remain there until the above movements have been completed.

8. O.C. "A" Coy. will be responsible for QUINNEY'S POST X.29.b.3.3. which will continue to be held by Lieut. QUINNEY and 1 platoon "B" Coy. 1/9th. Manchester R.

25/4/17.

(Sd) O.J. Sutton, Capt. for Adj.
1/9th. Bn. Manchester Regt.

| Copy No. 1. | "A" Coy. | Copy No 6. | 2nd. in Command. |
| 2. | "B" | 7. | War Diary. |
| 3. | "C" | 8. | do |
| 4. | "D" | 9. | Extra Copy. |
| 5. | C.O. | | |

Vol. XXI Appendix 3

## ATTACK ON OLD GERMAN TRENCH 26/4/17.

At 6-30 p.m. on the 26th April. 2 Platoons under Lieut. SHATWELL were ordered " to establish and consolidate " an old German Trench about 800 yards South East of PETIT PRIEL FARM.

At 12-30 a.m. on the 27th., 13 & 14 Platoons guided by 2/Lieut. THOMASON ( 1/4th East Lancs ) advanced in two lines, but were discovered by flares when about 70 yards from the enemy trenches.

Despite heavy rifle and M.G. fire, the advance continued to the Sunken Road running parrallel to and about 15 yards from the objective. Here Lieuts. FUGE and THOMASON were wounded, and enfilade M.G. and hostile artillery fire drove back the attack.

Two Officers and 9 men were wounded, and 6 men reported missing.

(Sd) H.G. SHATWELL,
Lieut.

Vol XXI  APPENDIX 4

1/9th. Battalion. MANCHESTER REGT. ORDER No.3.

Copy No...6...

APRIL 26th. 1917.

Para. 1.   The following relief will take place during the night 26/27th.
   (a). The 1/4th. Bn. East Lancs. Regt. will relieve 1/9th. Bn. Manchester Regiment in the Right Sector of the Brigade front. This relief must be completed before 12-0 Midnight.
   The relief of the line of resistance is to be completed before the relief of the trench in X.29.d. (held by Capt. STEPHENSON) is carried out.
   (b) The 1/5th. Bn. East Lancs. Regt. will relieve 1/10th. Bn. Manchester Regt. in the left Sector of the Brigade front
   This relief is to commence at Midnight. In addition the 1/5th. Bn. East Lancs. Regt. will relieve the post at X.23.c.9.6. (at present held by 1/9th. Bn. Manchester Regt. 2/Lieut. GRAY) which was not relieved on night 25/26th.

Para. 2.  (a)  The 1/9th. Bn. Manchester Regiment & 1/10th. Bn Manchester Regiment on relief in front line will take over the "BROWN LINE", surplus troops not required for the Garrison will be billeted at VILLERS-FAUCON and SAULCOURT respectively.
   (b)  Reference 126 Infantry Brigade Order No. 9. para' 6. the Garrison will not actually live in the posts, but in dug-outs behind. These must be added to until accommodation is adequate and sanitary arrangements require special attention.

Para. 3.   Completion of relief will be reported by wire to Brigade Headquarters.

Para. 4.   Guides for all posts will meet at CATELET COPSE at 9-30 p.m. except in the case of POST X.23.c.9.6. (2/Lieut GRAY) where the Guide will meet the 1/5th. Bn. East Lancs. Regt. at 9-0 p.m. at COPSE 13.

Para. 5.   Trench F.5.c.7.2. must be handed over as a day and night post.

Para. 6.   One Section R.E. will assist Infantry in wiring trench in X.29.d. to-night.   One Section R.E. will assist Infantry in wiring trench at PRIEL FARM, work begins about 9-0 p.m.

Para. 7.   Capt. G. MAKIN will provide guides for two Companies "A" & "D" at MALASSLES FARM at 10-0 p.m. for the "BROWN LINE".
   Companies "B" & "C" after relief effected will march to VILLERS-FAUCON and be there billeted.

Para. 8.   Battalion H.Q. for the night 26/27th inst. will be at EPEHY.

(Sd) O.J. Sutton, Capt.
for Adjutant,
1/9th. Bn. Manchester Regt.

DISTRIBUTION :-
Copy Nos. 1/4. O's C. Coys.
   5. 2nd in Command.
   6/7. War Diary.
   8. File.

APPENDIX 5.

1/9 Manchester Regt.

Casualty Report for April 1917

| Officers | | Other ranks | |
|---|---|---|---|
| Nº killed | — | Nº killed | 6 |
| " missing | — | " missing | *7 |
| " wounded | 1 | " wounded | 39 |
| " sick | 1 | " sick | 90 |
| Total | 2 | Total | 142 |

* Sgt. T.H. LEE included in this number since reported as being transferred to Nº 55 C.C.S. 30-4-17.

30/4/17

R. B. Howell
Major
Comdg. 1/9 Manchester Regt.

Vol 4

1/9th MANCHESTER REGT
WAR DIARY
May 1917
Vol. XXII.

# WAR DIARY
## or
## INTELLIGENCE SUMMARY.

Army Form. C. 2118.

1/9 MANCHESTER REGT.

Vol XII
Part 1.

Ref Map 20,000 Sheet 62cME.

Instructions regarding War Diaries and Intelligence Summaries are contained in F. S. Regs., Part II. and the Staff Manual respectively. Title pages will be prepared in manuscript.

(Erase heading not required.)

| Place | Date | Hour | Summary of Events and Information | Remarks and references to Appendices |
|---|---|---|---|---|
| MARQUAIX | May 1 | 8am | A Coy work on roads near TINCOURT (J24) Remaining Coys Training during morning and afternoon. | (1) |
| | | | Lt Col D.H.WADE inspected Town | |
| " | May 2 | | Coys engaged in fatigues and training. | |
| | | | 2/Lt H.H.KNIGHT proceeded to hospital sick. | |
| " | May 3 | 8am–4pm | B Coy works on roads near TINCOURT. Other Coys drilled with training under programme compiled by OC Coys. Rifle grenade practice. Wire, firing men 2/Lt RODWELL, 2/LIEUT J.H.RAWLINGS REGT. proceeded to hospital sick. CAPT O.J. SUTTON appointed adjutant. Major R.A. NOWELL and party of officers inspect front line held by 1/5 LANCS FUS. to be taken over by 1/9 MANCH R. (E18 c2) | (2) (3) |
| " | | 9am | Orders recd. that 1/9 MANCH R. will relieve 1/5 LANCS FUS. in night of 5/6/17 Hqrs on night of 3/4/17 | |
| " | | 5pm | Capt D.B. STEPHENSON and party of officers proceed to 1/5 LANCS FUS. for attachment in front line for night of 3/4/17. | (4) |

Army Form C. 2118.

Vol XII
Page 2

# WAR DIARY
## or
## INTELLIGENCE SUMMARY. 1/9 Manchester Regt.

Reference Map Sheet 62c N.E.

| Place | Date | Hour | Summary of Events and Information | Remarks and references to Appendices |
|---|---|---|---|---|
| MARQUAIX | 4/May/19 | 9 am | A Coy working party main drain ? TOM NAAR, PILLORS FAUCON (F.E.23) | |
| | | 4.30 pm | B Coy providing small fatigues & guards & remainder continue training | |
| | | 8 am | " " " " " " " - RONSSOY - EMILIE RLY | |
| | | 9 am | C Coy working party on roads | |
| | | 10 am | D Coy working party on roads - LONGAVESNES - EMILIE | |
| " " | 5/May | | Batt. relieves 1/5 LANCS FUSILIERS in front line & Rgt. Sub Sectr & right - C Coys & marquaix till next day | APPENDIX 1 O.O.5. |
| | | | Right picket commencing at Bois R. C Coys K marquaix till next day | |
| | | | Boundaries Right: North of MALASSISE FARM | APPENDIX T SKETCH M.P |
| | | | Left: Southern point of RONSSOY wood & the Brown Line as F.23.6.3.2 | |
| | | | There is no change to our Kings points 13 & A13 | |
| " " | 5/May | | Batt. H.Q. & at 62 N. STAFFS for a days. 'THO MAMET R. C. | |
| | | | Capt. HANDFORTH returned from Leave U.K. | |
| | | | 2Lt FRISSOMAN returned from course gunnery | |
| F25 c07 | 6/May | 10 pm | C Coy (Capt HANDFORTH) relieves right Coy 1/5 LANCS FUS. in front line. | |
| | | | 2/ W.N.BURY prcent. & course of Instruction at FOUQUESCOURT | |

# WAR DIARY or INTELLIGENCE SUMMARY

Army Form C. 2118.

R/Mf 20,000 63°N2 19 B-MANCHESTER REGT
62. M.M. VOL XVII Page 3

| Place | Date | Hour | Summary of Events and Information | Remarks and references to Appendices |
|---|---|---|---|---|
| F.23.c.0.7 | 6/7/M9 | | Boundary against enfilm. Rifle shoots F.17.6.10 to a straight line through A.13 central. BILLEMONT FARM and the Road over K.4/10 March R. | |
| | | | Raids mentioned in Special Instructions (App. 2) carried out. | APPENDIX 2 SPECIAL INSTRUCTIONS. |
| | | | Para. 1 by "C" Coy (Capt HANDFORTH) with 3 platoons. "D" Coy. This RIFLE PIT TRENCH mannedICI as far as F.24.6.85 without being interfered with. | APPENDIX 3 SPECIAL ORDERS... |
| | | | Para. 2 by Lieut R.J.M.DALE. No snipers in machine gun's seen. | |
| | | | Para. 3 by A Coy (MAJOR HOWORTH). This task met with Machine Gun fire & Rifle machine gun's & a number of shrapnel oversoll worship. Lt. C.E.COOKE wounded. Small posts for 3 men each established a and east of performed during night a compain in numbers notably by Pte A. HOLDEN 35007 and 350149 Pte KINSELLA and others. | |
| | | | Para. 6. by B Coy Scotty men. LT CROOKE almost complete. | |
| | 7 M4 | | LT C.E.COOKE to hospital wounded. | |

Army Form C. 2118.

# WAR DIARY or INTELLIGENCE SUMMARY.

1/9 Bn. MANCHESTER REGT

Ref Map 20.SW, 62cNB, 62SW.

(Erase heading not required.)

| Place | Date | Hour | Summary of Events and Information | Remarks and references to Appendices |
|---|---|---|---|---|
| F.23.c.07 | 8/9 May | | Bath outside (6 M. STAFFS) to attack trenches on our front and co-operate by advancing along RIFLE PIT TRENCH & bombing up. The Bath on right pushed to midnight objective, and patrols sent out by us went to obtain information for the main attack. Lt T. AINSWORTH in charge of patrol along RIFLE PIT TRENCH discovered it occupied by the enemy & after being on ran I him after killed a few yards from the enemy bomb & wounded. Lt H.G. SHUTTELL as liaison officer with the 6th M. STAFF gives difficulty in obtaining information. (See APPENDIX 4.) | APPENDIX 4. O.O. 6 |

Army Form C. 2118.

Re/Manch. War. Diary. 62° NE  
G.2.B.Nov. 1/2 Bn. MANCHESTER REGT. Vol xx".  
Page 5.

# WAR DIARY
## or
## INTELLIGENCE SUMMARY.
*(Erase heading not required.)*

Instructions regarding War Diaries and Intelligence Summaries are contained in F. S. Regs., Part II. and the Staff Manual respectively. Title pages will be prepared in manuscript.

| Place | Date | Hour | Summary of Events and Information | Remarks and references to Appendices |
|---|---|---|---|---|
| F.25.c.d.7 | 9/10 May | | Batn. relieved by 1/4 EAST LANCS REGT. & 46bn. on from 1/4 BATT LANCS in reserve at TEMPLEUX QUARRY. (G2. F.27.c.) B Coy. trestled reserve Coy. | (GP) |
| TEMPLEUX QUARRY | 10th May | | Batn in support. Night working parties amounting to 300 GR. found by Batn. | (GP) |
| | 11th | | Batn. in support. Night working party of 300 found by Batn. | (GP) |
| | 12th No.3/5 10/0/15 | | Batn in support. Night working parties & 300 provided. B Coy sent to reinforce 1/4 EAST LANCS. 10.30 pm. Coy to return 1.30 am but having been engaged. Lt. P.S. MARSDEN return from Zopital. Lt. GREENWOOD return from East U.K. | (GP) |
| | 13th | | 2/Lt in support. 2/Lt SHATRODE proceed to course at B.E.F. Gas School. 2/Lt CLARKE to course of Bombing. 2/Lt KNIGHT return from Zopital. Capt LILLIE proceed to leave to U.K. 2/Lt K. FUGG invalided home | (GP) |

Army Form C. 2118.

# WAR DIARY
## or
## INTELLIGENCE SUMMARY.
*(Erase heading not required.)*

Ref Map. 20,000. 62ˢ N.E. 4th Bn MANCHESTER REGT
62 B NW                                             Vol XXI
                                                    Page 6

| Place | Date | Hour | Summary of Events and Information | Remarks and references to Appendices |
|---|---|---|---|---|
| TEMPLEUX QUARRY | MAY 13/14 | | Bn relieves 1/4th EAST LANCS REGT. in Right Subsector 9/74 Right Secta commencing at dusk. Relief uninterrupted. The front line of the Bn was relieved line by the 1/4th EAST LANCS REGT. on orig20 of 9/102. Heavy downpour of rain about 3.30 a.m. making communication very difficult about posts and trenches. Much work done in clearing trenches. B was in training. Disposition of coys as per APPENDIX 5. 4 platoons in support line, 3 platoons in one strong point, 3 platoons in intermediate posts. | APPENDIX 5 O.O.7 |
| F.23.0.7 | 14/15 | | Patrols sent out by all coys. Work carried on until communication finel. RIFLE PIT TRENCH improving RIFLE PIT TRENCH & STGE. points A, B + C. also sap runs from "C" strong point. | |
| ,, | 15/16 | | Patrols sent out. 2 dead German bodies, identification of one reported. Work of German snipers continued. | |

# WAR DIARY or INTELLIGENCE SUMMARY

Army Form C. 2118.

1/9 MANCHESTER REGT.

Ref Map 1/20,000 62 c NE
 62 c NW

Vol XXII.
Page 1

| Place | Date | Hour | Summary of Events and Information | Remarks and references to Appendices |
|---|---|---|---|---|
| F.23.c.07 | 16/17th May | | Large hostile working party strongly about one company, discovered by patrol in R.E.L. ground in front of "B" Strong Point. Then attempts to surprise this party not being successful artillery was brought to bear on it about 3 a.m. | |
| F.23.c.07 | 17/5/18 | | Battn. relieved by 1/6th D.G. (Cameron's) & marches to billets in VILLERS FAUCON & that med at TEMPLEUX QUARRY. Relief completes about 11.30 p.m. on return of patrols which had been sent out by next Coy. | APPENDIX 1 O.O.8. |
| VILLERS-FAUCON | 18th | | Billets inspected by B.G.C. Gen TUFNELL. | |

# WAR DIARY or INTELLIGENCE SUMMARY

Army Form C. 2118.

1/9 MANCHESTER REGT

Ref. Map. 1/20,000 62c NE  57c SE

| Place | Date | Hour | Summary of Events and Information | Remarks and references to Appendices |
|---|---|---|---|---|
| VILLERS-FAUCON | May 19th | 4.50 pm | Depart VILLERS FAUCON. Arrive EQUANCOURT (57c S.E. V.10-B.8) 21 Tents + 68 Tarpaulins pitched by 1/4 East Lancs for use of 1/9 MANCH R. | APPENDIX 8 O.O.9 |
| EQUANCOURT | May 20th | 4 pm | Depart EQUANCOURT. Arrive BERTINCOURT (57c S.E. P.7.) & go into Billets chiefly ruined buildings. Latrines with tarpaulins & urinal dug by troops pending Sanitation arrival. | (9) (6A) |
| BERTINCOURT | May 21 | | Lt H. SHATNELL returns from Divl. Gas Course. | (9) |
| BERTINCOURT | May 22/22 10 pm | 7 pm | Depart BERTINCOURT. Billets to be taken over by 11th RIFLE BDE. Bn relieves 11th RIFLE BDE in Reserve S. W. of HAYRINCOURT WOOD. Bn HQ at 57c S.E. P.18 d.9.6. B + C Coy HQ in METZ (57 S.S.E. Q.20) A + D Coy H.Q. (57 S.S.E. P.19 C.) | APPENDIX 9 O.O. 10 (6A) |
| HAYRINCOURT WOOD P.18.d.9.6 | May 23 | | Lt QUINNEY return from leave U.K. | |
| HAYRINCOURT WOOD P.18 d 9.6 | May 28/24 | | Coys working from Back Trench on new reserve trenches between BEAUCAMP (Q.12.c) and TRESCAULT (S.q Q.4) and at A Coys new position in Q.17 a + c. A Coys trenches are now at Q.17 a + c. B Coys " " " " Q.21.c + Q.20.c to METZ-TRESCAULT road C Coys " " temporarily Q.20.c from METZ-TRESCAULT Rd to Q.14.c 3.4. D Coys " " Q.13 d.c. r.a. | (6A) |
| | | 9.30 pm 10.15 pm | Gas alarm. Gas alarm. | |

Ref Map 57 C S.E. 1/24,000

**WAR DIARY**
or
**INTELLIGENCE SUMMARY**
(Erase heading not required.)

Army Form C. 2118.
Vol XXII Page 9

| Place | Date | Hour | Summary of Events and Information | Remarks and references to Appendices |
|---|---|---|---|---|
| P 18 d 9.6 | May 24 | | LT T.G.HYDE proceeds on Leave to U.K. LT H.SHEATWELL returns from duties of 2/Lieutenant & wound his service. LT C.E.COOKE dies of wounds. LT RUTTENAU & LT LEWIS GUN COURSE. STAPLES. Boys working on trenches between BEAUCAMP and TRESCAULT and in Q.11.C and d. Numbers coming up in section P loyants. | |
| " | May 24/25 night | | | |
| 6 | May 25/26 | | Work continued from previous night. 350077 Pte A HOLDEN awarded Military Medal for gallantry on night of April 25/26 in bringing in wounded. (D.R.O. 24/5/17) | |
| | May 26/27 | | Bn. relieves 1/5 EAST LANCS RGT in Left Battn Sector. TRESCAULT-RIBECOURT Road. Q 4 + Q 5. Boundaries Right Q 4 a 49 to Q 4 a 4 o Punch R Q 4 c 0 0 - Q 4 central. Left Steam Q 4 a 49 to Q 4 a Q . B Coy (Capt KERSHAW) + D Coy (LT MADSDEN) in Front Line (See Appendix 7) C Coy (Capt KERSHAW) + D Coy (LT MADSDEN) in Front Line (See Appendix 7) Both A & C concentrated in front line & support line, but B East again much dispersing. | |
| HARINCOURT WOOD Q 14 d 19 | May 27 | | LT COL E.C.LLOYD. 13 R.I.R. again + taken over command of Battn. | Appendix 11 30.5.11 |

Army Form C. 2118.

1/9 MANCHESTER REGT.
BEXXIV
Page 10

# WAR DIARY or INTELLIGENCE SUMMARY.
(Erase heading not required.)

Ref Map Europe
57 c SE

| Place | Date | Hour | Summary of Events and Information | Remarks and references to Appendices |
|---|---|---|---|---|
| Q 14 a 19 | May 27/28 | | Situation quiet. Unit enumerated on front line A6.5 & B6.9 providing working parties for Reserve. | Appendix 10 SKETCH MAP. |
| " | 28/29 | 7 am | HARINCOURT CHATEAU (R 29 d.) blown up by enemy. Shots led there were in a German O.P. | (OP) |
| | | | Work continued on front line + supports + got parapets made. Patrols sent out, one with orders to visit German wire. This patrol is stopped by M.G. fire 600 + 700 yards from our line. | (OP) |
| " | " | | CAPT. W.H. LILLIE returns from leave U.K. & takes over command of right company subsector. | (OP) |
| " | 29/30 | 1 am | Work on front line & supports. Patrol consists of 2/Lt P.S. MARSDEN and 3 privates is fired on. 2/Lt P.S. MARSDEN and 1 of the men hit, both in the shoulder. The two unwounded privates drag Subn to shell hole + after some distance, & then return, a stretcher & some assistance is sent after he is brought in to the front some hours later. 2/Lt P.S. MARSDEN dies. | (OP) |
| " | 30 " | | 2/Lt RODWELL proceeds on leave U.K. Construction of new BATTH.Q. proceeded with at Q 14 £ 5.9 2/Lt O.S. NEEDHAM to course of instruction on Lewis gun. | (OP) |

# WAR DIARY or INTELLIGENCE SUMMARY

Army Form C. 2118.

Ref. Map 20.000 1/9 MANCHESTER REGT
57°c SE horex14
& 57°NE Page 11

| Place | Date | Hour | Summary of Events and Information | Remarks and references to Appendices |
|---|---|---|---|---|
| Q.14 d.1.9 | MAY 30/5/17 | | New line consolidated in front by 1/9 MANCH R & 4/5E LANCS REGT. With the view in tactic of making a front line running forward from the night of the left Battalion sector through FERN WOOD (57° NE. K 34 central). 1. Firing trench facing East Q.9 a 4.0.15 Q 5 a 4.3 wide T. Posts + wired. R Coy under Capt. HOWORTH. 2. T trench about 150 yards out with communication Trench Q 4 & 5.1 Any by 1/5 EAST LANCS. REGT. 3. T Road at Q.4 a.6.4. about 300 × out with ammunition Trench Dug by 1/5 EAST LANCS REGT. The rest of Trench were garrisoned + held during the day 31st most under O.C. B Coy. No's 2 & 3 under O.C. B Coy. On return of C Coy men 2nd Lt GREENWOOD relieves platoon of 1/10 MANCH R in front trench in Reserve Line Q.10 a 5.4 to Q.10 a. 7.3. | APPENDIX 12 6-5-17 |

# WAR DIARY
## or
## INTELLIGENCE SUMMARY.

Army Form C. 2118.

1/9 MANCHESTER REGT

Ref Map 20,000 57cSE & NW, 57cNE

Page 12

| Place | Date | Hour | Summary of Events and Information | Remarks and references to Appendices |
|---|---|---|---|---|
| O14 d.1.9. | 31/7/17 | | Work continued on the new Trench, covering parties covering everything. Battn M.G. Teams with L.G. Teams Reported much annoyance from ENEMY MGD. Officers patrol sent out to reestablish contact. B Company in FENNY WOOD. Unable to locate his position in FENNY WOOD owing to reports of 2nd BEDFORDS and 1/4 R.W.F. as to the position. Orders were along line running North from Q.4 central, up in to FENNY WOOD. Officers & agnts making party hole R.4.200. & the 59th Div FRONTAGE extended two points + thirst on the party, whence our own front was covered. TRENCHT twenty shells 77 & from about 10.2.30 pm. | APPENDIX 13 CASUALTY TABLE |

Redmond
Lieut Col.
Comm'g 1/9 Manchester Regt

1/9th Manchester Regt.

War Diary – Vol. XXII May 1917

Appendices – 1–6 Orders.
7 Sketch.
8–9 Orders
10 Trace
11–12 Orders
13 Casualty Return.

1/9th. Battalion. MANCHESTER REGT. ORDER No.5.

Vol XXII APPENDIX I.

SECRET.
Copy No. 5.
Map Reference, 1/20,000 .62.c.N.E.                    May 5/1917.

1. **RELIEF**. The Battalion will relieve the 1/5th. Lancs. Fusiliers on the night of 5/6th. in the Right Sub Sector of the Right Sector, commencing as soon as it is dusk.

2. **DISTRIBUTION**. The distribution will be as follows :—
    Right Coy.     "C" Coy.         Right Centre Coy.   "A"
    Left Centre    "B" Coy.         Left Coy.           "D"
    Coys. on the flanks will ensure that they are in touch with the flanking Coys. of adjacent units.
    Coy. Officers will report completion of relief and establishment of touch, on completion.

3. **PARADE-ROUTE**.
    The Battalion will parade at 6 p.m. Dress: Fighting Order, and march from MARQUAIX by platoons, in the following order "C","A","B","D" Coys. via ROISEL, and the ROISEL - ST. EMILIE Road to PLEASANT HOUSE, E.30.c.18., where guide from LANCS. FUSILIERS will meet the leading platoon at 7-30 p.m. Platoon guides will be met at TEMPLEUX Quarry, F.27.c.
    Officers chargers will be sent back from TEMPLEUX QUARRY.

4. **TOOLS, etc.** Each Coy. will take from TEMPLEUX Quarry, 26 spades, 17 picks, from tool limbers, which with limber for grenades will march in rear of the first platoon.
    Remainder of Tools, i.e. 6 spades & 8 picks will be taken to Bn.H.Q. under arrangements to be made by R.S.M.
    One box of rifle grenades per Coy. will also be taken from the Quarry. S.A.A. Mill's hand and rifle grenades, rockets, flares and lights will be handed over by Unit relieved, and receipts for these will be given as trench stores.(copy to be sent to Bn.H.Q.) The R.S.M. will take over S.A.A. and any other reserve trench stores at TEMPLEUX QUARRY, and will hand in copy of receipt to H.Q. at earliest opportunity.

5. **COOKERS AND WATER CARTS**. Cookers will follow their own Coys. and remain at TEMPLEUX Quarry. Water Carts will follow Bn.H.Q. One cart will remain at the Quarry, and the other will proceed to Bn. H.Q. Water Carts will return daily to ST. EMILIE Well - 62.c.E.24.b.04. to fill. Cookers will fill from Water Carts in the Quarry. Drinking water will be drawn from the Water Cart at Bn H.Q.

    The forward limber of the Cookers of "A" & "C" Coys will take meals for "A" Coy. & 3 platoons "C" Coy. to TOINE WOOD at 7 a.m., 1 p.m. & 6 p.m. daily. "D" Coy's Cooker will be used to cook "A" Coys. food.
    The forward limber of "B" Coys. Cooker, with meals for three platoons, will be at QUEUCHETTES WOOD at 7 a.m., 1 p.m. & 6 p.m. daily. Orderly men will meet their own Cookers at above places at the hours stated.
    "D" Coy's Dinners will be sent up to QUEUCHETTE WOOD at 11 p.m. nightly. They will be taken to the FARM by the reserve platoon of "B" Coy. One platoon "B" Coy. will be supplied with dinners in a similar way at the same time. This will be cooked in "D" Coys. Cooker.

( Continued.)

ORDER No.5. (Continued)                    (2)

- **COOKERS & WATER CARTS**(Continued). Dinners for the platoon of "C" Coy. in the Forward Quarry will be taken up at 11 p.m. from TOINE WOOD. The Transprt Officer will make arrangements for the necessary teams for these moves at TEMPLEUX QUARRY.

6. **RATIONS** . Rations will be drawn at a point to be notified later at 9-30 p.m. commencing 6th inst. Rations for the 6th. will be drawn to-night immediately after relief is completed .

7. **POSITIONS** . The REGT. Aid Post will be established near the Cross Roads about F.22.b.16. Bn. H.Q. will be established at F.23.c.07. The Brigade Transport Lines and Bn. Quartermaster's Stores will be at VILLERS FAUCON, E.27.d.

8. **GRENADES**. O.C. Coys. will draw 30 rounds blank ammunition for Hale's grenades & 6 Mill's cups from Q.M. Stores, MARQUAIX, at 10 a.m. to-day.

9. **TRENCH STORES.** O's C.Coys. will ensure that when leaving trenches all S.A.A. ,Tools, Petrol Tins, Grenade Cups, Blank Ammunition, etc taken in, are brought away . S.A.A. may be left in if necessary to leave sufficient reserve . Receipts for all Trench Stores handed over must be obtained and forwarded to Orderly Room, after relief .

10. **LOSSES** . All losses of equipment and material by shell fire will be reported immediately and the circumstances explained .

11. **PACKS & VALISES** . Packs will be ready for loading at Coy. Dumps at 8 a.m. Officers Valises to be ready for loading at Coy. H.Q.at 3 p.m.

12. **GUIDE** . On arrival at the new Bn. H.Q., a guide will be sent to report to Bde T.O. Lieut . BAXTER,126 b. to act as guide for reinforceforcements . He will live at the Transport Lines under orders of Bde. T.O.

13. **RETURNS & REPORTS** . Map mentioned by C.O. in letter to Officers attached to 1/5th LANC. FUSILIERS, and Statement showing work completed -- to be rendered on the morning on 6th inst.
    Situation Reports ------- 3 a.m. and 3.p.m.
    S.A.A., Bombs, Flares (showing size and colour) expended to be rendered 11 a.m.
    Intelligence Reports will be collected by Intelligence Officer at 6 a.m.
    Casualty , Nominal Roll..... 11 a.m.
    Casualty , estimated Numbers only....3 p.m.
    Work Report showing work done and work proposed....3 p.m.
    Parade State........... 7 p.m.
    Map . Bi-weekly . *Sunday & Wednesday 9 a.m.*

14. **NAMING OF POSTS** etc. Posts, Dug-outs, Trenches, Hd.Qrs. etc. must be named and numbered as the case may be, furnished with name boards and situations reported to H.Q.

                                        (Sd) O.J.Sutton , Capt,
                                                A/Adj ,
                                        1/9th.Bn.Manchester Regt.

Issued ...........
DISTRIBUTION :-
Copies Nos. 1/4 -    Coys.
            5.       O.C.
            6/7.     War Diary.
            8.       File .

Vol XXII Appendix 2

SECRET.

## SPECIAL INSTRUCTIONS TO
### O.C. 1/9th. Bn. Manchester Rgt.

The following tasks have to be carried out by your Battalion to-night as preparatory measures for further offensive operations on a larger scale.

(1)     The line of rifle pits, or what is sometimes described as "Rifle Pit Trench", running through F.29.b.30.a. and 30.c. will be occupied as far South as 30.a.0.1. and consolidated.
The Northern part of this trench is believed to be unoccupied, but as the advance proceeds bombing operations may be necessary. If opposition is not encountered up to that point, or the opposition is slight and can easily be overcome it will be a further advantage if the trench can be made good for an additional distance. i.e. up to any point possible as far as F.30.c.2.8.: but not beyond this.
     Whatever point is reached must be blocked; and whatever part of the trench you succeed in occupying must be consolidated at once and held.

(2)     Two banks shown running North East and South West in F.30.a. are reported to contain snipers with possibly one or more machine guns. A stealthy patrol should be sent out immediately after dark to-night with the object of verifying or refuting this. This patrol is to make every effort to avoid being seen; and it is essential that it should be back within the lines before midnight, as at that hour the artillery will commence firing on the ground where the banks are.

(3)     Two small posts are to be established on the road running from locality b. to QUENNEMONT FARM, one on either side of the road, and joined up. This should be undertaken as a very minor operation, with only sufficient men to dig a rifle pit on each side and then connect up. The object should be to advance these posts a short distance every night without attracting the enemy's attention; and connect them up from behind with a communication trench.

(4)     It is absolutely essential that all men taking part in enterprises should be ready to start before it is dark and that the start should be made the moment darkness allows, as the moon rises so early.

(5)     The results obtained and especially the exact distance for which "Rifle Pit Trench" is made good must be reported to Brigade Headquarters by 8 a.m. to-morrow, in order that the artillery may be informed.

(6)     To-night also the post you partially established about F.24.a.8.0. should be consolidated, held, and linked up with a communication trench.
     Please report frequently.

7/5/17.

(Sd) A.G.P.Heywood,
Captain,
A/Bde.Major,
126th. Infy. Bde.

Copies to 1/9th.Bn.Manchester Regt.
         42nd.Division.
         1/10th.Bn.Manchester Regt.

## SPECIAL ORDER No. 1.

O.C. A. COY.

I am directed by the Major General to convey to you and your company his gratification in the bearing and general good conduct of the N.C.O.s., and men in the recent attack on the enemy on the evening of the 6th. and 7th., of May

Will you please deliver this message to all ranks of your Company which behaved splendidly throughout.

Sdg. R.B. Newell, Major.
Comdg. 1/9 Bn. Manchester Regt.


O.C. Coy.

Above is passed to you for information. I trust that no other Coy., in the Battalion will be satisfied until a similar honour falls to its lot. Please circulate.

Sdg. R. B. Newell., Major.
Comdg. 1/9 Bn. Manchester Regt.

SECRET.

Vol XXII Appendix 6

Copy No. 6

## 9th Bn. Manchester Regt. Orders No. 8.

In the field.
17/5/17.

Para. 1.   The Battalion will be relieved in the Right sector to-night commencing at 9-0 p.m. by the 1/6th. D. G. (Carabineers).

2.   After relief the Battalion will march to VILLERS FAUCON and billet there. After dinner, to be provided at TEMPLEUX QUARRY after relief, platoons will march independently to VILLERS FAUCON. A guide for each platoon will be at Church, VILLERS FAUCON at 12 M N. to guide the platoon to its billets.
Officers chargers will be at the Quarry at 10-0 p.m.

3.   GUIDES.
Guides for A & B Strong Posts will be at Battn. H. Qrs. at 9-0 p.m. H. Qr. Runners will act as guides.
A guide for C Strong Post will be sent to QUEUCHETTE WOOD by O. C. "B" Coy. for 9-0 p.m.

4.   TOOLS.
Each Coy. will take 26 spades and 17 picks to be loaded on limbers. "A" & "C" Coys. limbers will be at Battn. H. Qrs., "B" & "D" Coys. limbers at QUEUCHETTE WOOD.
S. A. A., bombs and flares, &c, will be handed over in accordance with instructions sent to O. C. Coys.
Lewis Gun S. A. A. will be taken according to establishment, except "A" Coy. which will not take away its 7000 rounds of reserve S. A. A.

5.   LEWIS GUN LIMBERS.
Lewis Gun Limbers for "A" & "C" Coys. will be H. Qrs. and for "B" & "D" Coys. at QUEUCHETTE WOOD at 9-0 p.m. A guide will be sent by O. C. Coys. with each L. G. Limber. This guide will remain with the limber till arrival at VILLERS FAUCON.

6.   TRENCH STORES.
Receipts will be obtained on forms distributed to O. C. Coys. for all trench stores and sent to Battn. H. Qrs. on arrival at VILLERS FAUCON.

7.   O. C. Coys. will send platoon guides to Church at VILLERS FAUCON to rendezvous at 6-30 p.m. there. These guides will be met by Town Major there and will be instructed by Coy. Commdrs. to meet their platoons there on arrival from M N. onwards.

(Sd.) O. J. Sutton.
Captain & A/Adjutant,
1/9th Bn. Manchester Regt.

Copies
1 - 4 Coys.
   5 C. O.
6 - 7 War Diary.

Issued by Orderly at........

Vol XXII Appendix 7.

Scale 1/20,000

Sheet 62c NE    62B NW

Map labels:
- GUILLEMONT FM.
- L.G. POST.
- No 3. POST.
- M.G. 3.
- STRONG POST. C.
- SAP.
- CLARKES POST
- STRONG POST. B.
- PIT. No 1
- RIFLE PIT. TRENCH.
- M.G.
- STRONG POST A
- NEW ADVANCED POST.
- QUARRY POST.
- MALAKOFF. FM.

| Position | Strength |
|---|---|
| Quarry Post. | 1. Platoon. |
| New Advanced Post. | 2 Secs. |
| Rifle Pits Trench. | 2½ Platoons. |
| Trench. | 2 Platoons. |
| Strong Point A | 1 Platoon. |
| Pit. No 1. | 7. O.R. (by night) |
| Strong Point. B | 1 Platoon. |
| Clarkes Post. : Sap. | 2 Secs. |
| Barricade. | 2½ Platoons. |
| L.G. Post. | 1 Sec. |

SECRET.                                                    Copy No. 8

Vol XXII App 34

1/9th Bn. Manchester Regt. (Order No. 6. May 8th. 1917.)

Map Reference 1/20,000  62c N.a.

The Battalion on our right will attack the German trenches between
L. 6. a. 53 and F. 30. c. 0. 7 this evening. Zero hour is 9.30p.m.
"C" Coy. 9th Manchester Regt. will co-operate in the attack as follows:-
            A Lewis Gun will be located in position indicated
to Capt. HANDFORTH about F. 29. b. 65.
            A Section of Bombers and Bayonet men will remain in
readiness in RIFLE PIT TRENCH about F. 30.b.83. to co-operate
with the Battalion on our right in bombing RIFLE PIT TRENCH towards F.30.c.17.
            To avoid danger of our bombers and those of the 6th
Bn. N. STAFFORD Regt. (on our right) injuring one other Capt.
LILLY with small patrol will establish touch with O. C. left Coy.
6th Bn. N. STAFFORD Regt.  He will report to Capt. HANDFORTH at
his report centre at F. 29.d.49 for instructions issued verbally
to Capt. HANDFORTH.
            The Lewis Guns at Cross ROADS at F. 29.b.99 will
co-operate with fire in direction of MALAKOFF FARM and TRIANGLE
WOOD A.29.b.
            Two sections Rifle Grenadiers will occupy sunken
road from F.29.b.99 to its junction with RIFLE PIT TRENCH and
direct fire on the bank extending from F.30.a.29 to F.30.a.57.
            The flanks of these sections will be secured by
2 sections Riflemen in Sunken Road.
            Fire will be opened at ZERO hour.

2.         2 Platoons "D" Coy. under 2 Lieut. AINSWORTH,
attached to "C" Coy. will continue digging on Rifle pits towards
F.30.a.01. These will be withdrawn under cover temporarily at
ZERO hour until limits of danger from Barrage fire are determined.
O. C. "C" Coy. will arrange to draw bombs, ground flares, S. O. S.
and Very lights required from Battn. H. Q.

3.         Major T. S. HOWARTH will provide working party 100
strong for work between strong Points A & B, with 100 shovels
and 30 picks, and a carrying party of 75, using 2 platoons "D" Coy
attached "A" Coy. and support Platoon of Coy. attached from 1/6th.
Battn. EAST LANCS. REGT.
            Rendezvous Battn. H. Qrs. at 9-30 p.m.

4.         O. C. 126 T. M. Battery will direct fire with 2
L. T. Ms. from about F.29.b.99 on TRIANGLE WOOD and on banks on
F. 30a. paying special attention to more southerly of the two banks.

5.         O. C. "B" Coy. will detail one Officer and 33
other ranks to proceed with work on new trench and communication
trench in F. 24.a. Officer to report personally to Battn. H. Q.
for instructions immediately after relief within "B" Coy.
                                                             from
6.         4 M. Gs. will probably fire overhead fire with
F. 29. b. 88 against Spur East of MALAKOFF FARM. Instructions
for defensive action have been issued to O. C. Machine Gun in
GREEN LINE.

7.         Os. C. Coys. will warn their men of action as
detailed in paras 4 & 5.                              (contd.)

Order No. 6. (contd.)

8. Should the Battalion be ordered to take over the trench after capture, 2 Platoons "C" Coy. will take over New Trench from L 6 a 38 to F 30 c 43. "A" Coy. from F 30 c 43 to F 30 c 37 and "D" Coy. from F 30 c 37 to road crossing at F 29 b 75 and along sunken road to F 29 b 99.

2 Platoons "C" Coy will be in support in roads from F 29 d 43 to F 29 d 22 and F 29 d 72.

Repair and consolidation will be proceeded with immediately on taking over.

(Sd.) O. J. Sutton,
Captain & A/Adjutant,
1/9th Bn. Manchester Regt.

8/5/17.

Copies 1-4 Coys.
5 126 Infy. Bde.
6 6th Bn. N. Stafford Regt.
7-8 War Diary.
9 Spare Copy.

A.I.C. 257.

SECRET.

Reference 1/9th Bn. Manchester Regt. Order No. 6.

Zero hour will now be 9-50 (nine fifty) p. m. to-night.

There will be intense artillery barrage from Zero + 4 to Zero + 12 - medium from Zero + 12 to Zero + 30.

Slow from Zero + 30 to Zero + 60.

Infantry expect to reach their objective at Z + 8.

(Sd.) O. J. Sutton,
Captain & A/Adjutant,
1/9th Bn. Manchester Regt.

8-5-17.

SECRET.

Vol XXII App 5    War Diary
Copy 6

1/9 Battn. Manchester Regt. Order No. 7..

May 13th 1917.

Map Reference 1/20,000.

**Para 1.**
**Relief.** The Battn. will relieve the 1/4 Bn. EAST LANCS REGT. on the night of 13 / 14th May in the Right Sub Sector of the Right Sector, commencing at 10. p. m.

**Para 2.**
**Distribution.** The distribution will be as follows:-
Right Coy. "C" Coy ) "A" locality Nos 1 & 2 Outposts.
& 1. platoon "D" Coy)
Right Centre Coy. "A" Coy. R.P. Trench to left of "B" locality.
Left Centre Coy "D" Coy. (3 platoons) Left of "B" locality to right of "C" locality.
Left Coy. "B" Coy. "C" locality to Barricade and 2. Outposts S. of GILLEMONT FARM.

**Para 3..**
**Parade.** The Bn. will parade at 9-30. p.m. Dress:- Fighting Order, and will move in the following order:- C. A. D. B. Coys. to H.Q. 1/4 Bn. EAST LANCS REGT. where guides from the 1/4 Bn. EAST LANCS REGT. will be met ( 1. per platoon.)
The QUARRY Post No. 1. will be exchanged direct, 2 Sections "C" Coy taking over.

**Para 4.**
**Tools.** Each Coy will take b 26 spades and 17 picks from the Guard at TEMPLEUX QUARRY. Remainder of tools will be taken by Bn. H.Q. O. C. Coys will send back to new Bn. H.Q. after relief for :-
6 Boxes Grenades No. 5.
1 Box Hales Grenades No. 20.
1 Box Mills Rifle Grenades No. 23.
1. S.O.S. Flare.
                                                    from
Very Lights and other stores will be taken over 1/4 EAST LANCS REGT., and receipts given for these as trench stores.
Copies of these receipts will be sent to Bn. H. Q. at earliest opportunity.

**Para 5.**
**Cookers &** The Cookers will remain at TEMPLEUX QUARRY. One Water Cart
**Water Carts.** will remain at the QUARRY and the other will proceed to Bn. H.Q. From the 14th inst the Water Cart at Bn. H.Q. will be filled at 10. p. m.
As Cookers cannot leave TEMPLEUX QUARRY In daylight Os C. Coys. will arrange to have one hot meal served at night between 10 pm. and 11 pm. This must not be allowed to interfere with working parties. Teams for Cookers will be at TEMPLEUX QUARRY at 9-30 p. m.

**Para 6.**
**Positions.** The Regtl. Aid Post will be near Bn. H.Q. on BASSE BOULOGNE- MALAKOFF FARM Road about F.23.c.07.
Bn H.Q. will be at F.23.c.07.

**Para 7.**
**Trench Stores.** O.C. Coys will ensure that when leaving trenches all S.A.A. tools, Petrol tins, Grenade Cups, Blank Ammunition etc m taken in , are brought away.
Receipts must be obtained for all Trench Stores handed over and copies sent to Orderly Room after relief.

**Para 8.**
**Returns &** Situation Reports 3 a.m. and 3 p. m.
**Reports.** Intelligence Reports will be collected by Intelligence Officer at 6 a. m.
Casualty, Nominal Rolls 10 a. m.
S.A.A., Bombs, Flares, ( showing size and colour) expended 10a
Casualty, estimated numbers only 3 p. m.
Work report, showing work done and work proposed 10. a. m.
Parade State 7 p. m.

ORDER No. 7. (Continued.)

Para 8.
Continued.   Map and bi-weekly work report. Wednesday 10. a. m.
             It is important that these reports be rendered punctually.

Para 9.      As early as possible on the 14th inst a sketch map of the
             Trenches occupied by the Coy will be sent to H.Q.
             The names or numbers of all posts must be marked on this map.
                         (Dugouts, trenches, H.Qrs etc)


                            (Sgd) O.J.Sutton Captain.
                       A.Adj. 1/9th. Bn. Manchester Regt.


Distribution.
1/4 Coys.
 5.  C. O.
6/7 War Diary.

Vol XXII  Appendix 8

## 1/9th Bn. Manchester Regt. Order No.9.

Ref. Map 1/40000  Sheets 57c & 62c.

1. **Move.**

    The Battalion will march to Camp V 4 d EQUANCOURT to-morrow. Starting Point, Cross Roads at F22d7.6. at 4-25 am. Dress:- Full Marching Order. Helmets will be carried on the back of the valise, Greatcoats in valise, groundsheets will be worn under the flap of the valise. Coys. will be reported ready for moving at 4-0 am.
    The route will be LIERAMONT - NURLU - FINS.
    On the 20th May the march will be continued in the afternoon. Orders will be issued later.

2. **March.**

    100 yards distance will be maintained between platoons. The Battalion will march 400 yards in rear of Bde. H. Qrs. 25 yards distance will be kept between every 6 Transport vehicles. Transport arrangements are as follows:-
    "A" Line in rear of Battalion.
    1 Limber S. A. A.                4 Lewis Gun Limbers.
    1 Limber Grenades.               2 Limbers Tools,
    "B" Line in rear of Bde. H. Qr. Transports.
    2 Limbers S. A. A.               4 Field Kitchens.
    2 Watercarts.                    1 Maltese Cart.
    1 Officers Mess Cart.

3. **Discipline.**

    Particular attention will be paid to general march discipline, calling to attention before halts, keeping to right of road, equipment correct, brakesmen only behind wagons, chimneys of travelling kitchens to be properly stayed.

4. **Blankets, &c.**

    Blankets will be rolled in bundles of 10 and stacked ready for loading at 6-0 pm.
    Officers valises will be stacked ready for loading near old Q. Mrs. stores at 7-0 p.m.

5. **Billeting Party.**

    2nd. Lieut. B. FREEDMAN and 2 N. C. Os. will proceed as Billeting party by cycle in advance and will report to TOWN MAJOR EQUANCOURT.

6. **Rations.**

    Breakfast will be ready at 2-0 a.m.
    Unexpended portion of days ration will be carried on the man.

7. **Leave.**

    Party proceeding on leave on the 19th will remain at VILLERS FAUCON and report to Lieut. BUTTERWORTH at a time to be notified later. Parties proceeding on leave on the 20th & 21st. will proceed on Motor Lorries from EQUANCOURT to PERONNE on the afternoon of the 20th.

18/5/17.

(Sd.) O. J. Sutton,
Capt. & A/Adjt.
1/9th Bn. Manchester Regt.

Copies 6 & 7.
War Diary.

Copy No... 6.

Vol XXII. App. 9.

1/9th Bn. Manchester Regt. Order No. 10.

In the Field,
21st. May 1917.

1. The Battalion will relieve the 11th Rifle Brigade in the Reserve line to-day.
March via ROYAULCOURT to MILL FARM, P.24.b.5.9. "A" Coy. will pass the Starting Point, P. 8. a. 4. 8. Cross Roads at 3-15 p.m. followed by other Companies at 100 yards distance. Lewis Gun Limbers will follow their Companies. Tool Limbers, S. A. A., Cookers and Water Carts will follow behind Battalion.
Coy. Commdrs. will enquire for guides in accordance with allotment of Companies as per para. 1. Battalion Orders No. 55 d/20/5/17.
"B" Coy. 1/9th Bn. Manchr. Rgt. to relieve "D" Coy. 11th R. Bde.
"C" " " " " " " "C" " "
"D" " " " " " " "A" " "
"A" " " " " " " "B" " "

O. C. Advance party has been instructed to arrange for guides for Watercarts and Cookers which will be met at MILL FARM.

Dress:- Groundsheets will be worn under the flap of the haversack. Greatcoats rolled en Banderolle, passed round haversack and fastened tightly with valise strap.

2. Transport.
Transport Officer will arrange for accommodation of Horses, either in METZ or HAVRINCOURT Wood or both.

3. Tents.
Tents used by Companies in BERTINCOURT will be struck and handed in to TOWN MAJOR by 2-0 p.m.

(Sd.) O. J. Sutton,
Captain & A/Adjt.
1/9th Bn. Manchester Regt.

Distribution:-
Copies 1-4 Coys.
5 C. O.
6-7 War Diary.
Issued by Orderly at.....

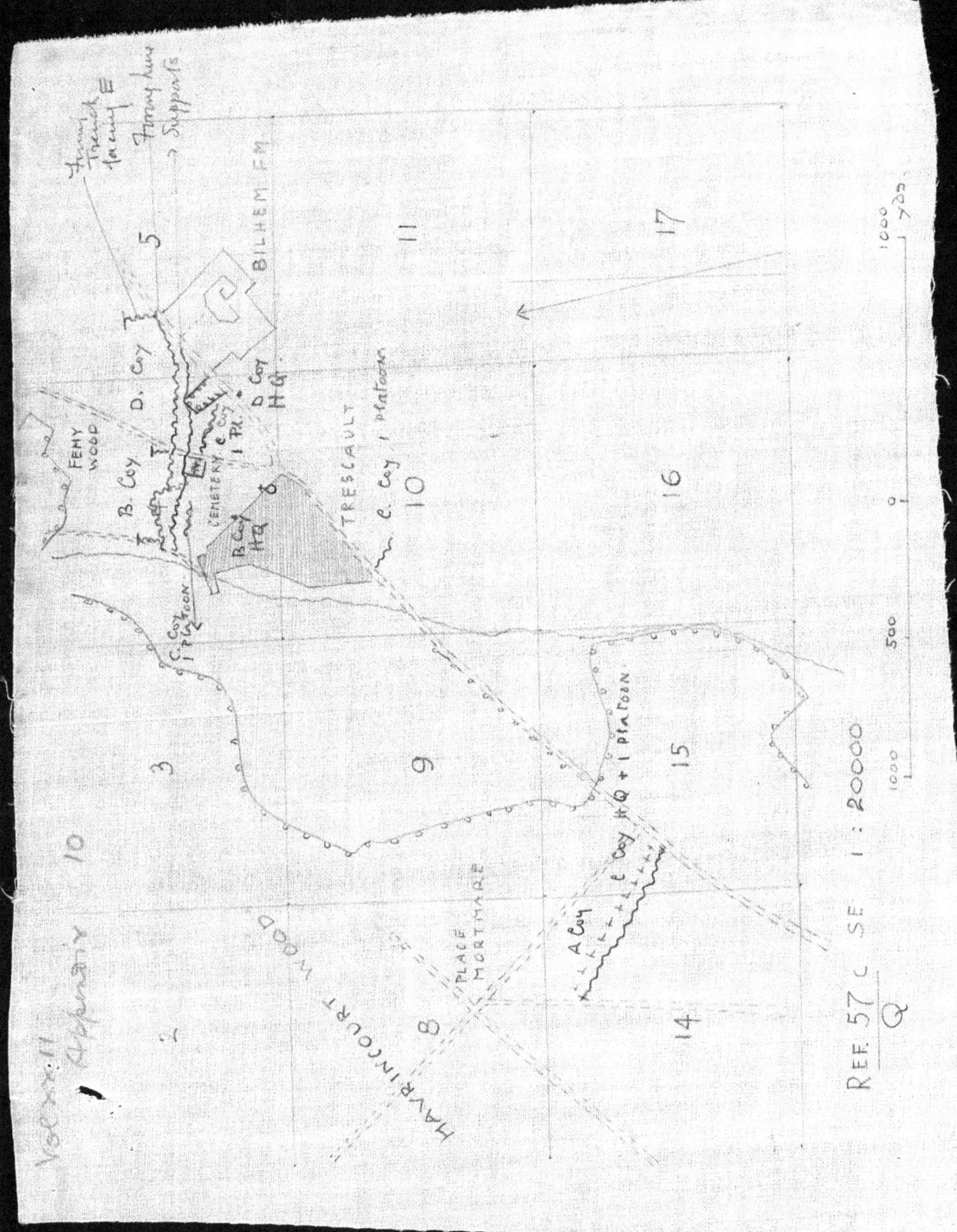

1/9th. BN. MANCHESTER REGT. ORDERS No. 11.

May 26th. 1917.                                         Copy No. 8

1. **RELIEFS.**   The Bn. will relieve B.126, in the left sub-sector this evening.
   "D" Coy. will make a preliminary relief of "B" Coy. D.126 in Q.15.a.5.4. to Q.15.b.0.4.   The Coy. will report to H.Q. D.126 at Q.15.c.4.8. at 2 p.m.
   Coys. of C.126 will relieve Coys. of B.126 of same letter.
   One platoon "C" Coy. will be in support on the right, and will be attached to "D" Coy.
   One platoon "C" Coy. will be in support on the left, and will be attached to "B" Coy.

2. **GUIDES.**   Five Guides ( 1 Coy H.Q., 1 per platoon per Coy.) B.126 will be at entrance of main road METZ - TRESCAULT into HAVRINCOURT WOOD at 9 p.m.
   Each Coy. C.126 will leave 5 Guides at the same point to guide Coys. of B.126 to positions vacated by us. These guides will be instructed to take Coys. B.126 as follows:—

   Guides "A" Coy. C.126 to take "A" Coy. B.126.
      "  "B"  "    "   "  "  "B"  "    "
      "  "C"  "    "   "  "  "D"  "    "
      "  "D"  "    "   "  "  "C"  "    "

3. **TOOLS and TRENCH STORES.**   Each Coy. will take its establishment of tools.   It will hand over all trench stores to the advance parties of B.126.   S.A.A., Bombs, etc., will be taken over from B.126.
   Bn.H.Q. will take the remainder of the Bn. establishment of tools.
   "B" & "D" Coys. will take with them 25 petrol tins, 17 for the trenches and 8 for the Cookers.   "D" Coy. will make up its numbers from "A" Coy.,- "B" Coy. if necessary, from "C" Coy.
   "A" Coy. will return to R.E's all tools, shovels, borrowed from them on the 23rd inst.

4. **COOKERS.**   The Cookers of "B" & "D" Coys. will remain Left of the Fork Roads Q.10.a.4.4.
   The Cookers of "A" & "C" Coys. will remain near their Coy. H.Q.
   Cooking for forward Coys. should commence about 6 p.m.

5. **WATER CARTS.**   Water Carts will proceed to forward Companies after dark, will go into TRESCAULT as far as the SECOND Crater where water bottles and petrol tins will be filled; they will then return to the Fork Roads Q.10.a.4.4. where Cookers will be filled; they will return to refill at 12 Midnight.
   One water cart when filled will then proceed to "A" Coy.H.Q. for use of "A" & "C", and the other to Bn.H.Q.
   They will return to refill at 9 a.m. returning to "A" Coy. & Bn. H.Q. respectively, about 12 Noon.

6. **RATIONS.**   Ration Limbers for "B" & "D" will reach Fork Roads about 10 p.m., will offload meat rations at Cookers, and then proceed to SECOND Crater in TRESCAULT.

7. **REPORTS etc.**   Completion of reliefs will be reported to Bn. H.Q. Copies of receipts for trench stores will be sent to Bn. H.Q. as soon as possible.

DISTRIBUTION :-                                   (Sd) O.J.Sutton, Capt &
Copies 1 - 4   Coys.                                                A/Adjt.
       5   C.O.                           1/9th. Bn. Manchester Regt.
       6   Qr.Mr.
  7 - 8   War Diary
       9   B.126
     10   File.

Vol XXII
APPENDIX 12                                    Copy No. 6

## 1/9th. Bn. MANCHESTER REGT. ORDERS. No. 12.

Reference Map :- 57.c. S.E.1/20,000 .           May 30th,1917 .

1. **RELIEF** .   1 Platoon "C" Coy. 1/9th. Bn. Manchester Regt. will relieve a Platoon of "A" Coy. 1/10th. Bn. Manchester Regiment, in section of Reserve trench ( about 50 yards ) running S.E. from Cross Roads in Q.16.d.4.4. on the night of 30/31st, May .

2. **GUIDE** .   A guide from this platoon of "A" Coy. 1/10th. Bn. Manchester Regt. will be sent by the officer in charge, - 2/Lieut. HORSFALL, to bifurcation of the road at Q. 15.a.7.5. at 10 p.m.

3. **TRENCH STORES** . Receipts for trench stores will be given to the Officer being relieved.   Copy of these receipts will be forwarded to Battalion Headquarters immediately after relief .   A certificate of cleanliness will be given to the officer relieved .

4. **COMPLETION OF RELIEF** . Completion of relief will be sent to Battalion H. Q., immediately after relief is completed .

5. **RATIONS, etc** .   This platoon of "C" Coy. will be attached to "D" Coy. for rations, water and for use of Field Kitchens.
   Arrangements will be made to take up an extra tank for the Field Kitchen, if required .
   Extra petrol tins will be taken up , if available .

                                                (Sd). S.J. Sutton,
                                                     Captain,
                                                     A/Adjt,
                                                1/9th.Bn. Manchester R.

DISTRIBUTION :-
   1 - 4.   O's C. Coys.
       5.   1/10th.Man. R.
   6 - 7.   War Diary .
       8.   File .

Issued by ............at    p.m.

1/9 Manchester Regt.

Casualty List for May 1917

| Killed | | Wounded | | Died of Wounds | |
|---|---|---|---|---|---|
| Officers | Other ranks | Officers | Other ranks | Officers | Other ranks |
| 1 | 13 | — | 18 | 1 | 4 |
| (a) | | | (b) | (b) | |

(a) Lieut. P.S. MARSDEN 30-5-17.
(b) " C.E. COOKE (Died in Hospital 24-5-17)

1/6/17

R Lloyd
Lieut. Colonel,
Comdg. 1/9 Bn Manchester Regiment

SECRET.

Vol 5

Cover for Documents.

War Diary.
1/9th MANCHESTER REGT.

June 1917

Vol. XXIII.

# WAR DIARY or INTELLIGENCE SUMMARY

Army Form C. 2118.

Ref Map 20,000 57 c SE / 57 c NE  19 Manchester Regt  Vol XXIII

| Place | Date | Hour | Summary of Events and Information | Remarks and references to Appendices |
|---|---|---|---|---|
| HAVRINCOURT WOOD Q.14.d.19 | May 1/2 | | Work continued on new trenches in front of our line. On the centre trench a new T head dug & advanced about 70 yards further out. 2/Lt CLARKE goes out to listen at Q FERNY WOOD & attempts stopped by being prevented by enemy fire. | |
| Q.15.a.07 | June 2 | 10 am | Bn HQ transfers to our position about Q.15.a.07 | |
| | June 2/3 | 6 pm | Scouts attempt to reach FERNY WOOD from right. Get as far as from right, to return. They succeed by crawling from old German Pdr about 200 yards short of western support trench. 2/Lt Peyton (12th R.S.L) & 2/Lt G. GRAY go out & throw 9.30 & occupy post 80 yards from FERNY WOOD. 2/Lt PEYTON comes in (2/Lt GRAY MISSING) about 2 am. Rest of patrol comes in 10/K safe. | Appendix 1 Sp. Order |
| Q.15.a.07 | June 3 | | 2/Lt H.E. BUTTERWORTH returns from leave to U.K. | |
| RUYAULCOURT | June 3 / 4 | 5 6 | Work continued as supra. 2/Lt MILLS takes forward party from Bn major Suttrn arrive at RUYAULCOURT from en route B.E.F. 2 AM Bn in tents outside RUYAULCOURT. Battalion rested. | Appendix 2 |

A5834 Wt. W4973/M687 750,000 8/16 D. D. & L. Ltd. Forms/C.2118/13.

Army Form C. 2118.

# WAR DIARY
## or
## INTELLIGENCE SUMMARY.
*(Erase heading not required.)*

1/9 Manchester Regt. Vol XXIII Page y.

Instructions regarding War Diaries and Intelligence Summaries are contained in F. S. Regs., Part II. and the Staff Manual respectively. Title pages will be prepared in manuscript.

MAP 57c S.E. 1/20000

| Place | Date | Hour | Summary of Events and Information | Remarks and references to Appendices |
|---|---|---|---|---|
| RUYAULCOURT P15 & 98 | 7 June | | Whole battalion on working parties. | |
| " | 8 | | B. C. & D. on working parties. A fatigue party in second line HAVRINCOURT WOOD | |
| " | 9 | | do | |
| " | 10 | | FATHER BULLOCK reports as R.C. Chaplain. A fatigue party on working parties. A fatigue party moves into second line left sector. Capt F.W. KERSHAW proceeds on leave. Gun Course to LE TOUQUET. 2/Lt PICKFORD do | APPENDIX III November 13 |
| " | 11 | | B.C. & D. on working parties. L/Cpl LILLIE attached to 126 Brigade Head Quarters. | |
| HAVRINCOURT WOOD P18A 73 | 12 | | B.C. & D. move into intermediate line night sector A move into second line night sector A Battn.H.Q. at Q18d 73 A Coy H.Q. " Q18d 45 B " " Q15a 45 C " " Q14a 95 D " " Q8d 62 | APPENDIX IV Operation Order 14 |
| " | 12/13 | | LT SMATHWAIT proceed to 42 Divisional Gas School as Instructor. 80 men preparing working parties METZ-TRESCAULT road 100 men digging ammunition trench METZ-TRESCAULT road Q9d - Q10a 2/Lt A. GRAY proceeds 3days leave to PARIS Working parties on communication trench METZ-TRESCAULT road | |
| " | 13/14 | | 2/Lt W.N.B. BURY rejoins Bgion from course 2/Lt G.E. RODMELL rejoins Bgion from course | |

Army Form C. 2118.

# WAR DIARY
## or
## INTELLIGENCE SUMMARY.
*(Erase heading not required.)*

1/9th Manchester Regt. Vol XVIII
Part 3

| Place | Date | Hour | Summary of Events and Information | Remarks and references to Appendices |
|---|---|---|---|---|
| HAVRINCOURT WOOD P18 & 13 | 15 June 1917 | | Capt REDMOND proceeds U.K. on 10 days Leave | APPENDIX 5. (Nos 1-15) |
| | 16 | | Relieved by 1/4 E.L. Regt. go into billets at YTRES | |
| YTRES P 26 a | 17 | | Church parade. Presentation of MILITARY MEDAL to Corpl EASTWOOD by MAJOR GENERAL MITFORD. 2/LT GREENWOOD proceeds 42nd DIV. Bombing School BUS. 2/LT D NEEDHAM rejoins from course. | |
| " | 18 | | Battalion in training 2/LT CAREY rejoins from hospital CAPT. O.J. SUTTON rejoins from leave to U.K. | |
| " | 19 | | 2/LT. A. GRAY rejoins from leave to PARIS A + B on rifle range YTRES P19b C + D training | |

Army Form C. 2118.

# WAR DIARY
## or
## INTELLIGENCE SUMMARY. 1/9 MANCHESTER RGT.

(Erase heading not required.)

Instructions regarding War Diaries and Intelligence Summaries are contained in F. S. Regs., Part II. and the Staff Manual respectively. Title pages will be prepared in manuscript.

Ref Map. 1/20,000.
57 C SE
57 C NE

Vol XXIII
Page 4

| Place | Date | Hour | Summary of Events and Information | Remarks and references to Appendices |
|---|---|---|---|---|
| YPRES | Jan 20 | | Battn training near Gillets. | O/C |
| " | Jan 21 | | 2 Lt E. TONER proceeds on short leave to U.K. | G/S |
| " | Jan 21 | 22 | Bn relieves 1/4 E LANCS RGT. as Regtl Reserve Battalion in HAVRINCOURT WOOD. Bn Headquarters Q 18 d 7.3. A Coy & C Coy Q 1 d & Q 6 d in camp. B & D Coy in INTERMEDIATE LINE, Q 6 d. All coys on working parties at night. B & D Coys and tracting front gn Enemy Rble. C Coy digging in FRITH ALLEY, Q 18 d 4.3. A Coy digging communication trench Q 2 d. | APPENDIX 6 O.N°15ᴿ G/S |
| HAVRINCOURT WOOD Q 18 d 7.3 | Jan 22 | | Capt F.H. KERSHAW and 2Lt PICKFORD & 2Lt H.DOTTERWORTH return from Course of Instruction. Report to scene of instruction. | G/S |
| " | Jan 22 | 23 | 3 Coys working on trenchwork in RAZOOZA AVENUE, Q 4 C 4.7 to Q 3 d 4.3. from 9.30 pm to 3 am. | |

# WAR DIARY or INTELLIGENCE SUMMARY

Army Form C. 2118.

19th Manchester Regt.
Vol XXVI
Page 5

| Place | Date | Hour | Summary of Events and Information | Remarks and references to Appendices |
|---|---|---|---|---|
| Q.16.d.10.70 | 23rd April 1917 | | Working parties continuing the trench [illegible]. Intense bombardment of enemy lines & CRITH [?] | Appendix 7. |
| | 24/25 | | Some hostile shelling of [illegible] positions during night. Enemy's front line to line Q.26. | @ S.O.O N°16 |
| | 25.26 | | Battalion relieved 1/5 East Lancs for a Right Outpost Batln. (relieving men of the Battalion at 1 hr. on 2 Bttns May 25-27) | @ G1 |
|  |  | | Dispositions of Coys: C, B, D in front line to [illegible] in support, A in reserve | @ G1 |
| | | | [illegible lines about trenches and operations] Lent HARTSHORN wounded & Cpl CROWE sent to Hospital. | @ G1 |
| | 26th | | Sick Casualties 21 [illegible] wind head ([illegible] MORRISON 3) = | |
| | | | on joining the Batln Officer Lieuts MARSH + BULL + | @ G1 |
| | | | Improving Saps B + C. Sent out patrols with a view to learn enemy positions. Also S/L 2/Lt BOOTH | @ G1 |
| | 27/5 | | Work carried on Saps [illegible] No 4 out 2 Patrols from Coys of 3 mn. | @ G1 |
| | | | 2/Lt HAUTTSMORTH returns from Course of Instruction | |

S.O.O N°17

Army Form C. 2118.

# WAR DIARY
## or
## INTELLIGENCE SUMMARY.
(Erase heading not required.)

Army Form C. 2118.

Ref M/AP/1/20,000  1/2 MANCHESTER REGT  Vol XXII
57 c NE                                   Page 6
57 b SE

| Place | Date | Hour | Summary of Events and Information | Remarks and references to Appendices |
|---|---|---|---|---|
| Gun-e-26/37/38/39 DK076 | | | Work of digging parties. Journey of fire covering & drawing carrying fatigue patrols. Drawing telecomms 5 roads energy gas sheets buy carried. | Appendix 9 Scheme war |
| | June 30/11 | | During last 3 enemy seeming Sunday and front line sweep up rifle fire at first the while fore. No Minenwerfer Patrol issued to No N.M.L. no injury. anti-craft fire of 1/10 Manual milling Class A.5 (NBN 653). Night quiet, all posts moving bottom answer. | APPENDIX 1 History plot |

R. Wind
Major
Comd 1/2 Manchester Regt

Vol XXIII, Appendix 1.

S P E C I A L   O R D E R ,
BY
Lieut.-Colonel, E.C. LLOYD,
Commanding, 1/9th. Bn. MANCHESTER REGT.

In the Field,
3rd. June 1917.

The Major General wishes to congratulate the Scouts and Platoon of "B" Company for their work last night.

(Sd.) O.J. Sutton,
Capt. & A/Adjt.,
1/9th. Bn. Manchester Regt.

VOL XXIII  Appendix 2
COPY No...9...

1/9th. Bn. MANCHESTER REGT. ORDER No. 32.

Map Reference – 57.c.S.E., 1/20,000.    June 5th.1917.

**RELIEF.** The Battalion will be relieved in the right battalion sub-sector, on night of 5/6th. June , by 1/7th. Bn. Lancashire Fusiliers .

After relief the platoons will march independently to RUYAULCOURT, via southern edge of HAVRINCOURT WOOD .

Guides will meet platoons at cross roads at entrance to RUYAULCOURT , P.10.c.9.5. at 2-0 a.m., 6th inst. , to guide platoons to their billets .

Officers chargers for "B" and "D" Coys. will be at Q.15. c.2.9. at 12 midnight ; for "A" & "C" Coys. at Company Hd. Qrs. at 11-0 p.m.

**GUIDES.** 4 Guides per Company will meet relieving Companies at cross roads Q.15 c.2.9., at 10-0 p.m.

In addition one guide from both "B" & "D" Coys. will meet Cookers of "A", "B" & "D" Coys. 1/7th.Bn. Lancashire Fusiliers , at the same place and time to guide Cookers, Ration Carts to Fork Roads TRESCAULT. and 1 guide from "A" Coy. to meet Cooker of "C" Coy. 1/7th.Bn. Lancashire Fusiliers , to guide it to Coy. H.Q.

**TOOLS .** Each Company will hand over the tools it took over , limbers for "B", "C" & "D" Coys. will be at cross roads in TRESCAULT at 10-0 p.m.; for "A" Coy. at Company H.Q. at 9-30 p.m.

**TRENCH STORES .** All trench stores including trench sketches, air photos, defence scheme and instructions re. work policy will be handed over.

"B" & "D" Coys. will also hand over all petrol tins surplus to 25 each .

Receipts for the whole will be obtained , and forwarded to Battn. H.Q. at RUYAULCOURT , by 12 Noon , 6th inst .

**LEWIS GUN LIMBERS .** Lewis Gun limbers for "B" "C" & "D" Coys. will be at first cross roads, TRESCAULT at 10-0 p.m., for "A" Coy. at Company Hd. Qrs. at 9-30 p.m.

A guide will be sent by O.'s C. Companies to each Lewis Gun limber, who will remain with it until arrival at RUYAULCOURT .

**COOKERS .** Teams for Cookers will be at cross roads TRESCAULT for "B" & "D" Coys. at 10-0 p.m., for "A" & "C" Coys. at 9-30 p.m. at Company Hd. Qrs.

**SANITATION .** Usual certificate of cleanliness will be obtained from relieving unit, and forwarded to Battn. H.Q. by 12 Noon, 6th inst .

**BILLETING .** 1 officer & 20 other ranks from "A" Coy. will proceed to RUYAULCOURT on 5th inst, as billeting party . The Officer will report to Battn. H.Q. at 1-0 p.m. for instructions .

**WATER .** All water carts will be filled at YTRES at P.33. C.. and all horses and mules will water at P.33.C.

**TRANSPORT .** All horses and mules will remain at YTRES, in Brigade Transport Lines .

**RATIONS .** Rations for 6th inst will be taken to RUYAULCOURT, and dumped there under charge of Coy. Q.M.S's prior to move .

**DISTRIBUTION :-**
```
 1 - 4  to Coys.                                (Sd.) Wm.G. Whitney,
 5 - 6  CO/Qr.Mr.                                    2/Lieut. for Adjt.
    7   1/7th. L.F.                            1/9th. Bn. Manchester Regt.
 8 - 9  War Diary.
   10.  File .
```

Vol XXIII Appendix 3.

1/9th. Bn. Manchester Rgt.

Move Orders No. 13.

By Lieut-Col. E.C. LLOYD. Commanding 1/9th Bn. Manchester Rgt.

In the Field.
10-6-17.

**Para 1. Move.** "A" Coy will move into the second line as part of permanent garrison to-day.
They will be responsible for line between F12.c.8.4. to Division left boundary of the canal J36a00.
1 Coy of 1/16th Bn. Manchester Rgt. will be on their right.

**Para 2. Parade.** Coy will move off at 5-30 p.m.

**Para 3. Limber.** Limber for Lewis Gun and tools will be at "A" Coy at 4p.m.

**Para 4. Cookers.** "A" Coy will take their Cooker, team for which will arrive at 4 p.m.

**Para 5. Rations.** O.C. "A" Coy will leave guides behind for water cart and ration limbers.

**Para 6. Work.** The Company will be employed on constructing iron shelters in or near the second line.

DISTRIBUTION :-
1 Copy to "A" Coy.
1 " " Qr.Mr./T.O.
2 " " War Diary.
1 " " File.

(Sd.) Wm. W. Quinney, 2/Lieut,
for A/Adjutant,
1/9th. Bn. Manchester Regt.

Vol. XXIII War Diary Appendix 4

1/9th. Bn. MANCHESTER REGT. ORDER No. 14.

Copy No ........

12th. June 1917.

**MOVE.** The 1/9th. Bn. Manchester Regt. ( less "A" Coy. ) will move into HAVRINCOURT WOOD to-day, June 12th.1917 , taking over accommodation vacated by the 1/7th. Bn. Lancashire Fusiliers and will become Brigade Reserve, 125th Infantry Brigade .

Each Company will take over from company of same letter of the 1/7th. Lancashire Fusiliers .

"A" COY. will take over from Coy. of 1/10th Battn. Manchester Regiment on its right in second line .
O.C. "A" Coy. will make all arrangements .

Battn. Hd. Qrs. will be at P.18.d.7.3.

**PARADE.**
"D" Coy. will parade at 6-0 p.m.
"B" " " " " 6-30 p.m.
"C" " " " " 7-0 p.m.
Bn. HQ. " " " 7-30 p.m.

All will march independantly to their positions .

**LIMBERS.** Limbers for Lewis Guns and Tools will be at Coy. Hd. Qrs. at 5-15 p.m.

**DRESS.** Packs will be worn with great coats bandolier fashion round packs .

**COOKERS.** Cookers will be taken up by their Coys.

**WATER CARTS.** One water cart will go with "B" Coy . and will supply "B" & "D" Coys. One will remain at Battn. H.Q. and will supply Bn. H.Q., "A" Coy. & "C" Coy .

**VALISES.** Valises will be taken .

**RATIONS.** All Coys. will send a guide to new Battn. H.Q. at P.18.d.7.3. to guide ration limbers to their Coys .

**TRENCH STORES.** Receipts for Trench Stores to be sent to Battn. H.Q. as soon as possible .

(Wm.W. Quinney, 2/Lieut.,
A/Adjutant ,
1/9th. Bn. Manchester Regt .

DISTRIBUTION . :-

Copies 1 to 4   Coys.
        5       T.O. & Qr.Mr.
    6 - 7       War Diary.
        8       File .

Vol XXIII   Appendix 5

## 1/9th. Bn. MANCHESTER REGT. ORDER No. 15.

Copy No. 7

16th. June, 1917.

---

**RELIEF.**  The Battalion will be relieved by the 1/4th. Battalion East Lancashire Regiment, about 5 p.m. this afternoon. 16th inst.
After relief, the platoons will march independently to Billets at YPRES, being met there by their C.Q.M.S.
Officers chargers will be at Bn. H.Q., and all Coy.H.Q. by 4 p.m.

**TOOLS.**  Each Company will bring out its own tools.

**TRENCH STORES.**  All trench stores will be handed over, and receipts obtained which will be forwarded to Battalion Hd. Qrs. as soon as possible.

**LIMBERS.**  Limbers for Lewis Guns, Tools etc., will be Coy. Hd.Qrs' at 4 p.m.

**COOKERS.**  Immediately after mid-day meal, Cookers and Water Carts will proceed to YPRES, and evening meal will be served on arrival of Companies.

**SANITATION.**  The usual certificates of cleanliness will be obtained from relieving unit, and forwarded to Battn. Hd. Qrs. as soon as possible.
All open latrines must be filled in.

**WORKING PARTIES.**  All instructions re. working parties will be handed over, and all permanent working parties will finish with shift ending 4 p.m. to-day.

DISTRIBUTION :-
Copies No. 1 - 4   Coys.
           5       Qr.Mr./T.O.
        6 - 7      War Diary.
           8       File.

(Sd.) Wm W. Quinney,
2/Lieut. for Adjutant,
1/9th. Bn. Manchester Regt.

Vol XXIII Appendix 6

1/9th Bn. Manchester Regt Orders No 15A    Copy No 8
June 20/1917

1. **RELIEF** The Battalion will relieve the 4th Bn East Lancashire Regt as the Right Reserve Battalion tomorrow.
   Relief to be completed by 6 pm.

2. **DISTRIBUTION** "B" & "D" Coys will relieve "B" & "D" Coys of 4th Bn East Lancashire Regt respectively in the Intermediate Line. "A" & "C" Coys will proceed to Q 14.a., and take over tents occupied by them when last in the Right Reserve. O.C. Coys will proceed to the Line tomorrow morning, and will guide their Coys when relief takes place.

3. **MOVE** Coys. will move off at the following times :—
   "D" Coy 3 pm     "B" Coy 3-15 pm     "C" Coy 3-30 pm
   "A" Coy 3-45 pm     Bn. Hd Qrs at 4 pm.
   Each Coy. will take its Field Kitchen, Lewis Gun Limber and 1 Limber for Tools and Officers Valises. These will move behind the Coys.

4. **DRESS.** Fighting Kit. Greatcoats rolled and fastened on belt.

5. **ROUTE** Generating Station P.27.a NEUVILLE — MILL FARM.

6. **PACKS** etc. Packs and superfluous kit will be dumped at Qr. Mr. Stores during the morning
   "A" Coy. 10 a.m.     "B" Coy. 10.30 am
   "C" Coy. 11 am     "D" Coy. 11.30 am.
   Bn. H.Q. 12 Noon.

7. **TRANSPORT.** Ride horses, Field Cookers, Lewis Gun Limbers, and one limber for Tools and Officers Valises will report to Coys. at the following times :—
   "D" & "B" Coys at 2-30 p.m.     "A" & "C" Coys at 3 pm
   2 G.S. Wagons, two limbers, Mess cart, and Medical cart will report at Bn H Qrs at 3 pm
   Ride Horses of C.O. & Adjutant will be at Bn H Q. at 3-30 pm.
   Ride Horses of C.O., 2nd in Command & Adjutant also 5 teams of 1 limbers will remain in HAVRINCOURT WOOD near Bn H.Q. under Transport N.C.O.

8. **WATER CART.** One water cart will be stationed at "A" Coy. for use of "A" & "C" Coys. and Bn H.Q. and one water cart at "D" Coy. for use of "B" & "D" Coys

(Continued)

## Battalion Orders (Continued) 2

**Watercarts**
(Continued) They will refill at METZ between the following hours:- 6-0 am to 7-0 am, 10 to 11 am and 4-0 to 5-0 pm.

9. **GUARD.** "C" Coy will relieve guard at Bde H Q at Q.14.d. at 6 pm 21st inst.

 O.C "C" Coy will ascertain number of men required for this guard.

10. **MARCH DISCIPLINE.** Strict attention must be paid to march discipline, and the saluting of General Officers.

 Attention is directed to Battn Orders No 64. dated 4-6-17 para. 8. Saluting.

 Correct intervals between platoons will be maintained.

11. **DUTIES.** Lieut. RUTTENAU will supervise the working of the Baths at METZ and look after the Brigade's interests at the METZ Well. The Baths are allotted to the 49th Battalion Manchester Regt. from 9 am to 1-0 pm on Tuesdays and Fridays and 8 am to 1-0 pm on other days.

 The R.S.M. will arrange to have a policeman on duty at METZ Well from 3-30 am to 8 pm daily to regulate traffic.

12. **TRENCH STORES.** Copies of receipts for trench stores will be sent to Bn H.Q. by 8 pm on the 21st inst.

13. **BATHS.** Baths at METZ will be allotted to "A" Coy from 9 to 11 am on the 22nd inst, and "B" Coy from 11 am to 1 pm. Clean clothing will be supplied at the Baths.

DISTRIBUTION:-
Copy No 1 - 4 Coys
5 T.O / A.M.
6 - 7 War Diary
8 File.

(Sd) O J Sutton
Captain, A/Adjutant
49th Bn Manchester Regt.

SECRET      1/9th Bn. Manchester Regt. Order No. 16     Vol XXIII Appendix 7.

24 June 1917                                                Copy No. 8

1. **Relief.** The Battalion will relieve the 1/4th Bn. East Lancashire Regt. in the right Bn. Sector on the night of the 25th/26th. Distribution as follows:- Front line from right to left 'C', 'A', 'D' Coys. Support Coy. 'B' Coy.    Bn. H.Q. 'C' about Q.4.d.7.2. (where 'D' Coy. was previously) 'A' Coy. in old firing line about Q.4.d.3.7. 'D' Coy. about Q.4.c.9.3. (where 'B' Coy. was previously.) 'B' Coy. near Q.4.a.4.4.

2. **Advance Party.** Advance party of 1 Officer per Coy. 1 N.C.O. per platoon, and 1 man per Lewis Gun will proceed to the line tonight, meeting guides at Cross Roads G.10.a.4.4. at 10 p.m. tonight. Coys. will relieve Coys. of the 1/5th East Lancs. Regt. of the same letter.

3. **Guides.** One guide per Coy. of 1/9th Bn. Manchester Regt. will be sent to Bde H.Q. for Advance parties of 1/5th East Lancashire Regt. at 11 a.m. tomorrow.
Tomorrow night, Companies of the 1/9th Bn. Manchester Regt. will meet guides at Cross Roads at 10.30 p.m. in the following order 'B' 'D' 'A' 'C'.

4. **Cookers.** Two Cookers only will be taken up. 'B' Coys. Cookers for the use of 'B' & 'A' Coys. 'D' Coy. will use its own cookers, and 'C' Coy. will use open fire-places constructed by the 1/5th Bn. East Lancashire Regt.

5. **Route.** Parties moving up to TRESCAULT should use the C.T. commencing near the threshing machine on the right of the METZ-TRESCAULT Road.

Further orders will be issued tomorrow.

                                             C.J. Stubbs
                                             Captain, Adjutant,
                                             1/9th Bn. Manchester Regiment.

SECRET                    VOL XXIII — APP. 8.
                                    Vol XXIII.

                1/9 Bn. Manchester Regt. Order No 17.

25th June 1917.                              Copy No 8

**1. Relief** — The 1/9th Bn Manchester Regt will relieve the
4/5 Bn East Lancashire Regt, in the front line
tonight, commencing at 10-30 pm.

**2. Distribution** — As stated in Order No 16.

**3. Guides** — 1 guide per platoon and 1 guide per Lewis
Gun from the 4/5 Bn East Lancs Regt will
meet Coys at Cross Roads Q.10.a.4.4. at 10-30pm
Coys will move to Trescault in the following
order B.D.A.C.

**4. Cookers** — B and D Coy cookers will remain in
TRESCAULT. Cookers from A + C Coys will
deposit the dannekins at the cross roads in
TRESCAULT and then return to Battn H. Qrs.

**5. Water Carts** — 1 Water cart will remain near cross roads
in TRESCAULT. and will be relieved by full
water cart each night. One water cart will be at
Bn H. Qrs

**6. Transport** — Teams for cookers, Lewis Gun limbers, 1 limber for
each Coy. for tools etc will report at Coys at
9-30 pm to night

**7. Valises** — Officers valises will be returned to Dump at YTRES
this morning

**8. Returns** — Situation Reports 3 am and 3 pm.
S.A.A Expended 7 pm.
Estimated Casualties 3 pm
Casualty Return. 7 am.
Work Report. 7 am.

**9. Command** — Lt SHATWELL will report to O.C.
C Coy. and take over command of
C Coy. after departure of Captain
HANDFORTH.


Distribution —:
    Copy 1-4 to Coys.
         5 Q.M./T.O.
         6. File
         7-8 War Diary

                            Captain a/a d/y.
                            1/9 Bn. Manchester Regt.

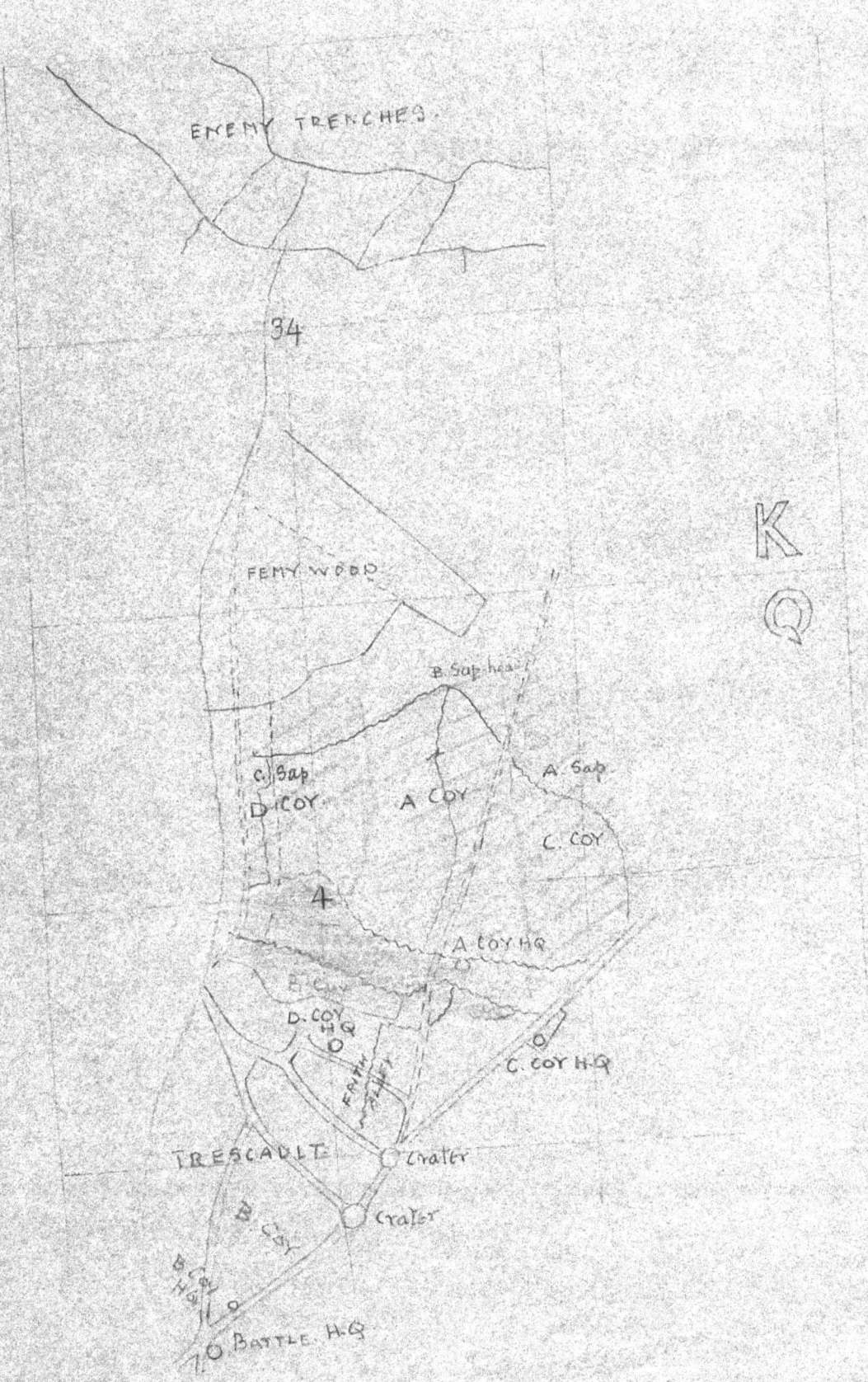

1/9th Bn. Manchester Regt.   VOL. XXIII  Appendix 10

## Casualty List for June 1917.

| KILLED | | WOUNDED | | DIED OF WOUNDS | |
|---|---|---|---|---|---|
| Officers | Other Ranks | Officers | Other Ranks | Officers | Other Ranks |
| — | 3 | 2 | 23 | — | 1 |

MAJOR T. E. HOWORTH. Wounded (Remaining at Duty)
2/Lieut GRAY. Wounded (Remaining at Duty)

30 June 1917

Commdg. 1/9th Bn. Manchester Regt.
Lieut Colonel

SECRET.

COVER FOR DOCUMENTS.

WAR DIARY
1/9TH MANCHESTER REGT.

July 1917

# WAR DIARY or INTELLIGENCE SUMMARY

Army Form C. 2118.

1/9 MANCHESTER REGT

Vol. XXIV.
Page 1.

| Place | Date | Hour | Summary of Events and Information | Remarks and references to Appendices |
|---|---|---|---|---|
| Q.18.d.7.5 Q.10.a.4.4 | July 1 | | Ref Map FRANCE 1/20,000 57 c NE, 57 c SE. Battn. Advance Headquarters at Q.10.a.4.4. Rear Headquarters in HARINCOURT WOOD Q.18.d.7.3. Lieut. & Adm. W. TARREY taken on strength 14/1/3. Capt T.G. HYDE relinquished appointment of Acting Q M R 30/6/17. 2/Lt GREENWOOD rejoins from 42nd Div. Bombing School, BUS. Revd. CAPT. C. BULLOCK, C.F. proceeds on attachment to 1/10 Manch R. Capt. RAYMOND attached to 1/9 MANCH R. Patrols sent out at night. | OP |
| " | July 2 | | 2/Lt M.L. PICKFORD to 210 Battery for attachment for 48 hours. Gas Shell bombardment of C Post (D Coy Capt STEPHENSON). Reports 300 gas shells sent over. He was has been unable to expect a bombardment within minutes, retired to no damage made to one man who has his gas mask torn away by a fragment of shell. | OP |
| " | July 3 | | B post (B Coy Capt KERIHAN) shelled by T.M. Battery. 2/Lt D. FREEDMAN + 3 OR kills. 2/Lt WOODARY rejoins from hospital. | OP |

Army Form C. 2118.

# WAR DIARY
## or
## INTELLIGENCE SUMMARY.

1/9 MANCHESTER REGT
Page 2

(Erase heading not required.)

| Place | Date | Hour | Summary of Events and Information | Remarks and references to Appendices |
|---|---|---|---|---|
| Q10 c 44 July 3/4 | | Ref Map FRANCE 1/20000 57c NE 57 &S6 | False gas alarm from Battalion on right. B Post main shelled by T. Mortar. DRESLINCOURT shelled by 4.2's. 2/Lt FREEDMAN burried at ROYULCOURT (P10 a 97) | CR |
| " | July 5 | | 2/Lt E.E. TOWLER rejoins from Corps L.K. & is attached to B Coy. Preparations made for taking A, B + C posts on Platoon Localities | CR |
| " | July 5/6 | | Working parties wired in front of A B + C posts, and work carried out on the communication trench to these posts. | CR CR |
| " | July 6/7 | | C post & D Coy (C Coy Post + supports) relieved by two patrols 1/4 EAST LANCS. REGT. APPENDIX 1. B Coy take over A+B posts as platoon posts. A + C Coys Battalion in INTERMEDIATE LINE REDOUBTS, relieving one Coy. | O.O. 18 |
| | | 11.10 P.M. | MARCH R. Quiet night, nothing unusual took place on the post. | CR |
| | July 7 | | A + C Coy Arrival to Bells at METZ. Enemy artillery active on DRESLINCOURT + HAYRINCOURT WOOD. | CR |

Army Form C. 2118.

# WAR DIARY
## or
## INTELLIGENCE SUMMARY.

(Erase heading not required.)

1/9 MANCHESTER REGT
Vol XIV
Page 3

| Place | Date July | Hour | Summary of Events and Information | Remarks and references to Appendices |
|---|---|---|---|---|
| Q10a4.4 | 7/8/17 | 2.30am | Ref Map 1/40000 57c. B Coy relieves in front line by 2/9 & 2/10 LONDON REGT. A Coy relieved in INTERMEDIATE LINE by 2/10 Bn LONDON REGT. Baton entrains at R14.c.21.c. Decauville Railway, detrains at BUS (O 24) & marches to BARASTRE (O 16). 2/Lt R.F ROBINSON struck off strength of Battalion (Auth ATD/3417:3.8.17) | APPENDIX 1 O.O. 18 APPENDIX 2 O.O. # 20 |
| BARASTRE | 9 | | Battn marches to BIHUCOURT AREA (518 c.entral) & camps under tarpaulins & canvas. Very dirty camp. | APPENDIX 3 O.O. 21 + ADDENDUM. |
| BIHUCOURT | 10 | | 2/Lt T. AINSWORTH rejoins from hospital & reports to 126 Bde L.T.M. Battery for attachment. 2/Lt KNIGHT rejoins from being on Draw Keys to BARASTRE LE TRANSLOY. Battalion engaged in inspection of kit & in bathing parties. | |
| " | 11 | 10 am | Battalion marches to COURCELLES, via BAPAUME & passes not billets in a M.N. portion of village. Billets in general dirty, many requiring ingoin to roofs out doors. CAPT. KERSHAW proceeds on leave to U.K. 2/LT GREY to hospital sick 2/LT PICKFORD & Coms. g Bomb. Camp. KNIGHT LONGSET. 2/LT H.M.KNIGHT takes over command g MTS Coy. | APPENDIX 4 O.O. 22 |

# WAR DIARY
## INTELLIGENCE SUMMARY

1/8 MANCHESTER REGT

| Place | Date | Hour | Summary of Events and Information | Remarks |
|---|---|---|---|---|
| COURCELLES | July 12 | Ref Map 1/40,000 57c | Battn. engaged in training. | |
| " | | | 2/Lt WILLIS rejoins Battalion from 42nd Div. Cements Party. | GP |
| " | | | 2/Lt O.S. NEEDHAM to Transport Course, ABBEVILLE | |
| " | 13 | | Battalion Training. | |
| " | | | Lt SHATWELL on leave to U.K. | GP |
| " | 14 | | Section training. | |
| " | | | 2/Lt DUNLOP rejoins 42nd Div Bombing School from leave U.K. | |
| " | | | Brigade Competition for Transport & for turn out of platoon in fighting kit. | |
| " | | | Battn. won in both. | |
| " | | | Battalion inoculated for Para-Typhoid. | |
| " | | | Four to AMIENS granted, six Officers per week, 2 O.R. per day, all return same day as leave given. | GP |
| " | 15 | | No church parade since a recount of inoculation | GP |

Army Form C. 2118.

# WAR DIARY
## or
## INTELLIGENCE SUMMARY.
1/9 MANCHESTER REGT
heavy
Page 5

(Erase heading not required.)

| Place | Date | Hour | Summary of Events and Information | Remarks and references to Appendices |
|---|---|---|---|---|
| COURCELLES | 16 | | Ref Map 1/40,000 57 c Section & platoon training + ceremonial. | |
| | 17 | | Platoon training + musketry. 2/Lt N.H.NARY to leave U.K. Capt RAYMOND C.F. rejoin from 42nd division. | GP GP |
| | 18 | | 2/Lt PICKFORD rejoin from Sniping Course. 2/Lt JOYNER proceeds to Sniping Course. Lt.Col. E.C.LLOYD takes over command of 126 Bde. On during absence of Brigadier General to leave. Bn training during morning. Afternoon occupied by company sports + football matches against Bde HQrs + 1/10 MANCH R. | GP |
| | 19 | | Platoon training & musketry. | GP |

Army Form C. 2118.

# WAR DIARY
or
# INTELLIGENCE SUMMARY.

(Erase heading not required.)

HQ MANCHESTER REGT
Page 6

| Place | Date | Hour | Summary of Events and Information | Remarks and references to Appendices |
|---|---|---|---|---|
| COURCELLES | July 20 | | Ref Map 1/40,000 57c.<br>Company Training.<br>Major HOWARTH to leave U.K.<br>CAPT HYDE takes over command S/A Coy during absence of Major HOWARTH | G/S |
| " " | 21 | | Battalion Drill + Platoon Training. Company recreation during afternoon. | G/S |
| " " | 22 | | Church parade in Concert Hall, COURCELLES.<br>CAPT. KERSHAW rejoins from leave U.K.<br>LT AGRAI invalid Kinjant dies. | G/S |
| " " | 23 | | Company Training. | G/S |
| " " | 24 | | Company Training.<br>LT COL LLOYD rejoins from 12th Bn<br>LT SHATWELL rejoins from leave U.K. | G/S |

Army Form C. 2118.

# WAR DIARY
## or
## INTELLIGENCE SUMMARY.  1/9 Manchester Regt

*(Erase heading not required.)*

Page 7

| Place | Date | Hour | Summary of Events and Information | Remarks and references to Appendices |
|---|---|---|---|---|
| COURCELLES | July 25 | Ref. Map. 1/40,000 57c | Battalion training.<br>2Lt J CARREY & 2nd Bomb Bombing Course<br>2Lt TONER rejoins from 42nd Div Bombing Course.<br>CAPT. T.G HYDE to General Course of Instruction, GIVENCHY LE NOBLE<br>Battalion wins Brigade Football Competition. | O/S |
| " | 26 | | Company training.<br>2 Lt KNIGHT proceeds on leave U.K. | O/S |
| " | 27 | | Battalion & platoon training.<br>Lt-Col E. LLOYD & Lt-Col GARR to PARIS<br>Major R.S. Newell takes over temporary command of Battalion.<br>2Lt DALE proceeds on leave to U.K.<br>Battalion reinforced (2 of Base) | O/S |
| " | 28 | | Training suspended on account of inoculation.<br>Sergt. A 45 reinforcements arrive.<br>2Lt HADSBURY rejoins from leave U.K. | O/S |

Army Form C. 2118.

WE XXIV
1/9 Manchester Regt
Page 8

# WAR DIARY
## or
## INTELLIGENCE SUMMARY.

(Erase heading not required.)

Instructions regarding War Diaries and Intelligence Summaries are contained in F. S. Regs., Part II. and the Staff Manual respectively. Title pages will be prepared in manuscript.

| Place | Date | Hour | Summary of Events and Information | Remarks and references to Appendices |
|---|---|---|---|---|
| COURCELLES | July 29 | | Ref Map 40,000 57c<br>Brigade Church Parade cancelled on account of bad weather.<br>2 Lt F. BEARD departs on leave U.K.<br>2 Lt S RUTTENAU to Musketry School, MARLOY. | C/S |
| " | 30 | | Battalion & Company training. Company Scheme tactical scheme set by Brigadier.<br>M Col E. CLLOYD upon from leave to PARIS.<br>42nd Divisional Sports. Carried out. B.Coy Practice General DUFNOH. | C.P.<br>C/S |
| " | 31 | | Company in the attack; and Company training.<br>New Staff inspects by the General. | C/S<br><br>APPENDIX 5<br>CASUALTY REPORT. |

R. Munchester Regt
C.O.

Vol XXIV. Appendix 5

## 1/9th Bn. Manchester Regt.

### Casualty List for July 1917

| KILLED | | WOUNDED | | DIED OF WOUNDS | |
|---|---|---|---|---|---|
| Officers | Other Ranks | Officers | Other Ranks | Officers | Other Ranks |
| 1 (a) | 4 | — | 13 | — | 1 (Gas) |

(a) 2/Lt. B. Freedman (killed in action) 3-7-17

31-7-17.

R. Lloyd.
Lieut. Colonel
Commanding 1/9th Bn. Manchester Regt.

Copy No. 6

1/9th Bn Manchester Regt Order No. 18

July 5/1917          V BE XXIV APPENDIX 1

1. **RELIEF.** The Battalion is being relieved in the Line on the night of 7th/8th inst.

2. **ADJUSTMENT. 6th/7th.** On the night of 6th/7th, the following adjustments will be made:—

   'C' Post will be taken over by a platoon of the 1/4th Bn East Lancashire Regt, which will have one platoon in support in TRESCAULT TRENCH.

   O.C. 'D' Coy will take one guide for the Company and one guide per platoon to meet 'D' Coy, 1/4th Bn East Lancashire Regt at the entrance to D Sap (Q.4.a.2½.1½.) at 10.30 p.m.

   D Coy will then place two platoons in TRESCAULT TRENCH to the left of B Sap, and 2 platoons in TRESCAULT SUPPORT.

   A & B Posts will be taken over by B Coy 1/9th Bn Manchester Regt with one platoon each. 'B' Coy will have 2 platoons in support in TRESCAULT TRENCH between A & B Saps.

   After relief of work for the night is completed A & C Coys will relieve one Coy of 1/10th Manchester Regt in the INTERMEDIATE LINE. 'A' Coy on left in trenches previously occupied by 'D' Coy, and 'C' Coy on right. O.C. 'A' Coy will take over all trench stores, and will send 1 N.C.O & 2 men in advance at 3 p.m. on the 6th inst, and 2 platoons at 10.30 p.m. O.C. 'C' Coy will send 1 N.C.O & 2 men in advance at 3 p.m. on the 6th inst.

   The N.C.O of 'A' Coy will report at 1/10th Bn Manchester Regt H.Q. at 3 p.m. The men will act as guides for the Coy & for the limbers.

   Lewis Gun Limbers for A & C Coy will be at CROSS ROADS, TRESCAULT (Q.10.a.4.4) at 11.30 p.m. Cookers for these 2 Coys will be sent up to TRESCAULT and will withdraw to HAVRINCOURT WOOD at 11.30 p.m.

   Receipts for all trench stores in possession must be obtained & sent to Bn H.Q the following day.

(Continued)

Orders (Continued)      2      Vol XXIV APPENDIX 1

3. On the night of 7th/8th 'B' Coy will be relieved by a Coy of the 2/9th Bn. London Regt. 'D' Coy will not be relieved but will withdraw to HAVRINCOURT WOOD at 10 p.m. After relief 'B' Coy will withdraw to HAVRINCOURT WOOD.

4. GUIDES.    O.C. 'B' Coy will send one guide per Company & one guide per platoon to meet the relieving Coy at ~~junction of track and railway Q.14.C.7.8.~~

Q 14 c 7.8    at 10.20 p.m. 7th inst.

'D' Coy will hand over Defence Scheme, Trench Sketch to relieving platoons. 'B' Coy will hand over Defence Schemes and Sketch Maps of A. B & C Coys to relieving Coy.

Lewis Gun limbers for D Coy will be at Q.10.a.4.4. at 10.30 p.m on the 7th inst, and for B Coy at 11.30 p.m. Cookers for these 2 Coys will withdraw to HAVRINCOURT WOOD at 11.30 p.m.

5. TRENCH STORES.    Trench Stores from H.Q. of 'A' & 'D' Coys will be moved to Battle H.Q as soon as possible. Trench stores from TRESCAULT SUPPORT will be taken to TRESCAULT TRENCH and handed over to B Coy. B Coy must obtain receipts for all trench stores in possession. Food Containers, Ayrton Fans, Snipers Camouflage Costume & Observer Screens will be handed over by B Coy.
Corpl Edwards will obtain receipts for Bn. H.Q. Stores in TRESCAULT. and for R.E. Dumps.

6. MOVE.    The Battalion will proceed by rail on the night of 7th/8th to Camp at O.16. entraining about Q.14.C.7.8 at times to be stated later.

7. TRANSPORT 7th/8th.    Lewis Gun limbers & teams for Cookers for all Coys will report to Coys as follows :—

         A & C    10.30 p.m. HAVRINCOURT WOOD
         D       10.30 p.m. TRESCAULT
         B       11.30 p.m. TRESCAULT
1 Limber for Tools A & C    10.30 p.m
1     "    "    B & D    11.30 p.m

(Continued)

Orders (Contd)

-3-

| TRANSPORT (Contd) | Maltese Cart | AID Station | 10.30 pm | TRESCAULT |
|---|---|---|---|---|
| | Mess Cart | H.Q. | 10.30 pm | HAVRINCOURT WOOD |
| | 2 Limbers | H.Q. | 11.30 pm | HAVRINCOURT WOOD |

Transport will be collected at MILL FARM and will proceed together from there to O.16.

8. WATER CART. The water cart in TRESCAULT will not be replaced in TRESCAULT on the night of 6/7th.

The 2 water carts will join the other transport at MILL FARM on that night.

9. COMPLETION OF RELIEF. Reliefs will be reported to Bn. H.Q. Code word for relief completed for 6, 7, 8th inst will be BOARDS.

Acknowledge.

Copies to:—
Nos 1-4   Coys
   5      Q.M.
  6-7     War Diary
   8      File

O. Sutton
Capt & Adjutant.
9th Bn. Manchester Regt.

SECRET.                                                          Vol XXIV APPENDIX 2

1/9th. Bn. Manchester Regiment OPERATION ORDER No. 20.

/ Operation Order No 19 cancelled/

JULY 7th. 1917.                                                  COPY No. 7

---

Map Reference :- 57 C. 1/40,000

1. On the night of 7th/8th., the Battalion will entrain at Q.14.c.2.1. O's C. Coys. will report with their Coys. to R.T.O. ( Capt. STOTT, 1/10 th. Bn. Manchester Regiment) at the following times :-

    "A" Coy.    ...    11-45 p.m.
    "C" Coy.    ...    10-45 p.m.
    "D" Coy.    ...    10-45 p.m.
    "B" Coy.    ...    After Relief.
    Hd. Qrs.    ...    2-0 a.m.

    Each truck will hold 30 other ranks. Each train has eight trucks, 5 trucks, will be allotted on first train to 1/9th. Bn. Manchester Regiment ; Second train allotted to 1/5th Bn. East Lancs. Regt. Remainder will be sent off by R.T.O. when loaded
    On detraining units will proceed by BUS BARASTRE to Camp at O.16. An officer of the 1/10th Bn. Manchester Regiment will point out the road.

2. Transport reporting at Battalion on the night 7th/8th will, after loading rendezvous at MILL FARM, and proceed to BARASTRE for Camp O.16., where it will be parked. Remainder of Transport will proceed to O.16, on the morning of the 8th inst. and be parked at O.16.

3. Ride horses will not be required to meet Battalion on detraining on the 8th inst.

4. Battalion will move by march route from BARASTRE on the 9th inst.

5. O's C. Coys. will ensure that sufficient guides are provided to place of entraining on the night of the 7th/8th.

6. "A" & "C" Coys will be relieved in the INTERMEDIATE LINE on the night 7th/8th, and will proceed from there to place of entraining.

7. Arrangements for motor transport and baggage wagons will be made by the Battalion Transport Officer, and the Quartermaster. The move of the Dump will be arranged by the Quartermaster.

(Sd.) O.J.Sutton,
Captain & Adjutant.
1/9th. Bn. Manchester Regt

DISTRIBUTION :-
    Copies No. 1/4 - Coys.
              5 - Q.M./T.O.
              6 - Dump.
              7/8 - War Diary.
              9 - File.

Copy No ..7....

## 1/9th. Bn. MANCHESTER REGT ( Orders No. 21.)

In the Field,
July 8th. 1917.

1. **Move.** The Battalion will march to BIHUCOURT area to-morrow. Parade :- 8-15 a.m. on ground East of Camp.
   Reveille :- 6-0 a.m.
   Breakfast :- 6-30 a.m.
   Dress :- Fighting Order. Steel Helmets will be worn.
   Greatcoats will be properly rolled and carried on the belt.

2. **Belts.** There will be half hourly halts, 10 minutes at the clock hour and 5 minutes at 30 minutes after the clock hour. Watches will be synchronised at 10 p.m. to-night.

3. **Order of March.** The Battalion will march closed up, with an interval of 400 yards between Battalions. Order of march Cylists, Signallers, Headquarters, A, B, C, and D, Companies.

4. **Discipline.** The points mentioned in circular sent round to O.C. Companies, relating to March Discipline, must be strictly adhered to, with the exception that platoon commanders must march in front of their platoons.
   Men must not carry buckets, extra sandbags or unauthorised articles. All officers servants will march with their Companies.

5. **Transport.** 1st Line Transport will march with Battalion closed up. Proper intervals between vehicles.
   No man must walk behind vehicles.
   All Cooks must be formed up in fours under the Master Cook behind the last Cooker. O.C. "D" Coy. will detail 1 Officer and 1 platoon to march behind transport.
   They will give assistance to Transport if required.
   Transport for loading will be at Q.M. Stores at 6-45 a.m.
   Lewis Gun Limbers must be reloaded to-day. O.C. Coys. will ensure that this is done.

6. **Fatigues.** O.C. "D" Coy. will detail fatigue party of XXX 1 N.C.O. and 20 men to report to Q.M. Stores for loading at 7-0 a.m.
   O.C. "C" Coy will detail party of 1 N.C.O. and 20 men for striking tents, to report to Q.M. at 7 a.m.

7. **Officers Valises.** Officers Valises will be dumped at 6-45 a.m. at Q.M. Stores.

8. **Rear Party.** O.C. "C" Coy. will detail 1 Officer and 1 Sergeant as rear party to march behind 430th Coy. A.S.C.

9. **Returns.** Returns will be rendered by 4-0 p.m. showing names of men who
   (a) Were carried in Ambulance Wagon.
   (b) Were stragglers, brought along by Officer detailed by O.C. "C" Coy. marching in rear of 430th Coy. A.S.C.
   (c) Were stragglers, not rejoined.

(Sd.) O.J. Sutton,
Captain & Adjutant,
1/9th. Bn. Manchester Regt.

COPY No. 7

Addendum No. 1 to 1/9th Bn. Manchester Regt. Orders No 21.

In the Field,
8th. July 1917.

Reference Sheet 57 c. 1/40,000.

1. REF: Para. 1. Parade 8-30 a.m.
   Greatcoats will be carried to BIHUCOURT on Motor Lorries. Greatcoats will be fastened in bundles of 10 and stacked at Q.M. Stores at 7 a.m.

2. Ref: para. 4. The Corps Commander will probably watch the Battalion march past at Road Junction O.10.c.O.3.
   Troops will be called to attention 50 yards before reaching this spot and the command " Eyes Right " ( or Left ) will be given. Troops will be given the command " March at Ease " 50 yards beyond this point.

3. Ref: para. 5. Special attention must be paid to the cleanliness of transport.

4. The Starting Point will be Road Junction O.16.a.1.2. Time 8-57 a.m.

5. The Route will be HAPLINCOURT – BANCOURT – BAPAUME.

6. Company Headquarters will fall-in in rear of the Company.

(Sd.) O.J. Sutton,
Captain & Adjutant,
1/9th. Bn. Manchester Regt.

vcxxiv. Appendix. 4

1/9th. Bn. MANCHESTER REGT. Order No 22.

JULY 10/1917.                                    Copy No ..6..

1. The Battalion will move to COURCELLES on the 11th inst; Breakfast 7-30 a.m.       Battalion will form up in mass at 9-30 a.m. on ground S.W. of Camp.
Starting Point G.6.c.2.1. will be passed at 10-10 a.m.

2. The Battalion will march closed up, 200 yards in rear of the 1/10th. Battalion Manchester Regt.   1st Line Transport will march closed up with the Battalion.

3. All tents & bivouac sheets will be struck and dumped at Q.M. Stores by 7-15 a.m.    O.C. "C" Coy. will detail party of 1 Officer & 20 other ranks to strike tents at 7 a.m.
12 Bivouac sheets will be taken.  19 Tents & 40 new bivouac sheets handed over to 1/4th Bn East Lancs Regt.
All drains will be filled in under Coy. arrangements.
O.C. "A" Coy. will detail 1 Officer & 10 other ranks to remain behind to load these tents and bivouac sheets under orders of Capt. T.G. HYDE.    This party will march to new area under Capt. T.G. HYDE.

4. O.C. "B" Coy. will leave rear party of half a company to clear the Camp, remove all manure, and fill up all latrines.
This party will report to the Field Officer of the Day at the present Bde. H.Q. when their Camps are thoroughly clean.
They will march under his orders as one body to COURCELLES.

5. An advance party of 2 other ranks from each Coy. will report to Lieut. W.G. GREENWOOD at 7-30 a.m.    This party will take over billets at 9 a.m. & guide Coys on arrival.
O.C. "A" Coy. will detail a loading party of 2 N.C.O's and 20 other ranks to report to Q.M. at 8 a.m.
Officers Valises will be dumped at Q.M. Stores at 8 a.m.

6. DRESS :-   Full marching order.

(Sd.) O.J. Sutton,
Capt. & Adjt.
1/9th. Bn. Manchester Regt.

DISTRIBUTION :-

Copy No 1 to 4.   Coys.
         5.       Q.R./T.O.
       6 - 7.     War Diary.
         8.       File.

*Confidential*

Army Form W.3091.

## Cover for Documents.

1/9th Bn Manchester Regt

Nature of Enclosures.

WAR DIARY
and
APPENDICES
AUGUST 1917.
VOLUME XXV.

Notes, or Letters written.

Army Form C. 2118.

Vol XXV
Page 1

# WAR DIARY 1/9 MANCHESTER REGT.
## or
## INTELLIGENCE SUMMARY.
(Erase heading not required.)

| Place | Date | Hour | Summary of Events and Information | Remarks and references to Appendices |
|---|---|---|---|---|
| COURCELLES | May 1 | | Ref Maps 1/40,000 57c | |
| | | | Battalion training. | |
| | | | 2/Lt CAREY rejoins from 42nd Div. Bombing School. | |
| | | | Capt. RAYMOND C.F. attached to 1/10 Manch R. | (G/8) |
| | 2 | | Draft of 30 O.R. arrive from 11th Border Regt. | |
| | | | 2/Lt N. WILKINSON arrives from 8th (Reserve) Manch R. taken on strength. | |
| | | | Posted to 'B' Coy | |
| | | | 2/Lt H.S. HUDSON taken on strength posted to 'B' Coy | |
| | | | Major HOWARTH rejoins from leave UK | |
| | | | Capt. HANDFORTH rejoins from course. | (G/9) |
| | | | 2/Lt BUTTERWORTH to course 42 Div Bombing School. | |
| | | | Battalion transport. | |
| | 3 | | Battalion training | |
| | | | Escort on Pte LEACH, M, 850,859 from Questa Du Tria 8.9 in T.S. | (G/c) |
| | 4 | | 2/Lt J.A.M. TARPEY to Forestry Course at ALBERT. | (G/c) |

Army Form C. 2118.

Vol XXV
Page 2

# WAR DIARY
or
# INTELLIGENCE SUMMARY.

1/9 Manchester Regt

(Erase heading not required.)

| Place | Date Aug | Hour | Summary of Events and Information | Remarks and references to Appendices |
|---|---|---|---|---|
| GOVRECHLES | 5 | | Ref Map 40,000 57 E. 2/Lt J.J.SB Orr. arriv from 2/7 Manch. R. & 2/Lt (T.Capt) H.E.L.Smith 2/Lt (T.Capt) T.Sayer taken on strength. Posted to "B" Coy. | O/S O/P |
| " | 6 | | Training. | O/P |
| " | 7 | | Brigade Scheme. Major R.R.Nowell for leave U.K. 2/Lt H.H.Knight rejoins from leave U.K. | O/P |
| " | 8 | | 2/Lt R.J.N.Dale rejoins from leave U.K. | O/P |
| " | 9 | | Lt H.B.Butterworth rejoins from Div. Bombing School. 2/Lt H.G.Willis proceeds to Div. Bombing School. 2/Lt & Q.M. Sarpey rejoins from course at ?????. Bn. engaged in forming Trench R/ Trench Attack. | O/P |
| " | 10 | | Coys engaged in Drill Firing. 2/Lt O.S.Needham joined from Comm. of Instruction ? Deomforce, Aldershot. | O/S |

# WAR DIARY
## or
## INTELLIGENCE SUMMARY.

*(Erase heading not required.)*

1/9 MANCHESTER REGT.

Army Form C. 2118.
Vol XXV
Page 3

| Place | Date | Hour | Summary of Events and Information | Remarks and references to Appendices |
|---|---|---|---|---|
| GOURBELLES | 11 | Ref Map 40,000 57c | CAPT. NELSON C.F. returns from leave U.K. & is attached to this Batt. 1/6 1&C Sports held in the afternoon. | G/1 |
| " | 12 | | Church Parade cancelled. Bttn Commander presents ribbon for Military Medal to 350149 Pte KINSELLA 7. 2/Lt PICKFORD to course at Sniping School. 3rd Army Musketry Course NAPON. Training w/ms from Musketry Course NAPON. Training. Trench to Trench attack. | G/1 |
| " | 13 | | Training by Coys in Trench to Trench attack. 2/Lt SCHOFIELD 1/10 Man.R attached to Batt as signalling officer. 2/Lt OBARD rejoin Bde Gun from U.K. | G/1 G/1 |
| " | 14 | | Training in Trench to Trench attack | G/1 |
| " | 15 | | Scheme with hostile Aeroplanes. 3 Officers arrive from 2nd (Reserve) Bn MANCHESTER REGT, taken on strength:- Posted to Coys as follows:- 2/Lt W.H. CRICK. C Coy 2/Lt B BURROWS. D Coy 1/8 Coy | G/1 G/1 |

Army Form C. 2118.

1/9 Bn. MANCHESTER REGT.
Vol XXV
Page 4

# WAR DIARY
## INTELLIGENCE SUMMARY.
*(Erase heading not required.)*

| Place | Date Aug | Hour | Summary of Events and Information | Remarks and references to Appendices |
|---|---|---|---|---|
| COURCELLES | 17 | | Ref. Map 1/40,000. 57c, 57d. Batten. Training. Divn'l & Bomb. attacks. 2/Lt H.G. MILLIS injured from H.M.S Div Bombing School. | |
| " | 18 | | Batten. Training. Warning order received for move. | |
| " | 19 | | Bath. Church Parade Service in CONCERT HALL | |
| " | 20 | | Bomber parties under 2Lt THATCHER & 2Lt CLARKE proceed by train. | |
| " | 21 | | Battalion proceed by march route to FORCEVILLE (K 32 d Sheet 57d), ms in billets & barns in the village. 2Lt CORRIE found on leave U.K. | App. 1 Bn Order No. 23 |
| FORCEVILLE | 22 | | Battalion less A Coy proceed to BEAUCOURT SUR ANCRE (Sheet 57d) entrains at 10 pm, departing at 11 pm. | App. 2 Bn Order No. 24 |

# WAR DIARY
## or
## INTELLIGENCE SUMMARY.

Army Form C. 2118.

1/9 MANCHESTER REGT

| Place | Date | Hour | Summary of Events and Information | Remarks and references to Appendices |
|---|---|---|---|---|
| WATOU K18 d.7.2 | Aug 23 | | Ref Map. Sheet 27 1/40,000 BELGIUM & FRANCE. Brigade PROVEN (F.7) marches via WATOU (K.4) to Camp at K 12 & 7.7 and billets at farm K 18 a.8.9. Bath HQ. at K 18 d.7.2. | |
| " | 24 | 10.30 | Capt HYDE rejoins from VI Corps School. A Coy dinner at billets K 18 a 8.9. Inspection of Camp and billets by Brigadier, 12 noon. 2Lt HUDSON proceeds on leave to U.K. | |
| " | 25 | | 2Lt WHERRICK attached 428 Battery R.E. until 26 ins. Route March. | |
| " | 26 | | Church Parade. Dinner at Camp. | |
| " | 27 | | Lt. KNIGHT & 2Lt BURT & 42 Div Divl Depot Battalion. 2Lt Viewers in attack on strongpoint on Battement. Warning Order to move to YPRES. | |
| " | 28 | | Training. attack on strongpoint by platoons. | |
| " | 29 | | Route March. | |

Army Form C. 2118.

1st XXV
1/9 Manch&r Regt
Page 6

# WAR DIARY
## or
## INTELLIGENCE SUMMARY.

(Erase heading not required.)

1/9 Manch&r Regt

Instructions regarding War Diaries and Intelligence Summaries are contained in F. S. Regs., Part II. and the Staff Manual respectively. Title pages will be prepared in manuscript.

| Place | Date | Hour | Summary of Events and Information | Remarks and references to Appendices |
|---|---|---|---|---|
| WATOU | Aug 30 | Ref Map 27 & 28 1/40,000 | March to POPERINGHE and entrain for YPRES arrive camp YPRES SOUTH | Appendix 3 O.O. 35 |
| YPRES H 19 D.4 | 31 | | Col LLOYD group 6 on the list & to taken over | |

R. Dunn
Lt Col Comdg
1/9 Manch&r Regt

APPENDIX 1.

1/9th. Battalion MANCHESTER REGIMENT Orders No 23.

Reference Map:-
1/40,000, 57.d.

Copy No...7......

20th August 1917.

The Battalion will move by march route to area MAILLY – MAILLET, BERTRANCOURT, FORCEVILLE, on the 21st inst.
Route :- via BUCQUOY – PUISIEUX – K.32.d.
Guides will meet battalion at Road Bifurcation near the Sugar Factory ( K.32.d.9.6. )

An interval of 400 yards will be kept between units. The 1st Line Transport will move closed up behind the Battalion. There will be halts from 10 minutes to the clock hour until the clock hour, and from 5 minutes to the half hour until the half hour.  During the 5 minutes halt equipment will not be removed.

Each Company and Battn.Hd.Qrs. will leave rear party of 1 reliable N.C.O. and 3 other ranks, to ensure that billets are left clean and in sanitary condition, and to hand over tents and bivouac sheets. LT HUDSON C.S.M. Birchall will remain with this party, and will obtain certificate from the Town Major that the area is left clean and sanitary. He will also obtain receipts for Tents and Bivouac sheets which will all be left standing.

These parties will leave Battn. Hd. Qrs., at 8-50 a.m., and will march behind 430th. Coy. A.S.C., which will pass Brigade Hd. Qrs., at 9-8 a.m.

REVEILLE :- 5-0 a.m.     BREAKFAST :- 5-30 a.m.
PARADE   :- 7-0 a.m.

DRESS :- Marching Order, Greatcoats and Caps in packs, Groundsheets and Mess Tins outside.  Helmets will be worn.

Lewis Gun limbers will be loaded this afternoon, and will remain loaded in Transport Lines.

Teams for Cookers will report at 6-30 a.m., and ride horses at 6-45 a.m.

Refilling point on 22nd inst is R.12.c.7.2., MAILLY – MAILLET.  Stores taken on lorries to-day will be dumped at Railhead at BEAUCOURT – SUR – ANCRE.

Officers valises will be dumped at H.Q. ( not Q.M. Stores) at 6-0 a.m.

DISTRIBUTION :-
Copy No. 1/4 to O.C., Coys.
         5  –  Q.M./T.O.
       6/7  –  War Diary.
         8  –  File.

(Sd.) O.J. Sutton,
Lieut. & Adjutant,
1/9th. Bn. Manchester R.

ISSUED by............AE...............

1/9th. Bn. Manchester Regt. ORDERS No. 23.

Copy No. 7

APPENDIX 1

## ADDENDUM No. 1.

20th August 1917.

1. <u>Baggage Wagons</u>.    After loading on the morning of the 21st inst, baggage wagons will be sent by Q.M. to meet an Officer of 430th. Coy. A.S.C. by 8-0 a.m., on the Football Ground, A.15.d.1.2.

    On arrival in New Area, the Q.M. will send a guide to fetch baggage and supply wagons from H.Q. of 430th. Coy. A.S.C., at MAILLY – MAILLET , P.12.c.7.2.

2. <u>Rear Party</u>.    The rear parties will ensure that no ammunition is left behind in the area. The party will report to Major R.B. NOWELL, at Battn. H.Q., and after he has inspected the billets and found them satisfactory will rendezvous at Town Major's Office, and proceed together to Brigade Hd. Qrs., BERTRANCOURT, where guides will meet them at 2-0 p.m.

    An Officer of the 1/4th Bn. East Lancs. Regt., and the Town Major will count tents and bivouac sheets to-morrow morning.    2/Lieut. H.S. HUDSON will arrange for a man from each Company to show the positions of tents and sheets to these Officers.

<u>DISTRIBUTION</u> :-

To all recipients of ORDERS No. 23.

(Sd.) O.J. Sutton,
Lieut. & Adjutant,
1/9th. Bn. Manchester Regt.

1/9th. Bn. Manchester Regt. ORDERS No. 24.

August 21st 1917.

1. The Battalion will be prepared to entrain any time after 8 p.m., 21st inst.

2. Entraining Station, BEAUCOURT - SUR - ANCRE.
Detraining Station, HOPOUTRE.

3. ACCOMMODATION. Each Truck will hold 40 O.R. No personnel or stores will be allowed in Brake Vans at each end of the Train. Stores may be loaded, if necessary, on the flats under vehicles, but care must be taken that these are carefully secured.

4. RATIONS. Arrangements will be made for a hot meal prior to entrainment, and men must carry haversack rations and waterbottles filled.

5. O.C., "B" Coy will be prepared to supply 1 platoon to go ahead as loading party to BEAUCOURT- SUR - ANCRE Station. This party will remain with baggage during the journey, and will offload it at the other end.

6. O.C., "A" & "C" Coys. will each be prepared to have an Officer's piquet for duty on the train to prevent men leaving the train.

(Sd.) O.J. Sutton,
Lieut. & Adjutant,
1/9th. Bn. Manchester Regt.

DISTRIBUTION :-

    O.C., Coys.
    M.O.
    T.O.
    Q.M.
    Sig. Officer.
    I.O.
2 Copies-War Diary.

1/9th. Bn. Manchester Regt. ORDERS No.25.

August 22nd.1917.

1.  The Battalion, less "A" Coy. will march to BEAUCOURT SUR ANCRE, and entrain there to-day.
    Parade 6-15 p.m.

2.  "A" Coy. with 1 Cooker and 1 ride horse will proceed to BEAUCOURT SUR ANCRE, and entrain there to-morrow. Train departs 3 p.m. Transport must report to entraining officer 3 hours before departure of train. Troops must arrive at Station 1½ hours before departure of train, and be fully entrained half an hour before departure of train.

3.  Lieut. H.H. KNIGHT will interview the MAIRE, and settle any claims made against the Battalion. The Interpreter will remain with "A" Coy. Lieut. H.H. KNIGHT will make necessary arrangements with O.C., Coys. and P.R.I.

4.  O's C., "B" & "D" Coys. will each have an Officers piquet, one at each end of the train. These will prevent men getting out of the train, except when allowed by orders. In case of a halt at a station where men are allowed to get out, a guard will be posted on buffets and on exits from the station

DISTRIBUTION :-

    O.C., Coys.
    R.S.M.
    Interpreter.
    Lieut. H.H. KNIGHT.
2 Copies.- War Diary.

(Sd.) O.J. Sutton,
    Lieut. & Adjutant,
1/9th. Bn. Manchester Regt.

APPENDIX 4

1/9 Bn Manchester Regt.

Summary of Casualties for Month Ending
August 31st 1917.

| NATURE | NO | RANK | NAME | DATE | REMARKS |
|---|---|---|---|---|---|
| KILLED | | | NIL | | |
| MISSING | | | NIL | | |
| WOUNDED | 357008 | Sgt. | FERNS J | 7-8-17 | Bayonet Wnd Accidentally |
| | 351542 | L/Cpl. | CLARE J | 7-8-17 | Shell. Fire. |
| | 350094 | Pte | BROADHURST A | 31-8-17 | Shell Fire. |

O J Scott Capt A/A
Commanding 1/9 Manchester Regt

Secret

1/9TH MANCHESTER RGT.
WAR DIARY
—
Vol XXVI
SEPT 1917

WAR

# WAR DIARY OR INTELLIGENCE SUMMARY

Army Form C. 2118.

1/9 Manchester Regt VOL XXVI PAGE 1

| Place | Date 1917 | Hour | Summary of Events and Information | Remarks and references to Appendices |
|---|---|---|---|---|
| YPRES Sept | 1 | | Ref sheet 28 NW & NE 1/40,000. Takes over front line relieving 142nd Brigade. A & B front line, C & D Support. Battalion HQ KIT & KAT T.1.A.5.8. Capt J.G. HYDE Transferred to M.F.C. 2/Lt G.E. RODMELL do. 2/Lt H.S. WILLIS to C.H.Q SENIS GUN SCHOOL LE TOUQUET. 2/Lt T. CAREY reports from leave to U.K. | APPEND I J.D. 2 |
| KIT+KAT T.1.D | 2 | | Movement proceeds. No.31 Lieut with 3 officers & 140 OR to Army School. 2/Lt PICKFORD reports from Intelligence officers course 3rd Army School. | |
| " | 3 | | 2/Lt H.H. GRICK from 428 Field Co. R.E. sick to hospital. Battalion relieved by 1/4 E.L. Regt. | App II |
| YPRES Sept | 4 | | March to camp at YPRES SOUTH H.18.a. 3 OR killed. 14 wounded. | C.O. 27 App III Map |
| " | 5 | | | |
| " | 6 | 1AM - 3AM | Operation bombardment. Mustard gas shells used. Both distinctly smelt & but respirators worn. Mr O.S. NEEDHAM reports from Transport course. C Company relieved 1 Coy 1/4 MANCHESTERS in hill in YPRES 18a 60. First one battery road repairing bike. | |

A5834 Wt W4973/M687 750,000 8/16 D. D. & L. Ltd. Forms/C.2118/13.

Army Form C. 2118.

Vol XXV/1
Page 2

# WAR DIARY
## of
## INTELLIGENCE SUMMARY.
*(Erase heading not required.)*

1/9 MANCHESTER REGT

| Place | Date | Hour | Summary of Events and Information | Remarks and references to Appendices |
|---|---|---|---|---|
| YPRES Sout. | Sept 4 | 1 a.m. | Map France 28 NE + NW 1/20,000. Gas shell bombardment; box respirators worn for 1/2 hour. 224 CARRET. T. R. HDS 127 C. R.E. 2nd Lt NEEDHAM rejoins from transport lines. | |
| " | 5 | | Capt M. HILLIS to hospital, jaundice. | GPS |
| " | 6/7 | | Battn relieves "15" East Lancs in support. | GPS |
| RAILWAY WOOD | 7" | | Dispositions A + B Coy the own dug-outs. C + D Coy remain in camp YPRES SOUTH 2nd Lt QUINNEY to Bde H.Q. Sent front & rear & front carrying parties Rampants, YPRES as ordered Staff Captain (telegram 8.9.17) | App 4 O.O. 28 GPS GPS |
| " | 8 | | 2/Lt HUDSON rejoins Battn from leave U.K. | GPS |
| " | 9 | | Gas Shell bombardment of BURR CROSS ROADS; 10 casualties in carrying party. | GPS |
| " | 10/11 | | Bn relieves "15" East Lancs in the front line. D Coy & ? L'TLE pond, A + C Coys front. C. Coy in mainsupport in cubbing mainworks (I6D) B Coy in 2 platoons at LOWE EARS. ( I12 B ) H.Q. at KIT KAT. 2 platoon of A Coy attached to "5" L'pool the front line. | App 5 O.O. 30 GPS |

# WAR DIARY or INTELLIGENCE SUMMARY

Army Form C. 2118.

1/9 Manchester Regt. Vol XXVI Pages

| Place | Date | Hour | Summary of Events and Information | Remarks and references to Appendices |
|---|---|---|---|---|
| KIT KAT J.1.D | 11/2 | 11.30pm | Map. Sheet 28 NE V.N. 1/10,000 (Capt Maddocks) C Coy attacked the "HUT" (26.D.1.8.) unsuccessfully. Objects to withdraw by OC Coy as the men prevented from advance by hostile M.G. & rifle ground fire. 2/Lt GREENWOOD wounded. 1 OR killed, 9 wounded, 1 missing. C Coy returns to trench near railway. (I6D) Gas shell bombardment 12 midnight to 5 am on KIT KAT. Battn Lewis Guns and Railway Automatic. (I6D) | |
| — // — | 12 | | 2/Lt EGTONIER to cover ? Instruction 2/x Corps School. | |
| — // — | 12/13 | | C & D Coy Nights in joining up No 1, 2 & 3 Posts. | |
| — // — | 13/4 | 2am | Battalion relieved on the night of 12/13/4 by R 1/4 East Lancs Regt 2/Lt D.N.E. Intelligence Officer to hospital sick. Battalion returned to No 3 Camp YPRES South (H18a) Battalion moved in evening SAR. Katie Retiring ctc to rest camp at KIT KAT from BIRR CROSS ROADS (I17a) Capt J.M. BIRCHALL & 10 OR wounded, 1 killed, 2 missing OR MAJOR MONTEITH (A/Lt. Col.) proceeds to rest camp for 12 days. | APR 1917 G.O. 31 |
| YPRES SOUTH | 14/15 | | | |
| — // — | 15/16 | | Casualist water, SAA & 18pr Shells from BIRR CROSS ROAD to KIT KAT. 2/Lt RICKFORD leave to U.K. 2/Lt W. NITTY and G.A. BIRKBY report for K.13 Cttee from "Artists Rifles". 2/Lt LLOYD takes over command 9 1st Bn in the field Brigade 6th JOHNSON wounded. Major French taken over command J. Battalion. | |

A 5634. Wt. W4973/M687. 750,000. 8/16. D.D. & L., Ltd. Forms/C.2118/13.

Army Form C. 2118.

# WAR DIARY
## or
## INTELLIGENCE SUMMARY.
(Erase heading not required.)

1/9 Manchester Regt

| Place | Date | Hour | Summary of Events and Information | Remarks and references to Appendices |
|---|---|---|---|---|
| YPRES South | Sept 16/3 | 8 pm | Battalion relieved in Reserve Trenches by 6" M.G.B. & move by march route to RED ROSE CAMP H.11.B.8.0. where men are billeted in huts. 2/Lt HAWKNEY rejoins from Divisional Depôt Battalion. Lt MACKWORTH rejoins from Brigade details. | G/s |
| H.11.B.8.0 | 17/18 | — | 2/Lt CAREY rejoins Battn. from 428 H.S.Coy R.E. 2/Lt T. NEEDHAM rejoins Battn. from 2nd E.O.R. | G/1 |
|  | 19 | 9.30 am | Bn. moves by march route to WINNEZEELE from No. 1 + goes into Camp vacated by 2/5 Scot. Staff. | APP. 8 O.O. 32 |
| WINNEZEELE | 20 |  | 2/Lt MILLS rejoins Battn. from Base of Instruction 5 August. |  |
|  | 22 |  | Battn. moves by march route to WORMHOUDT and 27 & 17 & 30 en route into billets. 2/Lt E. LLOYD joins Battn. C.O.R. on Camp 2/Lt E. LLOYD joins from TOTGHEM Bn. | G/1 |
| WORMHOUDT | 23 |  | Bn. moves by march route to UXEM (Sect DUNKERQUE) from new billets. Major R.B. NOBLE takes over temporary command from J Barlow | APP. 7 G.O. 34 |

Army Form C. 2118.

# WAR DIARY
## or
## INTELLIGENCE SUMMARY.

1/9 MANCHESTER REGT

(Erase heading not required.)

| Place | Date | Hour | Summary of Events and Information | Remarks and references to Appendices |
|---|---|---|---|---|
| OXEN | 23 | | Reply, Reigns Pole 11 Training. B.H.Q. moved in to LA PANNE (Sheet 11, W.I.S.G) from into Brig Camp | APP. 10 00.35 |
| | | | Capt G.N. HOWARTH sick to Eng hosp | |
| LA PANNE | 24 | | B. moved K C.SYDET-BANS & where as 24th Manch Regt in ST IDESBALD COAST DEFENCE Sector. Battns as "RECRUIT" N 6 & 3 B Coy on the left to Batts C on left out centre, A Coy on right reserve D Coy left reserve B.D Coy Relief 2 Coy DE DUNKIER See Sketch Map Appendix. | APP 11 |
| | | | 9.30 CONGREGATION & 2.5 O.R. attached to 428 F.C, R.B | |
| OXEN BARN | 25 | | 50 or R attd to 423rd Div R.E. Dumps Capt H.G. SHATWELL to Brig Gas School CHYVRIDE on Gas offcer (continued) Enemy aeroplanes — 6 GOTHA crossed noon on shore near Nos 2 Post 3 prisoners taken 10% and 2 O.R. Telephone party went after Enemy | |
| | 26 | | Boys training | |

Army Form C. 2118.

19 Manchester Regt
Volume XXVI
Page 6

# WAR DIARY
## or
## INTELLIGENCE SUMMARY.
(Erase heading not required.)

19 Manchester Regt 1914/1920

| Place | Date | Hour | Summary of Events and Information | Remarks and references to Appendices |
|---|---|---|---|---|
| COXYDE-BAINS | Sept 27 | | 2/Lt PICKFORD rejoins from Bn from E.V.R.<br>CAPT A.B. STEMBERTON proceed on leave U.K.<br>2/Lt R.J. NGALE reports on return from hospital shown R.T.O. detach W. Strength<br>4 Officers report from Reinforcement Camp & posted to Coys as follows<br>2/Lt A.J. MIDGLEY (3rd Reserve Manch 2) posted to K Coy<br>2/Lt A. E. STONE (8th Res Manch 2) posted to K Coy.<br>2/Lt N.M. AVINE (8th Res Manch 2) posted to C Coy.<br>2/Lt C. BARLOW (8th Res Manch 2) posted to A Coy.<br>Orders to strength 27/5/17 | |
| " | 28 | | 2/Lt HUDSON to Infantry Course # IV Army ELVERDINGT.<br>B Coy relieved by D Coy of support with 5 Day Relief. | APP. 12.<br>O.O.X. |
| " | 29 | | Major T.S. HOWORTH rejoin Battn from Y Army Summer Rest Camp. | |
| " | 30 | | Capt C.H.S. REDMOND, Lt C.P. NEEDHAM, Lt H. FORREST & Lt J.S. BRITT<br>Gen Return of 4 Day Course.<br>2/Lt A.E. STONE killed Div Bombing School. 2/Lt WILLIS & Kenn O.M. | |

R.B. Throstle
Major Command
1/9 Manchester Regt.

1/9th. Battn. MANCHESTER REGT. Orders No 26.
COPY No......

Ref: Map. 1/20,000, 28.N.W.
1/20,000, 28.N.E.
and ZILLEBEKE 1/10,000

1st September 1917.

1. The 126th Brigade will take over a portion of the front held by 142nd Brigade, to-night, 1/2nd September.

2. The right boundary of the Brigade will be the Cross Roads J.1.d.6.2., exclusive - South of JAFFA AVENUE - ZIEL HOUSE inclusive, except two dug-outs immediately South of ZIEL HOUSE - J.7.a.0.7. - I.12.a.85.50.- I.12.a.2.0.- I.11.d.1.5. - I.10.d.7.1.- HELL FIRE CORNER, thence along MENIN ROAD to I.9.c.70.55. - I.8.c.8.5. - I.8.c.0.2. - I.7.d.85.35. H 18 Central - H.17.c.80.25. - H.23.a.80.73. - H.15.Central.
The left boundary of the Brigade will be the YPRES - ROULERS Railway as far as HELL FIRE CORNER inclusive.

3. The Battalion will relieve the 21st Bn. London Regiment; "A" & "B" Coys in the Front Line. "A" Coy on the Left, "B" on the Right. "C" Coy. will be in support. "D" Coy. will be in Reserve taking over trenches from the 22nd London Regt at LAKE FARM.

4. Guides will be met at 10 p.m. at a point on the Duckboards, J.1.c.1.3., near track to Aid Post. Companies will move in the following order "A","B","C","D". Posts will be taken over in sequence from the left.

5. S.A.A. on the man will be made up to 170. An extra 50 in bandoliers will be taken over in the trenches.

6. The Battalion will proceed into the line with two days rations, plus the emergency Iron Ration. No further rations will be required until the Battalion moves into reserve.

7. Distances of 100 yards will be left between ½ platoons.

8. All S.A.A., Flares, Grenades etc., will be taken over, and copies of receipts sent to Battn. H.Q. to-night.

9. Regimental Aid Post will be near "C" Coy., about I.6.d.7.8. Battalion Hd.Qrs. will be at KIT & KAT, J.1.d.5.8.

10. Companies will each take in 25 Shovels.

11. Each Coy. will take from limbers at BIRR CROSS ROADS a proportion of petrol tins of water. Empty petrol tins must be returned to Battn. H.Q. as often as possible. "D" Coy. will arrange to supply water to the forward Companies from the night of the 2/3rd. T.O. will arrange to bring petrol tins of water loaded in limbers to the commencement of the Duck boards. O.C. "D" Coy. will supply guide at BIRR CROSS ROADS to-morrow at 10 p.m. to meet water limbers.

12. Maltese Cart will report at 6-30 p.m., and will proceed with Battalion. Mess Cart will not be required. 2 Limbers will report at 6-30 p.m. for Lewis Guns. 100 Shovels will be taken to BIRR CROSS ROADS, and distributed 25 to each Company by the Q.M.

( Continued.)

Orders No. 26 ( Contd.)         (2)

13. REPORTS .     Situation Report , 2 a.m. and 2 p.m.
                  Work Report .     4 a.m.
                  Estimated Casualties .    "A" & "B" Coys. 4 a.m.
                                            "C" & "D" Coys. 2 p.m.
                  Patrol Reports .  4 a.m.
                  Intelligence Reports.  4 a.m.
                  S.A.A. Expended.     "A" & "B" Coys.  4 a.m.
                                       "C" & "D" Coys.  6 a.m.

14.    Greatcoats of men proceeding to the line will be dumped at H.Q., rolled in bundles of 10 at 3 p.m.
       Officers valises will be dumped at H.Q. at 5 p.m.

15.    Details will proceed to Camp at G.11.d.3.5., under orders to be issued later, and will remain under command of Major. SIMON , 1/4th Bn. East Lancs. Regt .

16.    "A" Coy will move off at 7-30 p.m.

                                              (Sd.) O.J. Sutton,
                                                  Lieut. & Adjutant,
                                              1/9th. Bn. Manchester R.

DISTRIBUTION :-

Copies 1/4 -  O.C., Coys.
       5. -   T.O.
       6. -   Q.M.
       7/8 -  War Diary .
       9 -    File .

Issued by ............ at ...............

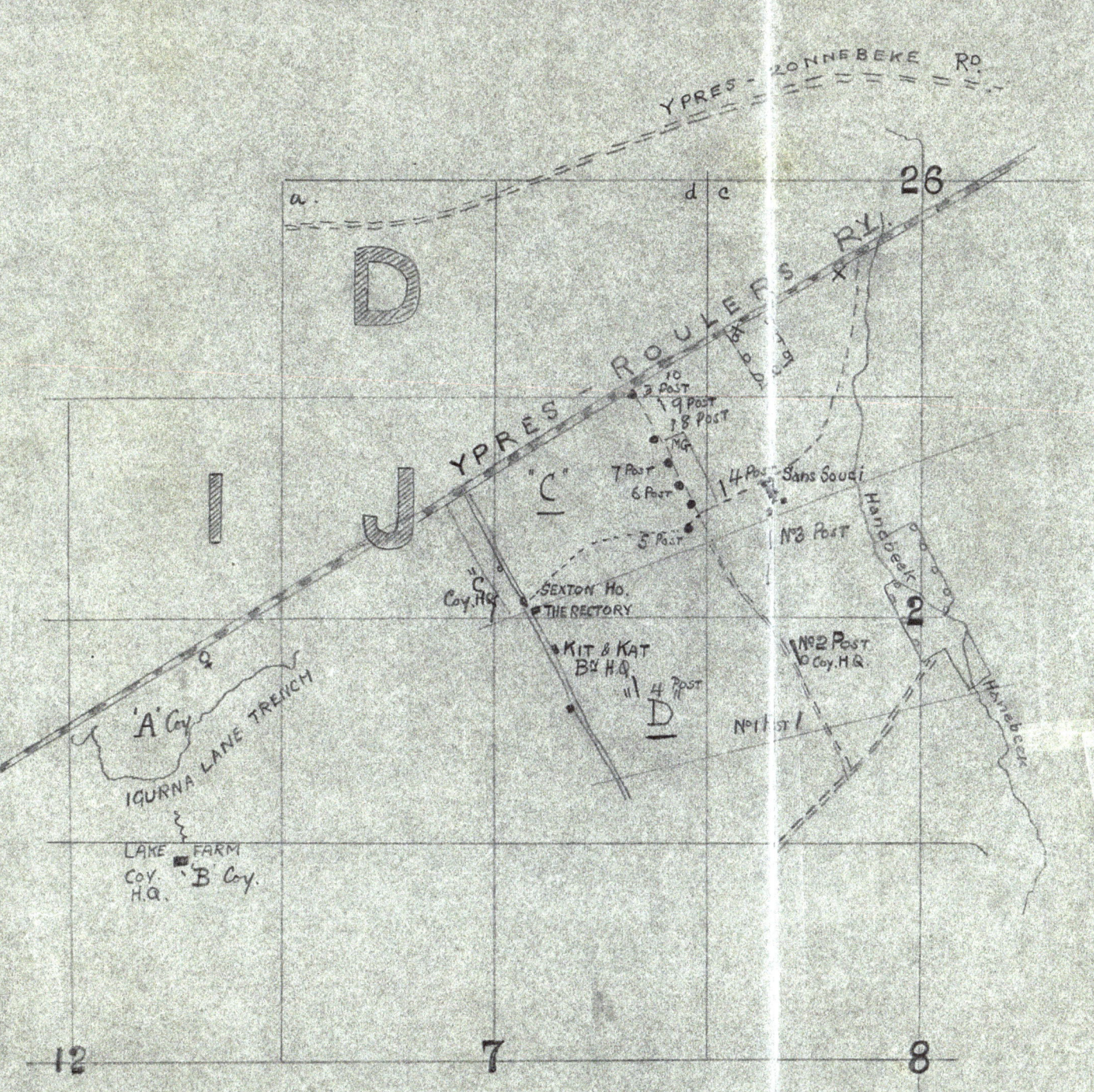

1/9th Battalion MANCHESTER REGT Orders No. 27.

Ref: Map – Sheet 28, N.W. & N.E., 1/20,000.   Copy No...7...

SEPTEMBER 2nd 1917.

1. **RELIEF.** The Battalion will be relieved in the Front Line to-morrow night 3/4th inst, by the 1/4th East Lancs. Regt.

2. **GUIDES.** 4 Guides per Company will rendezvous under Lieut. RUTTENAU at "D" Coy. H.Q. at 8 p.m. to-morrow. The guides from "A" & "B" Coys will report to him at "D" Coy before daybreak to-morrow. Further instructions re. guides will be issued to Lieut. RUTTENAU.
Posts will be taken over in sequence from left to right.

3. On relief the Battalion will return to camp at YPRES South Route by the Corduroy road used by the Battalion when relieving. 100 yards will be maintained between ½ platoons.

4. 25 Shovels per Coy will be taken down to dump near BIRR CROSS Roads where they will be collected by Transport at 2-30 a.m. L.G., S.A.A. will be dumped here also. Each Coy. will leave one Lewis Gunner to see these stores loaded.

5. 2/Lieut. QUINNEY will arrange to have a N.C.O. from each Coy. to prepare accommodation at the camp. A hot meal will be ready for the troops on arrival.
Officers valises will be brought to the camp.
Ride horses will be at a point on the WARRINGTON ROAD to be described to T.O. by 2/Lieut. QUINNEY.

6. **TRENCH STORES.** Receipts for Trench Stores handed over will be sent to Battn. H.Q. on the 4th inst.

7. The Signalling equipment & Medical Stores will be collected from BIRR CROSS Roads at 3 a.m. in the Maltese Cart. M.O. will detail a man to see this loaded.

2-9-17.
(Sd.) O.J. Sutton,
Capt. & Adjutant,
1/9th Bn. Manchester Regt.

DISTRIBUTION.
Copies 1 to 4  Coys.
       5       Q.M.
       6       T.O.
   7 / 8       War Diary.
       9       File.

Copy No......

1/9th Bn. Manchester Regt. (Orders No. 28.)

In The Field.
Sept. 7th. 1917.

1. The Battalion will relieve the 1/5th Bn. East Lancs. Regt. as Support Battalion on the night of the 7th/8th inst. "A" & "B" Coys. will be in Dug Out in RAILWAY WOOD, "C" Coy. in billets in YPRES and "D" Coy. at YPRES South.

2. "A" Coy. will move off at 8 p.m. followed by "B" Coy. and Battalion Headquarters.

3. Two days rations will be taken and water bottles filled.

4. Dress:- Fighting Order, less greatcoats, flares, bombs, rifle grenades and entrenching tools (i.e. picks & shovels).

5. Distance of 100 yards must be kept between half platoons.

6. Coy. Qar. Sgts. will take charge of greatcoats, haversacks and cookers belonging to "A" & "B" Coys.

7. Ride horses for C. O., Adjutant, M. O. and "A" & "B" Coys. will be at Battalion H. Qrs., YPRES South at 7-45 p.m. and H. Qrs. will be at

8. Guides for "A" & "B" Coys. will be at BIRR CROSS Roads at 10-10 p.m.

9. Advance parties from "A" & "B" Coys. will leave camp at 4-30 p.m. and duties will be taken over at 7 p.m.

10. 170 rounds S. A. A. will be carried on the man.

11. "A" & "B" Coys. will each take 2 Petrol tins. H.Q. 6 Petrol Tins. Water is obtainable in RAILWAY WOOD. These tins will be taken up empty by transport to BIRR CROSS ROADS and distributed to Coys. there. 1 Limber will be at H. Qrs. at 6-30 p.m.

12. When the Battalion is in Support and in the line, "B" Coy. will provide any carrying parties necessary.

13. Rations will be brought up on the nights of the 8th & 9th. On the night of the 9th, rations must be issued to the men by 5 p.m. The Q. Mr. will see that they are brought up in time for this.

14. List of returns required will be issued separately.

(Sd.) O. J. Sutton,
Captain & Adjutant,
1/9th Bn. Manchester Regt.

Issued to:-
Copy No...... O. C. "A" Coy.
  "   "  ...... "   " "B"  "
  "   "  ...... "   " "D"  "
  "   "  ......   ..............

1/9th. Battn. MANCHESTER REGIMENT Orders No. 30.

Copy No. 7

Vol XXVI App 5

Reference Map :- 1/20,000 28 Sheet. N.E. & N.W.

September 9th.1917.

Orders No. 29 are cancelled and the following substituted.

1. Relief.   The Battalion will relieve the 1/5th East Lancs. Regt. in the line on the 10/11th inst., with "A" & "D" Coys in the front line. "A" Coy on the left.   "C" Coy will be in support, and "B" Coy in reserve.

2.   "A" & "B" Coys will leave RAILWAY WOOD at 7-45 p.m. "C" & "D" Coys will meet guides at BIRR CROSS Roads at 9 p.m. "C" Coy will precede. "D" Coy will leave camp at 7-30 p.m. Posts in front line will be taken over from right to left.

3. Rations.   Two days rations will be carried on the man. "C" & "D" Coys will each pick up 14 petrol tins of water at BIRR CROSS Roads, which will be taken there by Q.M.   "A" & "B" Companies and H.Q. will each take forward petrol tins.   "A" Coy & H.Q. must have their tins full.   "B" Coy will fill at LAKE FARM before dawn. Water bottles must be full.
   When in the line "A" "C" & "D" Coys will be supplied with water by "B" Coy.   Empty tins must be returned daily to Battn. H.Q. or Res. as early as possible.   Water will be drawn from LAKE FARM, and Coy.H.Q. from water carts.

4. Cancelled.

5. No troops are allowed to use the Trench board track running from near Bde H.Q. through I.12.a. - 6.c. and d. to J.1.c.5.5., except stretcher bearers and runners.

6.   All runners must carry rifles.

7. Transport.   One limber for "C" Coy. and one for "D" Coy will report to those Coys. at 6 p.m., on the 10th inst., to proceed to BIRR CROSS ROADS.   Ride horses for these Coys at 7 p.m.

8.   Coy. Q.M. Sgts will arrange to collect greatcoats, haversacks and officer's valises after departure of these Coys from the camp, and will take the cookers to the Transport Lines.

9.   Route will be by WARRINGTON Road for "C" & "D" Coys.

10.   Distance of 100 yards will be left between half platoons.


9-9-17.
(Sd.) O.J. Sutton,
Captain & Adjutant,
1/9th Bn. Manchester Regt.

1/9th Battalion Manchester Regt. ORDERS No. 31.　　Copy No. 7

Reference Map, Sheet 28, 1/40,000　　　　　September 16/1917.

1. MOVE.   The Battalion will be relieved as Reserve Battalion by the 6th K.O.S.B., this evening, and will move to RED ROSE Camp, H.1.b.8.0., about 8 p.m.

2. TRANSPORT.   All transport will march under the B.T.O. starting at 5-30 p.m.   Baggage wagons will report to the Transport Lines under arrangements made by the B.T.O., and will collect Valises etc. at YPRES South Camp at 3-0 p.m.
   Lewis Gun limbers will be loaded and will leave Camp at 2 pm
   Maltese Cart will report at Camp at 4-30 p.m., and will move off loaded at 4-45 p.m.
   Ride horses for all but C.O. will be at Camp at 7-45 p.m.
   S.A.A., Grenades etc., will be correctly loaded on their limbers under arrangements to be made by the Q.M.
   Teams for Cookers will report at 4-15 p.m.
   No Motor transport is available.

3. 200 yards will be maintained between platoons on the march.

4. Officers valises will be dumped near Signal Officer's Tent at 3 p.m.

5. Men's tea will be at 4 p.m.

6. All copies of Map, FREZENBURG will be returned to Adjutant by 2 p.m.

7. Arrangements have been made by Major KERR to send parties to take over new areas. Each Company will send 1 N.C.O. to ascertain position & number of tents and bivouacs, and to meet Companies in VLAMERTINGHE.   2/Lieut. BURROWS will proceed with this party at 5-30 p.m., allot tents for Coys. and H.Q., and await arrival of Battalion in Camp.

8. T.O. will arrange to have transport for 14 shovels and 6 picks at Camp No.3. YPRES ( Battn. H.Q. ) at 8 p.m.

9. CLEANLINESS.   Care must be taken that the Camp is left thoroughly clean.   O.C. Coys will render a certificate by 8 p.m. that their Coy. Areas are in a clean and sanitary condition.

10. D.A.D.O.S. will remain in his present location.
    Bde. H.Q. will move to RIDGE CAMP, G.11.a.4.5. at 6 a.m., on the 17th inst.

11. Coys will report present or otherwise on arrival of H.Qrs in new Camp.

12. Time of departure will depend on relief and will be notified later.

13. Details from Bde Details Camp will rejoin at New Camp'. Details attached to R.E's will rejoin on the 19th inst.

14. ACKNOWLEDGE.

　　　　　　　　　　　　　　　　　　　　(Sd). O.J. Sutton,
　　　　　　　　　　　　　　　　　　　　　Capt. & Adjutant,
Issued at 11-30 a.m.　　　　　　　　　1/9th Bn. Manchester Regt.
Copies to O's C. Coys. Nos.1/4
　　　　　T.O.　　　　5
　　　　　Q.M.　　　　6
　　　　　File.　　　　7
　　　　　War Diary.　　8/9.

1/9th Bn Manchester Regt Orders
No 31   ADDENDUM   App 7.

Sept 16/17

1. Dress   Dress for move tonight will be fighting order with haversacks instead of valises. Ground sheets & mess tins will be taken.

2. Packs will be dumped near Signal Officers Tent at 5 pm. RSM will place a guard of 1 NCO & 3 OR over this dump. This guard will proceed by motor with the Packs to the final destination of the Battalion. They will take rations up till the 19th inst inclusive.

3. Lorries will be instructed to return to DADOS after completion of journey.

4. A loading party of 1 Officer (2/Lt HUDSON) & 10 OR of B Coy will remain at this camp to load lorries. This party will rejoin Battalion, RED ROSE Camp tomorrow morning.

Issued 2 pm                     (sd) O.J Sutton
Distribution - As for O.O.N°31          Capt & adjt
                                1/9th Bn Manchester Regt.

1/9th. Bn. MANCHESTER REGT. Orders No.32.

Copy No. 7

September 18/1917.

1. The Battalion will move by march route to WINNEZEELE Area No. 1. on the 19th inst.
Route will be via SWITCH Road, North of POPERINGHE, Road Junction L.4.b.8.2., WATOU, and DROGLANDT.

2. The Battalion will pass the starting point, cross roads G.5.c.5.2., at 6-43 a.m.

3. Reveille 4-30 a.m.
Breakfast 4-45 a.m.
Fall in, Coys independantly at 5-45 a.m.

4. H.Q. will move off at 6 a.m., followed at 3 minutes interval by "A" Coy. 'B','C' & 'D' Coys will follow in succession maintaining 300 yards distance between each Coy.
After passing Cross Roads L.4.b.8.2., the Battalion will halt for 20 minutes at the first clock hour, and close up.
A distance of at least 500 yards will then be maintained behind the 1/10th Bn. Manchester Regt.

5. Halts will be observed as follows, from 10 minutes to the clock hour until the clock hour, and from 5 minutes to the half hour, until the half hour.

6. The strictest attention will be paid to march discipline.

7. Only one man must march behind each vehicle. Cooks, with the exception of one cook per Coy. will march with their Coy.

8. Lieut. O.S. NEEDHAM, and one N.C.O. to be detailed by O.C., 'B' Coy., will march behind the Field Ambulance and march all men of the Battalion who have been given permission to fall behind (but not admitted to F. Ambulance) in a formed body to the destination.

9. Transport will march under orders to be issued by the B.T.O.

10. Officers valises will be dumped near H.Q. Mess ready for loading at 5-15 a.m. Baggage wagons will report there at that time.

11. Ride horses will be required at 5-30 a.m., and watches synchronised at the same hour.

12. All packs will be brought on by motor lorry.

13. Returns will be rendered by 2 p.m. showing names of men who :-
    (a) Were carried in Ambulance Wagons.
    (b) Were stragglers, brought along by Lieut. O.S. NEEDHAM.
    (c) Others not rejoined.

19-9-17.
Issued at 8 p.m.

(Sd) O.J. Sutton,
Capt. & Adjt.,
1/9th.Bn. Manchester Regt.

DISTRIBUTION :- Normal.

1/9th. Bn. MANCHESTER REGT. ORDERS No.31.

Copy No. 7

ADDENDUM. 2.

Ref. Map, 1/40,000, 27, 28.  September 18th, 1917.

1. **TRANSPORT**. One motor lorry will be available at Bde. H.Q. at 6-45 a.m. on the 19th inst, to carry surplus stores, and remaining packs to the new area. The Q.M. will send guide to bring this lorry. The lorry must be loaded at once, sent in charge of a guide to the new area. The men remaining at the old dump in charge of the surplus baggage will load this lorry at the dump, and will then proceed with the lorry to unload at the destination.

    After unloading this lorry, (serial number "B") will return with guide from 1/10th Bn. Manchester Regt to 1/10th Manchesters Camp or dump for use of 1/10th Bn. Manchester Regiment.

    2/Lieut. H.S. HUDSON will proceed with this lorry, and guide it to the new destination (see Para.4.)

2. **REAR PARTY**. A rear party composed of Lieut. S. RUTTENAU and 2 Men per Company will be left to clear the camp after the departure of the Battalion. This party will proceed by march route to the new destination. Lieut. S. RUTTENAU will obtain receipts for tents and area stores, & obtain certificate of cleanliness from incoming battalion, or from the Camp caretaker.

3. **ADVANCE PARTY**. An advance party of 2/Lieut. W.E. LEAVER and 1 N.C.O. from H.Q. and each Company will rendezvous at R.S.M's tent at 2-30 a.m. on the morning of the 19th inst. They will meet the Staff Captain at the cross roads, G.5.d.0.2. at 3 a.m. The party will be mounted on horses or cycles by arrangement to be made by Lieut. LEAVER with the T.O. and Signalling Officer.

    After being shown their billeting areas, this advanced party will meet the Battalion at the road junctions at DROGLANDT, J.12.b.8.7., and guide the Companies to the billets. Staff Captain will advise as to time.

4. **BILLETING AREA**. The approximate location is as follows :-
    1/9th. Bn. Manchester Regt.     J.11.c.3.6. & J.6.c.6.0.
    Brigade H.Q.                    J.17.b.7.9.
    430th Coy. A.S.C.               J.12.b.7.3.
    1/2nd Field Ambulance.          J.17.c.3.5.
    428th Coy. R.E's.               J.6.a.1.7 etc.
    1/4th East Lancs. Regt.         J.11.a.9.4.
    1/5th  "    "     "             J.11.b.6.4. etc.
    1/10th. Bn. Manchester Regt.    J.11.a.8.1. etc.

5. **BATHS**. Baths at J.11.b.4.4. are allotted to the Brigade on the afternoon of the 20th, and the morning of the 21st inst. They will take 200 men an hour.

6. **LEAVE PARTIES**. Will continue to entrain at POPERINGHE.

(Sd.) O.J. Sutton,
Captain & Adjutant,
1/9th. Bn. Manchester Regt.

ISSUED at ..........

DISTRIBUTION :-
    As for O.O. No. 31.

Sgt. ~~H~~ ... M.D. 907
~~2nd~~ ~~Coy~~ App. 9
O.O. 34

The Battalion will move by march route to TETEGHEM tomorrow. Parade ready to move 9 am. in the Grand Place. "B" Coy. nearest to the Church, next in succession A, D, C & H. Qrs. H. Qrs. will move off first.

Route will be by WINDEN Les CINQS CHEMINS, the Cross Roads, O. 17 & 19. '25, GAEGHOECK to TETEGHEN.

The usual hourly halts will be observed. In addition there will be a halt of one hour and a half from noon to 1-30 pm. for the mid-day meal. Cookers will not be brought up from the rear in such a way as to block the road. Horses will be fed and watered, the petrol tins carried in the limbers being employed for the

CON TO. (2)

latter purpose.

REAR PARTY. Lieut. RUTTENAU and 1 man per Coy. will remain behind and obtain certificates of cleanliness from the Area Commandant.

This party will rendezvous at the Church at 9-15 am.

Lieut. RUTTENAU will also complete the arrangements with regards to billetting and ascertain from the Town Major if there are any claims against the Battalion. Lieut. RUTTENAU will report to Adjutant before 8 am. for instructions.

Ride horses, etc.

Ride horses will be required at 8.30 am.

Teams for water carts will parade at the same hour.

21-9-17    (sd) O.T. Sutton.
10.45 pm.    Capt. +adjt.
                  1/9 Bn. Manchr. Regt.

Vol XXVI App. 10

1/9th Battalion MANCHESTER REGT Orders No.35

Copy No. 7

September 23rd 1917.

1. Battalion will move to LA PANNE Area today, 23rd inst.

2. Parade ready to move at 6-45 a.m., on road running N.E. from cross roads UXEM, in the following order, - H.Q., 'A', 'B', 'C', 'D'. The tail of 'D' Coy at the cross roads.

3. Ride horses will report at 6-15 a.m. Teams for cookers at 6-15 a.m.

4. Officers valises will be collected at 5-0 a.m. Os C. Coys 'A', 'C', & 'D', will send a guide to cross roads, UXEM at 4-45 a.m. to guide transport for these valises. The transport must be sent with valises as soon as possible with a guide to Q.M. Stores.

5. HALTS. The usual hourly halts will be observed. In addition, there will be a halt of one hour at a time to be notified on the line of march.

6. Advance party will rendezvous at H.Q. as ordered.

7. Rear Party consisting of Lieut O.S. NEEDHAM & 1 man per Coy., will remain behind, and will meet at cross roads, UXEM at 8 a.m.

8. Q.M. will send guides for Motor Lorries to be at Bde. H.Q. near TETEGHEM at 6 a.m.

9. Baggage wagons will report at 5 a.m. to H.Q.

10. All transport, including Cookers, Water Carts, Mess & Maltese Carts & Baggage Wagons must report to T.O., as early as possible before 6-50 a.m.

ACKNOWLEDGE.

23-9-17.

(Sd.) O.J. Sutton,
Capt. & Adjt.,
1/9th.Bn. Manchester Regt.

DISTRIBUTION :- Normal.

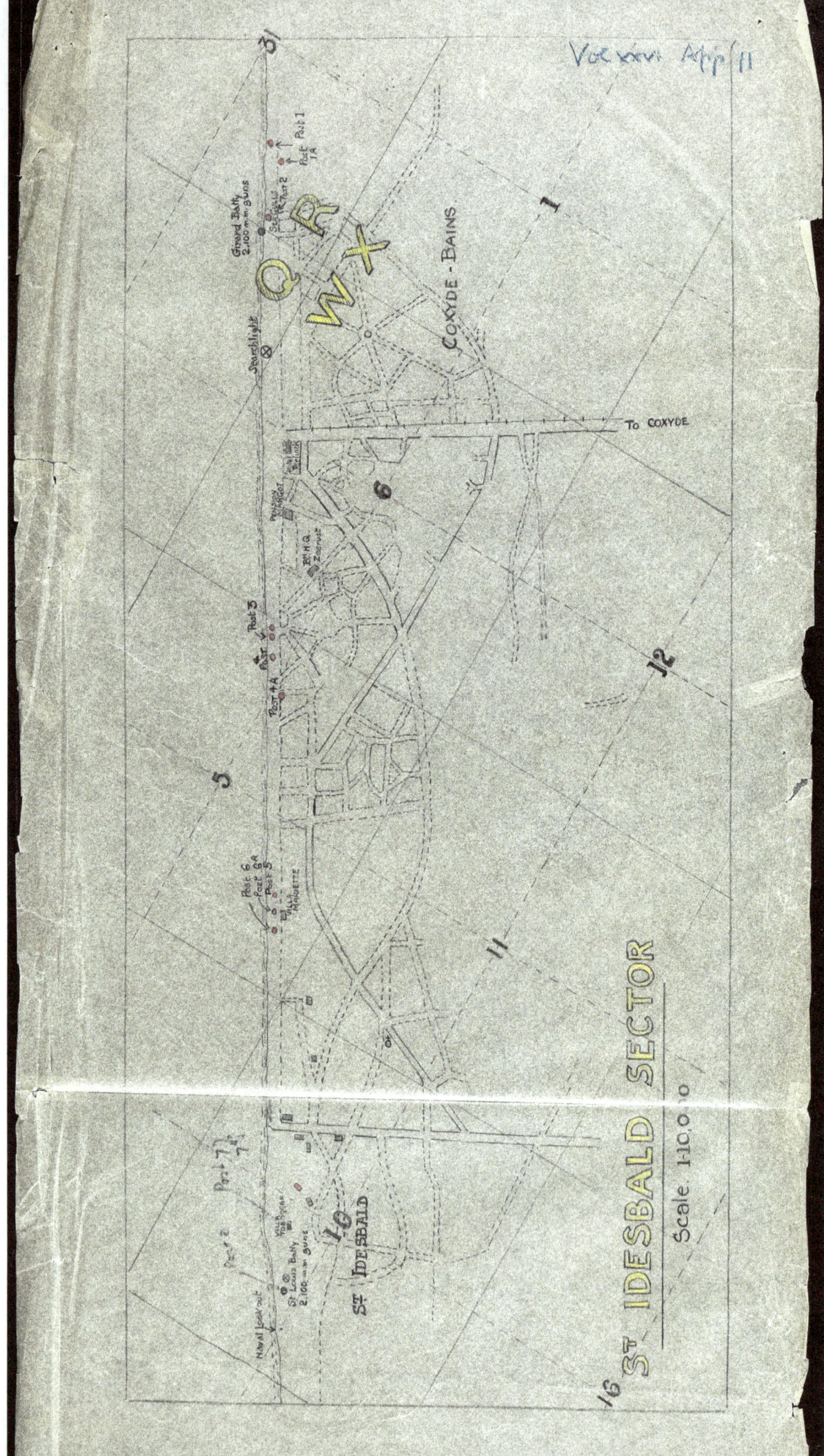

WCXXVI APP 12

1/9th. Battn. MANCHESTER REGT. Orders No 36

Reference Map, BELGIUM Sheet 11,    September 27th.1917.
                1/40,000.

  "D" Coy. will relieve "B" Coy in the Right Sector,
ST. IDESBALD Coast Defences to-morrow morning, 28th inst.

  Relief to be completed by 10 a.m.

  All arrangements to be made between O's C Coys concerned.

  "B" Coy. will hand over Lewis Guns at present in
their possession belonging to "A" & "HQ" Coys., and 1 Gun
belonging to "D" Coy.

  Trench Stores, Maps, Orders, etc., will be handed over,
and receipts sent to Battalion Headquarters by 7 p.m.


27-9-17.                    (Sd.) C.L. Sutton,
                              Capt. & Adjutant,
                            1/9th Bn. Manchester Regt.

WAR DIARY
VOL. XXVI   APPENDIX. 13.

## 1/9th. BATTALION MANCHESTER REGT.

Summary of casualties for month ending Sept 30th. 1917.

| Nature. | Officers. | Other Ranks. |
|---|---|---|
| Killed. | Nil. | 13. |
| Missing. | Nil. | 2. |
| Wounded. | 3. | 92. |
| Totals. | 3. | 107. |

O. Sutton
Capt. & Adjt.

Major.
30-9-17.                Commanding 1/9th. Battn. Manchester Regt.

CONFIDENTIAL  M9

WAR DIARY
of
119th Manchester Regt
from
1/10/17 to 31/10/17

Volume XXVII

# WAR DIARY or INTELLIGENCE SUMMARY

Army Form C. 2118.

1/9 MANCHESTER REGT

Vol XXVII
Page 1

| Place | Date | Hour | Summary of Events and Information | Remarks and references to Appendices |
|---|---|---|---|---|
| COXYDE BAINS | Oct. 7 to 6 | | Ref Map. BELGIUM Sht. 11 40,000. Batt remains on coast defences. Coast defences established. Battn. in camp on "Avenue de la mer". Slight shelling during the afternoon but no casualties. | |
| | Oct 3 | | Advance Billeting party from Batt + three men arrived of R.G.C. at Binern. | |
| " | Oct 6 | 12 noon | Battn moves to CANADA CAMP COXYDE (X.13.a.6.9) en Bus from K BZN Division Reliens in corps reserve by 2nd Bn Royal Fusiliers. | App 1 O.O. 37 |
| M.36.a.7.4 | | | Battn relieves the 15th Bn H.L.I. as the Right Subsector. NIEUPORT sector. 1/10th Bn on left, Belgians on right. Frontier details taken over along the Yseré canal. H.Q. at M.36.a.7.4. | |
| -"- | 6-10 | | Four coys in the line. Light shelling with no casualties. Patrols sent out each night over NIEWLAND POLDER. Take and enemy post from the enemy. Dump + mist spraction reported to regiment & Bings note. Relieved by the Cheetham Rifle + Inniskill Fusils. + Frontier Detail | |
| -"- | 10/11 | | Remains in R.E. fatigue work and DEICAR HUTSE. (X11d) 6N 3 6 ship (M35-13) | App 2 O.O. 38 |
| NIEUPORT | 11-14 | | 8 Billets at NIEUPSW. Enemy carries on to bith's no or almost town. Shells during day on village. 11 mpn Bombarden. No shelling during stay in village. Carrying parties of T.S or Nilrish smithly to Battn on lip. Battn of N. Zone (1/5 Lane Fus. Rep) | App 3 O.O. 40 |
| | 13 | | B Coy (Co Butterworth) reliev. B Co (Lt Holloway) in DEICAR HOUSE | |

1/9 MANCHESTER REGT
Folder VII
Page 2

Army Form C. 2118.

# WAR DIARY
## or
## INTELLIGENCE SUMMARY.
*(Erase heading not required.)*

| Place | Date | Hour | Summary of Events and Information | Remarks and references to Appendices |
|---|---|---|---|---|
| NOLPEN | Oct 14/15 | | Bn relieves 1/4 East Lancs in 10th Section C & D Coys in the Line. | APP. 4 S.O. + P |
| M26 a 7.4 M36 a 7.4 | Oct 15 15.12 | | "A" Coy still short 9/50 O.R. detached to 127 Bde HQ. (British Amelopen to 4th Div) & R.E. Dump. Lt Col LLOYD rejoins from 126 Bde HQ. British Amelopen burnt down in bombard | APP 5 Ops M26 a Ops PISTOL MAP. APP. 6 |
| | Oct 15 | | 4 Coys in the line. Repairing D Buoy Bombards v. | |
| | | | Battn relieved in the Right Bn & Sector by the IV Batt. East Lanc. Regt. | |
| OOST DUNKERQUE | | | Remained in reserve in OOST DUNKERQUE. Thunderstorm during march to out Sector. | |
| | Oct 18 | | 4 Officer report for duty. 2/Lieuts A.B. JACKLYN, 2/Lieuts R.E. ROWE 2/Lieuts W. HUGHES and 2/Lieut F. HUNT from 2/R. (Man) Bn. MANCHESTER REGT. Taken on the strength of the Battalion. | |
| | 21. | | 2nd Lieut W. WITTY Proceeds on leave to U.K. | |
| OOST DUNKERQUE | 19-22 | | Battn in Billets at OOST DUNKERQUE, clothing weight checked daily in villages. Battalion | |

WAR DIARY 1/9th Bn Manchester Regt
or
INTELLIGENCE SUMMARY.
(Erase heading not required.)

Army Form C. 2118.
Vol. XXVII
Page 3.

| Place | Date | Hour | Summary of Events and Information | Remarks and references to Appendices |
|---|---|---|---|---|
| M.30.A.7.4. | Oct 26 | | The Battalion was relieved by the 1/4 East Lancs Regiment with the exception of B Company which remained at WHITE HOUSE were engaged on R.E. fatigues. The remainder proceeded to WULPEN. | APP. 8. O.O. 44. |
| WULPEN | 27-30 | | Battalion on refit duties at WULPEN. Supplied (A) Carrying party 1 Officer & 50 O.R. reporting to Lieut ECHIN at TIRAM Dump 7 P.M. (B) Party of 1 Officer & 50 O.R. reporting to Lieut ECHIN at TRICAR DUMP at 8 P.M. (C) Party of 2 Officers & 100 O.R. reporting to Left Relief Headquarters for carrying rations to front line. These 3 fatigues were supplied nightly. No cheering known stay in village. Reaching parades by companies daily. | APP. 9. |
| M.36.A.7.4. | Oct 30 | | Battalion relieved 1/4 Bn EAST LANCS REGT in the front line right Battalion Sub-Sector, North. Reliefs were active throughout the day. | O.O. 45. |
| -do- | 31 | | 2/Lieut A.E. WROE attached to 428 Field Coy R.E. | |
| -do- | | | 2/Lieut A.P. JACKSON present to GLASGOW R.E. Dump | |
| -a-" | | | Lieut H.H KNIGHT rejoined Battalion from Course of Instruction (VAUX en AMIENOIS). | |

(contd)

# WAR DIARY
## or
## INTELLIGENCE SUMMARY.

(Erase heading not required.)

Army Form C. 2118.

Vol. XXVII
Page 4.

1/9 Bn. Manchester Regt.

| Place | Date 1917 | Hour | Summary of Events and Information | Remarks and references to Appendices |
|---|---|---|---|---|
| COXYDE BAINS | Oct. 2 | | Lieut S. RUTTENAU to Course of Instrn. 42nd DIV. Signalling School. | |
| -do- | - 3 | | 2/Lieut W.W. AVINS to Hospital (Sick) | |
| -do- | - 4 | | Lieut H.H. KNIGHT rejoined Battalion from 42nd DIV. DEPOT BATTN. | |
| -do- | - 5 | | Lieut J. BROADBENT proceeded on leave to UK. | |
| | | | Capt. G.W. HANDFORTH rejoined Battn. from Hospital | |
| | | | 2/Lieut. W. WITTY to Course of Instrn. 42nd DIV. GAS SCHOOL | |
| | | | Capt. C.H.S. REDMOND - Lieut. O.S. NEEDHAM - 2/Lieut H. GORST rejoined from 42 DIV. GAS SCHOOL. | |
| -do- | - 6 | | Capt. F.W. KERSHAW to Hospital (Sick) | |
| M.36.a.7.4 | - 8 | | Capt. D.B. STEPHENSON rejoined Battalion from leave U.K. | |
| | | | 2/Lieut. W.H. CRICK rejoined Battalion from Hospital | |
| | | - 10 | 2/Lieut. A.E. STONE rejoined Battalion from 42 DIV. Bombing School. | |
| | | | 2/Lieut. W. WITTY rejoined Battalion from 42 DIV. Gas School. | |
| WULPEN | - 11 | | 2/Lieut. W.H. CRICK proceeded to 42 DIV. Bombing School | |
| | | | 2/Lieut. G.A. BARTRAM to Course of Instr. IV Corps School LA PLAINE. | |
| -do- | - 12 | | 2/Lieut. E.E. TOWLER rejoined Battalion from XIX Corps School. | |
| | | | Lieut H.H. KNIGHT to Fourth Army School of Mortars, VAUX en AMIENOIS. | |
| | | | Lieut. W.N.B. BURY attached to BELGIAN PROVETE | |
| | | | Lieut. W.E. LEAVER proceeded to 42 DIV. Gas School (Course of Instruction) | |
| -do- | - 13 | | 2/Lieut H.G. WILLIS rejoined Battalion from leave to UK | |
| | | | Capt. W.H. LILLIE rejoined Battalion from Hospital and Sick leave UK | |
| -do- | - 14 | | Rev. Capt. WELBON proceeded to 11th Division to take over duties as senior Chaplain C of E. | |
| | | | A/Capt. H. BURROW attached to Battalion as interpreter. Chaplain proceeded to 42nd Div. | |
| | | | 2/Lieut E.E. TOWLER to Hospital (Sick) Capt F.W. KERSHAW rejoined from Hospital | |
| | | | Lieut O.S. NEEDHAM to Veterinary Course NEUFL CHATEL | |
| M.36.a.7.4 | - 15 | | Lieut-Colonel rejoined Battalion from 126 Bde H.Q. (Lieut. Comnd.) | |
| | | - 16 | 2/Lieut B. BURROW to IV Army Infantry Sanitary Inspection School BOUCHON | |
| OOST DUNKERKE | - 18 | | Lieut J. BROADBENT rejoined Battn. from leave UK Adjutant (Capt. O.V. SUTTON proceeds on leave UK | |
| | | | Lieut W.H. LILLIE & 2/Lieut H.G. WILLIS to Course of Instructor 42 DIV. Gas School Lieut W.E. LEAVER rejoined Bn from 42 DIV. Gas School | |
| | | | Capt. F.W. KERSHAW to Fourth Army Musketry Camp PONT REMY (Course of Instn.) from 42 DIV Gas School | |
| M.36.a.7.4 | - 23 | | 2/Lieut H.G. WILLIS rejoins Bn. from 42 DIV. Gas School Lieut W.H. LILLIE proceed to Fourth Army Gas School MALO (Course of Instr.) | |
| | | - 25 | Capt. H.E. BUTTERWORTH proceeds on leave UK Capt. G.W. HANDFORTH rejoined from leave UK | |
| WULPEN | - 27 | | 2/Lieut G.A. BARTRAM rejoins from 15th Corps School | |
| do. | - 28 | | Lieut O.S. NEEDHAM rejoined from Veterinary Course | |
| | | | 2/Lieut R.J. BADDELEY reported for duty from 8th Reserve Manchester Regt. taken on strength and posted to C Coy. | |
| | | - 29 | Lieut W.H. LILLIE rejoined from Fourth Army Gas School. | |

Commanding 1/9 Bn. Manchester Regt.

1/9th BN. MANCHESTER REGT Orders No. 37.    COPY No..

War Diary

October 5th 1917

1. The Battalion will be relieved in the COXYDE BAINS COAST Defence Sector by the 26th Battn. ROYAL FUSILIERS on the 6th inst. Relief to be completed by 12 Noon.

2. On completion of relief the Battalion will move to CANADA CAMP, COXYDE, X.13.A.6.9., as Divisional Reserve to 32nd Division. Companies will march there as relieved, and report for accommodation to Officer sent in advance.

3. On the night, 6th/7th, the Battalion will relieve the 13th Battn. H.L.I., in the Line, Right Sub-sector, NIEUPORT SECTOR, Battalion H.Q. will be at M.36.a.7.5.

4. Route will be OOST-DUNKERKE – WULPEN BRIDGE – S.8.b.2.3. – S.9.a.3.6. – S.9.a.9.9. – thence via RAMSCAPELLE Road to S.10.b.45.25. – by Track to S.11.a.9.9. thence North up the Main Road.    Distances of 200 yards will be maintained between platoons.

5. Advance party of 1 Officer from H.Q., 1 Officer per Company, and 1 N.C.O. per platoon will be at Battn. H.Q. at 6-15 pm to-day, and will proceed to the line, reporting at H.Q. 13th H.L.I. at 10 p.m., and will remain in the Line until the relief.    They will take rations for two days.

6. 'B' Coy. will be relieved on the 5th inst., reliefs arriving at 4 p.m.    'B' Coy will leave 1 N.C.O. per platoon 5th inst at WULPEN BRIDGE to await advance party at 8 p.m., and proceed with it to the Line. Two days rations will be taken. The 50 ORs of 'A' Coy at R.E. Dump will remain permanently detached.

7. TRANSPORT.    Q.M. will send guide to 430th Coy. A.S.C. for Baggage Wagons at 7-30 a.m. on the 6th inst. They will be returned after unloading at final destination.
    No motor transport is available.    A second journey will have to be performed with 1st Line Transport.

8. GUIDES.    1 Guide from each Coy, 1 from H.Q., and 1 from Transport will be at Cross Roads, ST IDESBALD, W.10.d.9.6., at 9-30 a.m. on the 6th inst.    'C' Coy will have guides for posts at Coy.H.Q.    Company Commanders of 'A', 'B', and 'D' Coys will meet relieving Coys with guides at the Cross Roads, near the TERLINCK HOTEL.    O.C., 'D' Coy., will have a guide at this point for each post in his sector.

9. WATER.    Battalion in the line are handing over a adequate supply of petrol tins as Trench Stores, and these can be filled at the Pump at WHITE HOUSE, M.35.b.9.3.

10. MEDICAL ARRANGEMENTS.    Casualties are evacuated from Regtl. Aid Posts to Advanced Dressing Station at M.34.a.6.6.

11. BURIALS.    Bodies are to be sent by Regtl. Transport to the Mortuary at COXYDE Military Cemetery.

12. RATIONS.    Cooking arrangements exist for Battalions in the front line at MAISON TRICAR and WHITE HOUSE DUMP. Food is taken forward by hot food containers.    Each Battalion will receive about 25 tins of solidified alcohol daily.
    Rations will be taken up by transport to MAISON TRICAR DUMP, M.35.b.6.3.    The best route is via S.17.a.9.8. – S.3.c.7.5. and RAMSCAPELLE.

(Continued.)

ORDERS No. 37 (Continued.)   SHEET II

RATIONS (Contd.)
　　　　The Area S. of the Canal is in the Belgian Command and the road at B.5. central is narrow, and vehicles cannot pass each other. The alternative route is via PELICAN BRIDGE and ALBERT and ELIZABETH BRIDGES. The former route is much less subject to shell fire, but requires traffic control at the narrow points.

13. TRENCH STORES. All S.A.A., etc. will be handed over and taken over, and receipts sent to H.Q. as soon as possible. Improvised L.G., A.A. mountings will be handed over.
　　　　No maps to be handed over, except marked copies necessary for relieving Battalion.

　　　　　　　　　　　　　　　　　　(Sd.) O.J. Sutton,
　　　　　　　　　　　　　　　　　　　Captain & Adjutant,
　　　　　　　　　　　　　　　　1/9th. Battn. MANCHESTER REGT.

DISTRIBUTION :-

　　Copies Nos. 1 - 4   O.C., Coys.
　　　　　　　　  5.   Q.M.
　　　　　　　　  6.   T.O.
　　　　　　　7 - 8   War Diary.
　　　　　　　　  9   File.

ISSUED at ................
BY .....................

SECRET.
1/9th Bn. MANCHESTER REGT Orders No.37.           Copy No.......

## ADDENDA   CORRIGENDA.

Reference, Map:- NIEUPORT Sheet.                October 5th 1917.

1. Ref: Para.3. Battalion will relieve the 15th Battn. H.L.I. and not the 13th as stated.

2. Ref: Para.9. All water will be drawn in dixies and water bottles from WHITE HOUSE, M.35.b.9.3.

3. Ref: Para.12.  Tanks from the Cookers will be taken up in a limber to-morrow evening to the corner house, M.35.b.7.3. and redrawn by Coys.

4. : BLANKETS etc.   Officers Baggage and men's blankets will be retained at Q.M. Stores, OOST DUNKERKE, X.4.c.4.4.
   Blankets of 'A' 'B' 'D' Coys & H.Q. will be dumped at Q.M. Stores properly rolled in bundles of 10 before 8 a.m.
   Officers valises at Q.M. Stores by 9 a.m.

5. Ref: para.4.    ROUTE.    The road running from S.8.b.2.3. to S.9.a.9.9. will not be used. Platoons will proceed from the former point along the canal to S.3.c.7.3., turning to their right from the canal along the camouflaged road.
   While on main road from RAMSCAPELLE to Front Line wherever duckboarding exists beside the road it will be used.

6. In the Line, 'D' Coy will take up NICE ALLEY, 'C' Coy NEGRO trench.    These two Coys are in the Front Line.
   'B' Coy will occupy NASTY AVENUE in Battalion Support.

7. GUIDES.    Five guides per Coy and a guide for H.Q. will meet Coys at 8-30 p.m. at HOOGE BRIDGE HOUSE, M.35.d.4.5.

8. Regimental Aid Post, M.36.a.30.35.

9. Lieut. W.L. PICKFORD will be attached to Battn H.Q. while in the front line.

10. DRESS.  Fighting Order with greatcoat in pack.

11. Move off in the following order 'D','C','B', H.Q.,'A', commencing 5-30 p.m.

12. Transport.   Ride horses will be sent for when required in the morning.    For move from CANADA CAMP they will parade at 5-15 p.m.   Horses for L.G. limbers, Mess Cart & Maltese Cart at same time.
    L.G. limbers will remain at CANADA CAMP till the Coys move off from there.

13. Refilling will be at W.17.d.6.3.

    RELIEF.
14. The usual certificate of cleanliness will be obtained from relieving Coys, and will be sent to Battn. H.Q.

15. 1 OR from each Coy., and 1 from H.Q. will meet at Bn. H.Q. at 10 a.m., and proceed with 2/Lieut. H. GORST to CANADA CAMP, X.13.a.6.9.

(Continued.)

ADDENDA CORRIGENDA (Contd.)  SHEET 2.

16. Leave parties will rendezvous at 10th Battn. Manchester Regt. Transport Lines, X.13.d.1.4. at 9 a.m. daily. Packs will be carried from there to ST IDESBALD Station, F.1.a.3.5. with a guide provided by Lieut. TRUEMAN, 1/10th Bn. Manch. Regt. These parties will report to R.T.O., ST IDESBALD Station by 11-30 a.m., two days prior to departure of leave boat.

17. Salvage Dump, OOST DUNKERKE, X.4.c.4.4.

18. ACKNOWLEDGE.

DISTRIBUTION :-
    As for Orders No. 37.

(Sd.) O.J. Sutton,
    Capt. & Adjt.,
1/9th Bn. Manchester Regt.

ISSUED at ..................
BY ......................

Vol xxvii
App. 2

1/9 Bn Manchester Regt Orders
No. 38.

1. **Relief.** The Battalion will be relieved in the Right Battalion Section by the 1/4 East Lancs Regt on the night of the 10th/11th October.

2. **Guides.** Guides for relieving Battalion will be at end of camouflage in junction of RAMSCAPPELL Road & track to Belgian [Lines S10 B6.3] at 6.30 pm. They will rendezvous at Bn Hd. at 5.40 pm. when Lt PICKFORD will take charge of them and take them to place of meeting. Each guide must be provided with chit stating nature of Coy i.e. 1. Right Coy 2. Left Coy 3. Support Coy 4. Reserve Coy.

3. **Advance Party.** Advance party of 1 NCO from each Coy & Hd. will rendezvous at Bn HQ at 1.30 pm reporting to Lt BUSBY & proceeding with him to WULPEN to take over billets. Reporting to Hd. 1/4 E Lancs Regt at 3 pm.

4. **Bn Party.** Each Coy will have

behind & MO & remain in the
line till the afternoon of the 11th
inst. Each MO. will leave
one runner. They will be
relieved by 1/4 East Lancs Regt.

5. Transport. Dumps for L.Gs. &c
for loading onto limbers will
be made on the Ramscapelle Road
near junction with BRUGES Road
& suitable loading parties left. The
limbers of the 1/4 East Lancs Regt
will be used. Mess Cart, 1 half limber
for equipm. stores [crossed out]
Maltese Cart will be required
at Bn. HQ. at 18.30 p.m. Ride Horses at junction
of track and RAMSCAPELLE RD at 12 MN.
A & B Coys' horses to be at above point at 10 p.m.

6. Trench Stores. All Trench Stores
& sketch maps, défense schemes,
aeroplane photos etc will be taken
over & receipts given to Bn. HQ
by 1 p.m. 11th inst. Certificates of
cleanliness will be obtained &
forwarded at the same time.

7. Completion of relief to be
reported immediately.

8.   7 O.R. from Divl Salvage Coy
billeted with Reserve Coy, will remain
in the lines and will be rationed by
Bde H.Q.
        60 O.R. from Reserve Battn may
be sent up at 12 hours notice to
occupy dugouts with Reserve Coy.

9.     Coys will take over billets in
WULPEN of the same letter.

                                    T. Sutton
                                    Capt & Adjt
                                    1/9 Manch R

Copies HQ A B C D Coys
    5  4 Stores
    6  T.O. & Q.M.
    7.  M.O.
    9   Spare

     Q.M. will send Q.M. Sgts to report to
2Lt BURY at WULPEN H.Q. 1/4 S. Lancs R.
     Q.M. will arrange for hot meals for
A & B Coys at 11·30 pm. & Remainder
of Bn at 12·30 pm.
                                    O.S.
     T.O. will arrange transport for 2 cycles
which will cannot be pushed    O.S.

War Diary Vol XVII App 3.

1/9 Bn Manchester Bn Orders
No. 40.
13th OCT. 1917

1. Duties.   'C' Coy will
relieve 'B' Coy tonight as
party working under R.E.

2. 'C' Coy will move off at
5.30 pm.
'B' Coy will have guides
at corner of BRUGES road
+ RAMSCAPPELLE road at
7 pm.

3. 'B' Coy will leave behind
4 N.C.Os to show 'C'
Coy the work to be done.
These N.C.Os will be
rationed with 'C' Coy
and will remain with
that Coy.

4. 'C' Coy will hand over
to N.C.O of 'B' Coy in
WULPEN 2 Lewis Guns
(less spare parts) and
(amca.)

(Contd.)

48 magazines. 'B' Coy. will hand over to 'C' Coy. on relief similar articles.

5. COOKING. 'C' Coy. will take over necessary cooking utensils from 'B' Coy. and will leave behind for the use of 'B' Coy. and for the party of 'C' Coy. remaining in HUNPEN. These utensils will be regained by their Coys. on relief from the line.

6. Billets. 'B' Coy. will take over 'C' Coys. billets under arrangements to be made by Lieut. WINNIS. 'C' Coy. will leave guides to conduct 'B' Coy. to its billets.

7. Hot soup will be
(Contd.)

2 (contd.)

provided for 'B' Coy. at 10-0 pm. by soup kitchen under management of Rev. RAYMOND.

8.
T.O. and Q.M. will conjointly arrange to have one limber for 'C' Coys. rations and 2 Lewis guns to be at 'C' Coy. H.Q. at 6-45 pm. This limber will be available for use of 'B' Coy. for return journey.

9.
Lieut. BUTTERWORTH. will report to Lieut. ECKLIN. R. Es. — TRICAR Dump at 7.30 pm

10.
Baths. Arrangements will be made for use of Baths for 'B' Coy. at KEMMEL tomorrow morning.
Q.M. will arrange for clean shirts and socks.

(contd.)

(Cont'd.)

11) A. M.R. will arrange to supply dry socks to 'C' Coy. tomorrow night.

12) Acknowledge. (C + B Coys & M.R. + T.O.)

13/10/14

Capt. & Adjt.
1/9 Bn Manchester Regt.

Issued by orderly
at 4 pm M.G.
5.10. O.C.W.

WAR DIARY. VOL XXVII APP 4.
M.D.1570

Bn Marching Orders
No 4

1. The Battalion will relieve the
4 [?] [?] in the Right
Battalion Sector to-night at [?]

2. Coys will take up the positions
now occupied presently i.e.
C Coy Right D Coy Left
B Coy in support. A Coy
in reserve.

3. Coys will move out in the
following order C. D. B. A. H.Q.
C Coy passing A-M-U at
6 pm. Guides will meet Coys
at corner of HAMSCOPPEL Rd. - BRUGES at 7.30pm.

4. C Coy will be relieved by
a party from the 15 Div Lancers
under Cpl. CARTER.

5. Lewis Gun Limbers &
Transport for Cooker & Dixies
will be at WOODEN Bridge (B
Coy HQ) at 5.30 pm.
[?] [?] a Wood and Cart will
be at Bn HQ at 6 pm.
Riding horses will be required at 5.45 pm.

6. Advance parties from Coys & HdQr will leave WULPEN at 3 pm.

7. 2Lt WILLIS will hand over billets & OR & Eq portion to Advance Party of 1/5 East Lancs Regt.

8. Trench Stores will be taken over, receipts obtained & sent to Bn HQ. as soon as possible

9. OC Coys will send to Bn HQ. early in the morning following relief a rough sketch map showing areas occupied by platoons.

10. Completion of relief will be wired to Bn HQ.

11. B Coy will supply all ration parties.

12. The Quartermaster will arrange to supply clean socks as often as possible while the Bn is in the line.

13. Acknowledge

Distribution "A" list

Cp Sutton
Cp 1/5 Manch

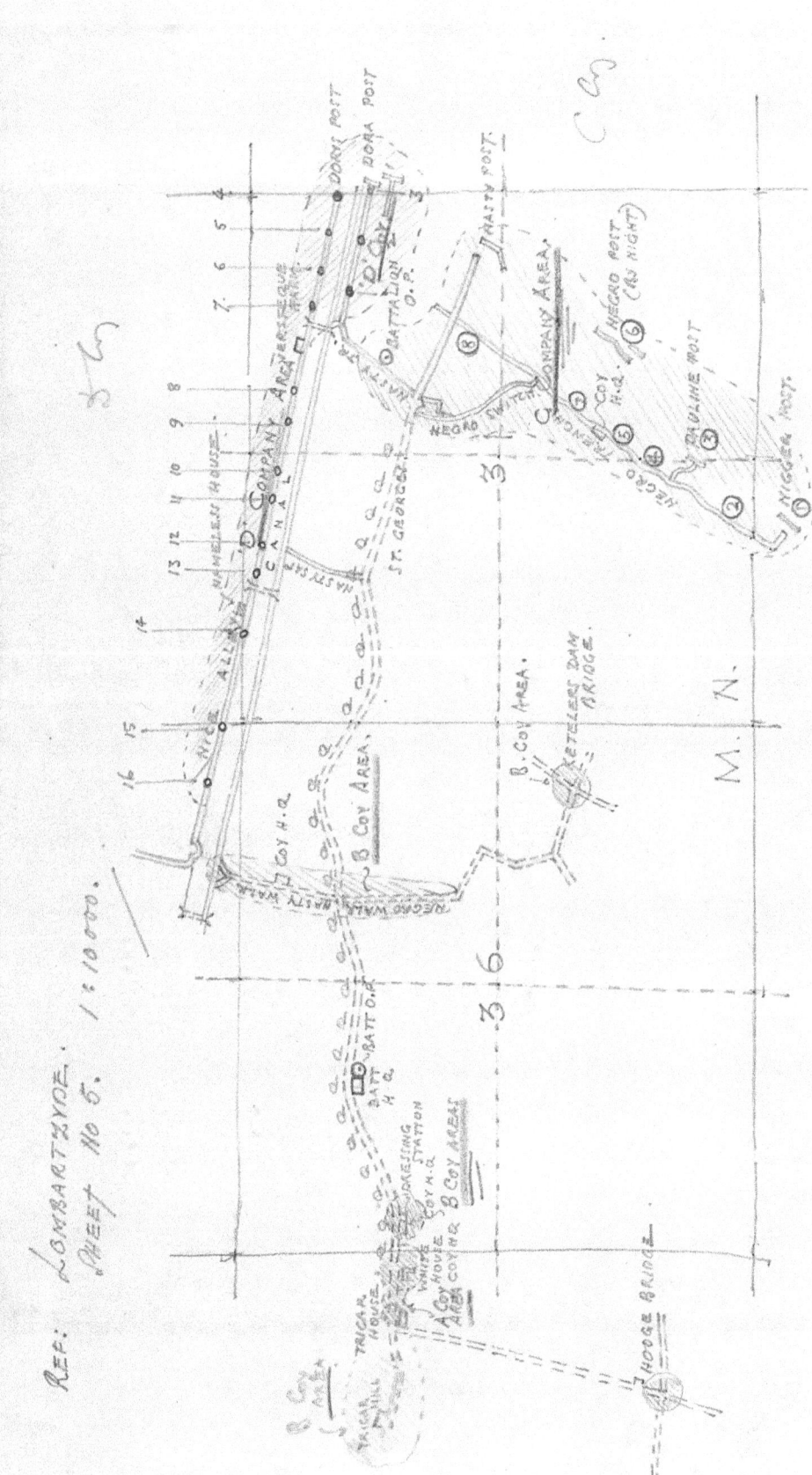

19th Bn. Manchester Regt.  WAR DIARY. VOL XXVII APP. 6

Orders No. 42.     Oct. 18th/17.

Ref. map LOMBARTZYDE. (1/20000)

1. **RELIEF.** The Battalion will be relieved in the Right Battalion Sector by the 1/4th East Lancs Rgt. on the night of 18/19th October. On relief companies will move to OOST DUNKERKE.

2. **GUIDES.** No guides will be required.

3. **ADVANCE PARTY.** Advance party consisting of 1 N.C.O. from each company and 1 from H.Q. will rendezvous at 12-30 p.m. at "B" Coy H.Q. and proceed with officer detailed by O.C. "B" Coy to take over billets from 1/4th East Lancs Rgt. at OOST DUNKERKE.

4. **TRANSPORT.** Dumps for L.Gs etc. for loading on limbers will be made on the RAMSCAPELLE Road near junction of BRUGES Road and suitable loading parties left. The limbers of the 1/4th East Lancs. Rgt will be used. Mess cart, half limber for mess stores and maltese cart will be required at Battn. H.Qrs. at 8-0 p.m. and rede horses for "A" & "B" Coys at 9-0 p.m. remainder at 10-30 p.m.

4 contd.      at junction of track and
              RAMSCAPELLE Road.

5. BLANKETS.  Q.m. will arrange to have
              blankets, haversacks and
              Officers valises at the billets

6. TRENCH STORES.   All trench stores, sketch
                    maps, defence schemes, aeroplane
              photographs etc will be taken over
              and receipts sent to Bn. H.Qrs by
              1-0 p.m. 19th inst. certificates of
              cleanliness will be obtained and
              forwarded at the same time.

7. Completion of relief to be reported
   immediately.

8. Acknowledge.            W. Winford
                           Lieut
                           for Lt. Col.
                           Cmg. 1/9 Manchesters

Copies:-
    1 - 4   "A" to "D" Coys
    5.      1/4th E. Lancs Regt.
    6.      T.O. & Q.M.
    7 - 8.  War Diary.
    9       Spare.

WAR DIARY. Vol. XXVII APP. 7

1/9th Battalion MANCHESTER REGT Operation Order No.43.

COPY No. 7

October 21st, 1917.

(1). The Battalion will relieve the 1/4th Bn. East Lancs. Regt in the front line - Right Subsector, on the night 22/23 Octr.

(2). Companies will take up the position they occupied formerly, 'C' Coy. right, 'D' Coy. left, 'B' Coy in support, 'A' Coy in reserve.

(3). Companies will move up in the following order :- C, D, B, A, H.Q.

(4). 'C' Coy will pass Cross roads, X.4.c. Central, Junction OOST-DUNKERQUE BAINS and COXYDE, NIEUPORT Road at 4-45 p.m. Platoon intervals to be maintained.

(5). Lewis Gun limbers, transport for Dechsies will be at Q.M. Stores at 4 p.m. Mess cart and Maltese cart at Battn. H.Q. at 4-30 p.m.

(6). Advance parties from Companies will leave OOST DUNKERQUE at 2-30 p.m.

(7). 2/Lieut. H. GORST will hand over A.A. and Lewis Gun positions and Billets to advance party of 1/5th Bn. East Lancs Regt.

(8) Trench Stores will be taken over and receipts obtained.

(9) A rough sketch of areas occupied by platoons will be submitted on morning of 23rd inst.

(10). Completion of relief will be wired to Battn. H.Q.

(11). 'B' Coy will supply all ration parties.

DISTRIBUTION :-
Copies No.1/4 - Coys.
5 - T.O/Q.M.
6/7 - War Diary.
8 - ~~File~~ . 1/4 EAST LANCS.

(Sd) E.C. LLOYD,
Lieut. Colonel,
Commdg. 1/9th Bn. Manchester Regt.

ISSUED by ............ at .......

War Diary. Vol XXVII  App. 8
Copy No. 7

1/9th. Bn. Manchester Regt. Orders No. 44.
26th October 1917.

1. "RESCUE" will take over from REBATE on the night of 26th/27th inst.

2. "A" "B" Companies will remain at WHITE HOUSE under Lieut. N. WILKINSON, for day work under R.E's, as before.

3. All Trench Stores will be taken and handed over, and receipts sent to Bn. H.Q. on completion of relief, which will be notified to Bn. H.Q. by the word "GAS".

4. Billeting Parties.

1 N.C.O. from "C" and "D" Companies and 1 from H.Q. under 2/Lieut. C. BARLOW will leave H.Q. at 12.30 P.M. and proceed to WULPEN to take over from sister company "RESCUE" and obtain receipts for any stores etc. in the Area.

5. "RESCUE" will on completion of relief convey Lewis Guns and Stores of "REBATE" to WULPEN.

6. Rids Horses will be at junction of CAMOUFLAGE Road and track leading to Belgian Support at 11 P.M. less "B" Coy.

(Sd) W.H.Pickford
2/Lieut.
for Lieut.-Colonel
Commandg. 1/9 Bn. Manchester Regt.

ACKNOWLEDGE.
Distribution:—
Copies 1-4   A.B.C.D. Coys.
       5.    Q.M. and T.O.
       6.    1/4 Bn. E. Lancs
       7-8.  War Diary
       9.    R.S.M.

WAR DIARY. VOL. XXVII   APP. 9

1/9th Bn. MANCHESTER REGT. ( Orders No. 46) Copy No......

In the Field,
30th October 1917.

1. "REBATE" will relieve " RESCUE " in the right Battn. Sector to-night.

2. Advance Party.
An Advance Party of 1 Officer & 1 N.C.O. per Company and 1 N.C.O from Battn H.Qrs will leave WULPEN at 2-0 p.m. and proceed to the line to take over.
"D" Coy in the left sector, "C" Coy. right, "B" Coy. Support "A" Coy. Reserve.

3. The Battalion will move off in the following order "C", "B" "A", Battn. H.Q.   The first platoon of "C" Coy will pass Battn. H.Qrs., WULPEN at 5-30 p.m.
"D" Coy will relieve the Left Company Sector independantly at 6-30 p.m.

4. All trench stores will be taken over and receipts sent to Battn. H.Q. on completion of relief which will be notified by the word " TART ".

5. Transport.
Transport Officer will arrange for transport.
Mess Cart will be at H.Q. Mess at 7-30 p.m. and Maltese Cart at 2-0 p.m.
Ride Horses are required for Company officers at 5-15 p.m., and remainder at Battn. H. Qrs., at 7-0 p.m.

(Sd) W.L. Pickford, 2/Lieut.,
for Adjutant,
1/9th Battn. Manchester Regt.

DISTRIBUTION :-

Coys.
1/4th.Bn. E. Lancs. R.
1/5th Bn. E. Lancs. R.
T.O./Q.M.
War Diary.
File.

WAR DIARY.

WAR DIARY. Vol. XXVII APP. 10

1/9th Battalion MANCHESTER REGIMENT.

SUMMARY of CASUALTIES for the MONTH OF OCTOBER 1917.

| Nature of Casualty | OFFICERS | OTHER RANKS | |
|---|---|---|---|
| KILLED | Nil. | 3 | |
| WOUNDED | Nil. | 12 | |
| MISSING | Nil. | | |

31-10-17.

Lieut. Colonel,
Commdg. 1/9th Bn. Manchester Regt.

~~Confidential~~

# WAR DIARY

1/9 MANCHESTER REGT.

NOVEMBER
1917.
Volume XXVIII

# WAR DIARY
## or
## INTELLIGENCE SUMMARY.

(Erase heading not required.)

1/9 Bn MANCHESTER Regt       Army Form C. 2118.

Vol XVIII
Page 1

| Place | Date | Hour | Summary of Events and Information | Remarks and references to Appendices |
|---|---|---|---|---|
| HOUT N36 A7 b4 ST GEORGES | Nov 1. -2 | | Report on BELGIUM Sheet 11 1/40,000 LOMBARTZYDE. In the line. Enemy airplanes active over the line. Shelling slight. | (over) |
| " | Nov 3 | | Left front Coy post shelled. 2 or killed at stand-to. Battalion relieved by the East Kent Regt at 9.30 pm | APPENDIX 1 S.O. 46 (over) |
| OOST DUNKERQUE | Nov 4-5 | | In BILLETS at OOST DUNKERQUE. Many civilians left here. Many civilians being returned in to Battalion area & billets. Shelling occurred. Battalion finds small working parties. Own troops and [enemy?] for Anti Aircraft [Lewis?] gun positions. Cleaning, bathing & [parades?] when Coy Commanders [arranged?] | (over) |
| " | Nov 6-7 | | Battalion relieved 1/4 East Kent Regt in the same area in bivouac (ST GEORGES). | APPENDIX 2 S.O. 47 (over) |
| ST GEORGES | 8 | | Enemy OUT DUNKERQUE at 4 pm. 5 ONY's in the line. Occasional shelling on front line & supports. Enemy airplane active. | (over) |
| " | Nov 9 | Dawn | Relieved by the East Kent Regt & yorks billets at NIEUPORT. Rain. | |
| | | | B Coy (STOCKPORT) company at WHITE HOUSE blown up by enemy 4.2's. After what all available men used for working parties. Many arm at the billet about 4 am eating TS. | APPENDIX 3 S.O. 48 |
| NIEUPORT | Nov 13 -16 | | In billets at NIEUPORT. All available men sent up to line and supt to Left Battalion (1/5 East Kent Regt) or the RE. From parties for carrying materials | |

# WAR DIARY
## or
## INTELLIGENCE SUMMARY

Army Form C. 2118.

1/9 Bn. Manchester Regt.

Vol. 26
Page 2

| Place | Date | Hour | Summary of Events and Information | Remarks and references to Appendices |
|---|---|---|---|---|
| " " | Nov 16 | | Bn Hd Qrs DUNKERQUE (700,000)<br>B Coy Capt STEPHENSON relieved C Coy at WHITE HOUSE on entraini front. (GPS) | App. 4<br>O.O. 49 |
| " " | Nov 17 | 4.30 pm | Relieved in WILDEN by Battalion of French Marines, 133rd Armd Division & move (less D Coy) to WELLINGTON CAMP, OOST DUNKERQUE. (GP)<br>Billeting parties found as usual. Orders received for a few days rest. Bn MCLKINSON proceeds to Corner and WILDIS zone before army. | App. 5<br>Working Parties<br>App. 6<br>O.O. 50 |
| WELLINGTON CAMP | | | D Coy rejoins, also Lt Col from Bn. R.O. & N.C. officer reconnoitring to Rs? R Coy from Bn GARRISON (C.R.E.) Dumps, COXYDE, which is taken over by Bn Instead. (GP)<br>Major HUNWORTH detailed to examine billets in BITTERNE & DIVISIONAL Con Camp. Proposal of 2 Companies to clean up the Marsh & collect sea Grenades. Headman's I request, & by 1/9 Br Manchester Regt. One Coy 1/10 Bn MANCHESTER REGT & Garrison for the 1/9th 1/10th Lodgings. 2 Bn from July 16 to coven billets in BITTERNE Con, OOST DUNKERQUE under the 21st November. Rear to region tiles inspection by Battalion. (GP) |  |
| | | 4 pm | Battalion (less Artillery) march to COXYDE & proceeds from Cam by rollin way in convoy of 27 for 12 Omnibus to St. Box via DUNKERQUE where it is Billeted, chiefly in farms, for the night | (GP) |

# WAR DIARY or INTELLIGENCE SUMMARY

Army Form C. 2118.

1/9 B. MANCHESTER REGT.

No. 2.5
Page 3

| Place | Date | Hour | Summary of Events and Information | Remarks and references to Appendices |
|---|---|---|---|---|
| ST. POL | Nov 19 | 8.15 am | Enroute DUNKERQUE 3/11/05.00 HAZEBROUCK. 70 ORs marched to NORTHBOURT (Room A). Billets in NORTHBOURT & a farm S.E. of town. Fairly good. Other billets in town. | APP. 7 O.O. 51 (C.P.) |
| NORTHBOURT | Nov 20 | 1.30 pm | 70 ORs marched to RIETVELD. Coy arrived safety billeted 1.30 pm - 2 pm. Most of about 1½ miles. Recognized in town. Terrain reconnoitered for Officers. | APP. 8 O.O. 51A (C.P.) |
| RIETVELD | Nov 21 | 7.45 am | March route to LONGUE CROIX between STAPLES & HOUDEGHEM. Billets in billets MAZE CASSEL, ST MARIE CAPPEL, HOUDEGHEM. Roll ? very scattered, at 3 from B. H.Q. not CERF Bros, LONGUE CROIX. | APP. 9 O.O. 52 (C.P.) |
| LONGUE CROIX WITTES | Nov 22 | 9.30 am | March route to WITTES, 2 miles N. of AIRE. Route via WALLON CAPPEL, LYNDE, BLARINGHEM, WITTES. Good billets in twos, threes in men Coys. Accommodation for Officers. Inhabitants very friendly with us on the first billet. Troops for some months. Bath, break & meal one butter supplied with their clothing. Photos tracing Difficulties west to trust the road. Continued state.) 128 ORs in reserve 24 ORs sent on leave. | APP. 10 O.O. 53 (C.P.) |
|  | 25 |  | Warning Order received re H.Q.I. Division is taking over from 25th Division in the neighbourhood of GIVENCHY, LA BASSÉE about N.27 centre to S.28a (BETHUNE) | (C.P.) |
|  | 26 |  | A Coy (Major HOWORTH) reforms battalion at WITTES. Orders received for move to ROBECQ M.27A & BETHUNE Area (MT. BERENCHUN) on 28.5 | (C.P.) |

**WAR DIARY**
or
**INTELLIGENCE SUMMARY**

Army Form C. 2118.

Vol 28
Part 4

1/9 B. Manchester Regt

Summary of Events and Information
(Erase heading not required.)

| Place | Date | Hour | Summary of Events and Information | Remarks and references to Appendices |
|---|---|---|---|---|
| WITTES | Nov 27 | 9.am | Refugees arrive. BETHUNE COMBINED WORKSHOPS. Route march to ROBECQ by Company. AIRE & BUSNES. Rained 1.30pm. Fair weather. Gas instruction for Officers. | APP. 11 O.O. 54 |
| ROBECQ | Nov 28 | 10.30 | Route march to MT BERNENCHON about 2 miles. During the week of Nov 18th Nov to 28th much discipline has been good (only 2 men fell out) – advance party allotted non-Com. Pickets – To check have been well. | |
| MT BERNENCHON | Nov 29 | | Platoon training at MT BERNENCHON – LES HERBOIRES. Battn. Arrived Nov. 28 may be required to support 1/9 Manch R. if ordered to reinforce units on 1/4 East Lanca Bn. of that Battn. in event of withdrawal Givenchy section – if either of these Battalion given or withdrawn flank, & may be required when one or both Obs gaps is open Battalion in reserve forward trenches in MT to be to reinforce the Givenchy Sector. | APP. 12 CASUALTY LIST |

Army Form C. 2118.

1/9 MANCHESTER Regt
Vol 28
Page 5

# WAR DIARY
## or
## INTELLIGENCE SUMMARY.
*(Erase heading not required.)*

| Place | Date | Hour | Summary of Events and Information | Remarks and references to Appendices |
|---|---|---|---|---|
| ACW | April | | Lieut N.H. LITTLE to Base. 29/10/12 PRECAUTIONARY as Gas Instructor | (1) |
| | 1 | | Pte WILLIS to A/Capt. seconded from 1st Batt | |
| | 2 | | 2/Lt MIDDLEY & 2/Lt BYNG Gas Instr course | |
| | | | Capt. MYATT & LUTTON rejoin from Leave UK | |
| | 4 | | 2/Lt DOUGH rejoin from Hospital | |
| | | | 2/Lt BUSHBY R & Bn Lewis Gunner | |
| | 5 | | 2/Lt NAMEYER John Bn Trench Gun Mortar – to RSR B.S. | |
| | | | 2/Lt H. NITTY rejoin from Leave UK | |
| | | | 2/Lt WILLIS rejoin | |
| | 6 | | 2/Lt BURROWS admitted to 3/4 Army Infantry School, FLIXECOURT | |
| | | | 2/Lt WESLEY rejoin | |
| | 7 | | Lt. QM DOROFY to Leave UK | |
| | 8 | | Lt LONGER to Hospital Sick | |
| | 9 | | 2/Lt STONE to 3rd Army Infantry School (Arras) | |
| | 11 | | 2/Lt ROXY to Leave UK | |
| | | | Capt OUTTERWORTH from Leave UK | |
| | 12 | | 2/Lt NITTY to Conv 4th Army Infantry School | |
| | 13 | | 2/Lt RERRIHON rejoin from 132 Brow Batts Mortar School | |
| | | | 2/Lt ROSSMIN rejoin from Course UK | |
| | 14 | | Capt PERGUAN to Leave UK | |
| | 15 | | 2/Lt BATES John from 2/7 MANCR & in posts to B Coy | |
| | | | 2/Lt BARTRAN rejoin from Leave UK | |
| | 16 | | 2/Lt NORWOOD to Corps SHQ team for Final Lewis Gun Course | |
| | 17 | | 2/Lt BUTCHARD rejoin from Bn Lewis Sig't Course | |

# WAR DIARY
## or
## INTELLIGENCE SUMMARY.

*(Erase heading not required.)*

Army Form C. 2118.

1/7 Manchester Regt

| Place | Date | Hour | Summary of Events and Information | Remarks and references to Appendices |
|---|---|---|---|---|
| | Nov 18 | | 2Lt Boddeley rejoins | |
| | Nov 22 | | 2Lt Gurney proceeds to leave U.K. | 61 |
| | 23 | | Lt Jackson rejoins from R.E. Camp | 61 |
| | | | 2Lt Carrey rejoins from R.E. | |
| | 24 | | Capt Redmond, M.O. proceeds to leave U.K. | |
| | | | 2Lt Q.M. Darby rejoins from leave UK | 61 |
| | | | 2Lt H.G.Chatham appointed O.M.S Officer — 53rd Division in place of Lieut. R. Heaton | |
| | 26 | | 2Lt Dunlop proceeds to leave U.K. | 61 |
| | | | 2Lt Bartram to command 1/5 Corps Infantry School | 61 |
| | 27 | | Lt J. Drodgsent sick to hospital | 61 |
| | 28 | | 2Lt Pickfors to attached Stockport area school. | 61 |
| | 29 | | 2Lt Hilkinson rejoins from course | |

O Innes
Lieut Col
1/7 Manchester Regt

Secret

WAR DIARY Vol. XXVIII APP. 1    Copy No. 1

**1/9th Bn. Manchester Regt. Orders No. 46.**

Reference Map: LOMBARTZYDE (1/20,000)                November 3rd 1917

1. **RELIEF.** The Battalion will be relieved in the right Battalion sector by the 4th Bn East Lancs Regt. on the night of 3rd/4th November. On relief the Battalion will move to billets in OOST DUNKERKE.

2. **GUIDES.** No guides will be required by relieving unit.

3. **ADVANCE PARTY.** Advance party, consisting of 1 N.C.O. from each Coy. and 1 from H.Q. will rendezvous at 1 p.m. at "B" Coy. H.Q. and proceed with 2/Lieut. A.E. STONE to take over billets from 4th Bn. East Lancs. Regt. at OOST DUNKERKE.

4. **TRANSPORT.** Transport for conveyance of Lewis Guns, Medical Stores etc. will be provided by 4th Bn. East Lancs. Regt. Men carts of 1/9th Bn. Manchester Regt. will be required at 8 p.m. Ride horses for A & B Coys. at 8.30 p.m. Remainder at 10 p.m. Water carts will not be required.

5. **TRENCH STORES.** All trench stores, sketch maps, defence schemes, aeroplane photos, details of work in hand etc. will be handed over & receipts sent to Bn. H.Q. by 1 p.m. on the 4th inst. Certificates of cleanliness will be obtained and forwarded at the same time.

6. Completion of relief will be reported immediately. Code word will be "SUGAR".

7. **BLANKETS.** The Q.M. will arrange to have blankets, haversacks and officers valises at the billets.

8. **LEWIS GUN positions.** "B" Coy will relieve 3 Lewis guns of "A" Coy. Two Lewis guns in OOST DUNKERKE & NIEUPORT. One man per gun will rendezvous at "B" Coy. H.Q. under N.C.O. to be detailed by O.C. "B" Coy. at 11-30 am & proceed to H.Q. 4th Bn. East Lancs Regt. to take over positions. O.C. "B" Coy. will send written instructions with the N.C.O.

9. **BATHS.** 2/Lieut. A.E. STONE will make arrangements at the Baths at QUEVELAND camp for use by the Battalion on the 4th inst.

10. Acknowledge.

DISTRIBUTION:—
  Normal,
  4th Bn. East Lancs Regt.

(Sd) C.J. Sutton
Capt & Adjt.,
1/9th Bn. Manchester Regt.

SECRET 9  WAR DIARY No XXVIII APP. 2

1/9th Battn. MANCHESTER REGT. Orders No. 47.   Copy No. 9

NOVEMBER 7th, 1917.

1. **RELIEF.** The Battalion will relieve the 1/4th Bn. East Lancs Regiment in the Right Battalion Sector on the night 7th/8th inst.

2. **DISPOSITIONS.** Companies will take up the positions they occupied formerly, "C" Coy. Right ; "D" Coy. Left ; "B" Coy. Support ; and "A" Coy. Reserve.

3. Companies will move up in the following order. "D", "C", "B", "A" & H.Q.   "D" Coy moving off at 4-30 p.m.   No guides will be required.

4. **ADVANCE PARTY.** One Officer and 1 N.C.O. per Company from "C" & "D" Coys and 1 N.C.O. from "A" & "B" Coys will report at the Line at 3 p.m.

5. **BILLETS.** 2/Lieut. E.E. TOWLER will hand over billets and A.A., L.G. positions to advance party of Battalion taking over in OOST DUNKERQUE. "B" Coy will provide guides for the A.A., L.G. positions when required.

6. **TRENCH STORES.** Trench stores will be taken over and receipts sent to Battn H.Q. after relief.

7. Relief will be notified to Battn. H.Q. by the word " CAKE "

8. 8' C' Coys' will send to Battn. H.Q. early in the morning a sketch map of dispositions and shewing areas occupied by platoons.

9. **TRANSPORT.** T.O. will arrange for necessary transport. Lewis gun limbers & Maltese cart will be required at 3-30 p.m.   Company ride horses will be required at 3-45 p.m. Water cart will proceed at time to be arranged by T.O.

10. "B" Coy. will provide all ration parties in the line.

11. The Q.M. will arrange to supply clean socks as often as possible.

12. **ACKNOWLEDGE.**

(Sd) O.J. Sutton,
Capt. & Adjt.,
1/9th Bn. Manchester Regt.

DISTRIBUTION.
Copy No. 1 - 4   O.C. Coys.
         5.   Q.M.
         6.   T.O.
       7 - 8   War Diary.
         9.   File
        10.   1/4th Bn. E. Lancs. Regt.

ISSUED at 9.45 by

WAR DIARY. Vol XXVIII   APP. 3.   No 10

1/9 B. Manchester Regt Orders.
           No. 48                    Nov. 12/17

1. Relief   The Battalion will be relieved
   in the Right Battalion Sector by the
   1/4 East Lancs Regt. to-morrow night, 12th
   inst, & will proceed to billets in
   WULPEN.

2.          B Coy will relieve Coy of
   1/4 East Lancs near IRICAR MILL.
   O.C. B Coy will make all arrangements
   with the Officer commanding this Coy.

3. Billets  The a/Quartermaster will take
   over billets in WULPEN with the
   Quartermaster Sergeants during the
   morning & will arrange to have
   blankets, packs & officers' valises
   at the billets.

4. Lewis Guns  A Coy will take over
   Lewis Gun positions in WULPEN.

5. Transport  Transport will be provided
   by 1/4 East Lancs Regt. Rifle Lorries
   will be required as follows. A Coy
   7.30 p.m. C & D Coys 9.30 p.m. &
   H.Q. at 9.45 p.m. at usual place
   near the gap in the camouflage
   at end of track.

6.          Lt Knight will report
   at H.Q. 1/4 East Lancs Regt at 2.30

APP 3

pm to take over stores, papers, etc.

7. Working Parties. O.C. C Coy & O.C. D Coy will each detail parties of 2 officers & 50 o.r. to report to Lt ECHLIN at TRICKR DUMP as soon as possible after relief. O.C. B Coy will detail 1 officer & 60 o.r. to report to Capt THOMAS Special Coy R.E. at 6.30 pm at M 36 a 7.5.

8. Trench Stores. Receipts for Trench Stores & certificates of cleanliness will be forwarded to Orderly Room by noon on the 13th inst.

9. Completion of relief will be notified immediately by the word MOLASSES.

10. Acknowledge.

O. Sutton
Capt & Adjt
1/9 Bn Manchester Regt

Distribution.
1-4   Coys
5     Q.M.
6     T.O.
7     1/4 East Lancs Regt
8-9   War Diary
10    File

War Diary Vol XXVIII   App. 4

1/9th Bn. Manchester Regt.

Order No 49     18th Nov. 1917.

1.   "D" Coy. will relieve "B" Coy. as working party
     under R.E. at TRICAR DUMP to-night.
     "B" Coy. will move to "D" Coys. billets in VULPEN as
     soon as work is completed for the day.
     "C" Coy. will supply working parties to-night as ordered.

2.   "B" Coy. will leave 1 officer and 25 O.Rs. to proving
     draining party under Lieut. ECKLIN to-morrow, 19th inst.
     This party will move to VULPEN after completion of work.

3.   "D" Coy. will commence day work under R. E. on the
     19th inst.

4.   "B" Coy. officers chargers will be required at 8-15 a.m.
     Rations for "B" Coy. will be sent with Kubl limber which will
     take up "B" Coys. Lewis Guns.

     Acknowledge.

DISTRIBUTION :-
     O.C. "B" & "D" Coys.                    (Sd.) G. J. Sutton,
     T.O. & Q.Mr.                            Capt. & Adjt.
     Lieut. ECKLIN.                          1/9th Bn. Manchester Regt.

WAR DIARY Vol XXVIII APP 5

## 1/9th Bn. Manchester Regt.

### Working Parties.

15th November 1917.

                                2Lt CRICK.

1. O.C. "C" Coy. will detail ~~1 Officer~~ & 50 O.Rs. (Working Strength) & 2 stretcher bearers. This party will carry rations for the Left Battn. Move off at 6-0 p.m. The Officer in charge will report to the Battn. Headquarters at the SARDINERIE on arrival. This party will also do one journey carrying R.E. material for 1/5th Bn. East Lancs. Regt.

2. The following party of 50 O.Rs. will parade at Battn. H.Qrs. at 4-50pm. and move off at 5-0 p.m. The Officer in charge will report to Lieut. ECKLIN at TRICAR DUMP at 6-30 p.m.

       "C" Coy.  20 O.Rs.
       "B" "     10 "   and 2 stretcher
       "A" "      4 "           bearers.
       H. Qrs.    8 "
       "D" Coy.   8 to ~~report~~ join party
at TRICAR DUMP at 6-30 p.m.
1 Officer from "A" Coy.
1 Officer from "C" Coy. Capt. BUTTERWORTH.
                        2 Lt MELLOR.

3. O.C. "B" Coy. will detail a party of 1 Officer and 50 O.Rs. (Working strength) and 2 stretcher bearers. This party to report to Lieut. ECKLIN at 7-0 p.m. Move off at 5-30 pm.

Names of Officers detailed to be reported to Bn. H. Qrs.

ACKNOWLEDGE.                 (Sd.) O. J. Sutton,
O. C. Coys.                      Captain & Adjutant,
O.C. 1/5th E. Lancs.     1/9th Bn. Manchester Regt.
Lieut. ECKLIN.

WAR DIARY Vol XXVIII APP.C.

Secret

1/9th. Bn. Manchester Regt.            Copy No. 9
Orders No. 20.
                                       Nov. 15th. 1917.

1.
    The 42nd. Division is being relieved and is moving out of the XV Corps Area to the First Army Area via WORMHOUDT.
    The 1/9th Bn. Manchester Regt. is being relieved by Battalion of the 133rd. French Division and will move to WELLINGTON CAMP on the evening of November 16th 1917.

2.
    The British S.O.S. Rifle Grenade will remain in force until 12-0 noon, 19th November.

3.
    On relief in WULPEN, Coys. will move to WELLINGTON CAMP in parties not larger than platoons at 200 yards distance. Guides will meet Coys. and H. Qrs. in OOST DUNKERKE at corner of WULPEN - OOST DUNKERKE Road and OOST DUNKERKE - NIEUPORT Road at 5-0 p.m. The Q.Mr. will ensure that the guides are informed of the nearest way to WELLINGTON CAMP.
    Guides will be provided by Coys. for their working parties returning from the line.

4.
    "D" Coy. will return from the line on the 17th inst. Details from GLASGOW DUMP about 4-30 p.m. on the 17th inst. and details from 428 Field Coy. R.E. at the same time.

5.
    On the 18th inst. the Battalion will move to the SYNTHE Area by Motor lorries from the COXYDE - COXYDE BAINS Road between 4-30 and 5-0 p.m. On the 19th inst. the 126th Bde. will move to the WORMHOUDT Area "A" via DUNKERKE and BERGUES.

6.
    "A" Coy. under Major HOWORTH will remain behind when the Battalion moves and will be located in BRISBANE CAMP.

7.
    Transport will pass the Cross Roads, COXYDE at 9-11 a.m. on the 18th inst.

8.
    Advance party consisting of 2/Lieut. HUGHES, and 1 N.C.O. from Battalion H. Qrs. and one from "B", "C" and "D" Coys. will meet the Staff Captain at the Town Major's Office, OOST DUNKERKE at 7-30 a.m. November 17th. The Party will be mounted on cycles. Officer's kit and N.C.Os' Blankets and packs will be taken to Town Major's Office, OOST DUNKERKE and loaded on G.S. Wagon at 7-30 a.m., November 17th. This Advance party will sleep at Q.Mr. Stores to-night. Rations for 17th and 18th inst. will be carried.

9.
    Transport for move to WELLINGTON CAMP will be at WULPEN at 4-30 p.m. 16th inst.

                            (Sd.) O. J. Sutton,
                                Captain & Adjutant,
DISTRIBUTION:-                    1/9th Bn. Manchester Regt.
Copies 1 - 4. Coys.
       5. T. O.
       6. Q.M.
       7 File.
       8 & 9 War Diary.

SECRET.   1/9th. Bn. Manchester Regt.   COPY No. 4
          Orders No. 50. Addendum 1.        Nov. 16th. 1917.

1. **Supplies.**
The Divisional Supply Column lorries will deliver rations to a Ration Dump in each Brigade Area daily, and the Battalion will draw the following days rations on arrival with their own transport. The lorries allotted to the Battalion may be used for this purpose after unloading.   Officers proceeding in advance, must ascertain from the Staff Captain, the exact position of this dump, and the time at which their Unit draw.   Units will move with the unexpended portion of the days ration only.

2. **TRANSPORT.**
(1) Baggage Waggons.
Baggage waggons will be sent to Quartermasters Dumps at 6-30 a.m. on the morning of the 18th inst.
(2) Extra transport for the Battalion.
The following allotment of extra transport has been made:-
Each Battalion.   1 Motor Lorry   2 G.S. Waggons.
The G.S. Waggons will be sent to the Battalion by 6-30 a.m. on the morning of the 18th. inst.   Arrangements as to the distribution of motor lorries will be issued later.
(3) Any baggage which cannot be carried on the lorries or G.S. waggons provided, must be sent to ST. IDESBALDE Railhead by 6-0 pm. on the 17th inst.   O.C. 1/10th. Manchester Regt. will detail one Officer to be there at that time to receive baggage, and to see that it is properly stacked ready for loading. The time at which trucks will be ready for loading on the 18th. will be notified later and O.C. / 1/10 Bn. Manchester Regt. will arrange to provide 1 Officer and 20 men as loading party.

3. **AMMUNITION.**
The Battalion will move with complete establishment of Mobile Reserve of S.A.A., Grenades, etc. "A"

4. —
"A" Coy will remain behind and will be located at BRIGANDE CAMP.   Two G.S. waggons are being sent from the Divisional Train for the use of this party.
"A" Coy will retain its Field Cooker and Officer's charger.

5. **LEAVE PARTY.**
The leave party sailing on the 20th inst will report to R.T.O. DUNKIRK by 7-0 a.m. on the 19th. inst.   Further instructions will be issued.

6. **BUSSES.**
A separate timetable will be issued of the busses or lorries for the conveyance of dismounted personnel.   The em-bussing at COXYDE will take place under the supervision of Major H.L.PADDOCK 1/4th. Bn. East Lancs Regt

7. **SANITATION.**
All rubbish and refuse is to be incinerated before departure from camps or billets, and incinerators are to be cleared and not left piled up with unburned rubbish.   If necessary, rear parties in charge of an Officer will be left to see that vacated camps and billets are left clean.

(Sd.) O.J. Sutton.
Capt & Adjt.
1/9th. Bn. Manchester Regt.

Distribution:-
Copy No. 1. O.C. "A" "B" & "C" Coy.
  "    2. O.C. "D" Coy.
  "    3. Q.M. & T.O.
  "    4. & 5. War Diary.
  "    6. File.

SECRET.  1/9th Battalion MANCHESTER REGT Orders No. 50.   Copy No....

ADDENDUM   No. 2.

Reference Maps FRANCE & BELGIUM, 11, 1/40,000  OOST DUNKERQUE and
        Sheet 19 BELGIUM, 1/100000 DUNKERQUE
            -  ditto  -   HAZEBROUCK.

November 17/1917.

1. **SUPPLIES.**  Supplies will be drawn at 3 p.m. daily by the Motor Lorries allotted to the Battalion for the conveyance of surplus baggage.

2. **TRANSPORT.**  The extra G.S. Wagon ( see ADDENDUM No. 1. ) and also the baggage wagons will remain with the Battalion, and will move with 1st Line Transport until the completion of the move.

3. **ADVANCE PARTIES.**  The advance party under 2/Lieut. W.H. CRICK to-day proceeded to the SYNTHE AREA by Motor Lorry. A further advance party will proceed to-morrow under 2/Lieut. W.L. PICKFORD.  One N.C.O. from Battn. H.Q. & one N.C.O. from "B", "C" & "D" Coys will report to 2/Lieut. PICKFORD at 9-30 a.m.  They will then proceed to Q.M. Stores where cycles are available for them.
This party will remain in SYNTHE on the night of the 18th. Billets will be arranged for them by 2/Lieut. CRICK. On the morning of the 19th, they will proceed to Area Commandant's Office, WORMHOUDT AREA "A".
Further orders will be issued later.

4. **LEAVE PARTY.**   Ref : OO. No. 50 ADD. 1. Para. 5. -
The party sailing on the 23rd inst will consist of 1 Officer and 17 OR of the 1/9th Bn. Manchester Regt, and will proceed from HAZEBROUK Station, reporting to the R.T.O., there by 9 a.m. on the 22nd inst.

5. **BUSSES.**  Busses for conveying personnel of the Battalion will be on COXYDE BAINS Road, North of COXYDE at 5 p.m. on the 18th inst.   The lorries are being supplied on a basis of one lorry per 25 of strength.

6. **TRANSPORT**  Field Cookers and Water Carts will be moved to Transport Lines at 7 a.m.   Maltese Cart & Mess Cart will be loaded at 6-30 a.m.   Blankets & Officers valises will be dumped near road at entrance to camp ready for loading on G.S. Wagons on OOST DUNKERQUE - NIEUPORT BAINS Road, North of Camp at 6 a.m.   R.S.M. will have loading party ready at that time.
Q.M. will send guide for 1 Motor Lorry to Q.M.S. Howard at Bde. Hd Qrs. Transport Lines, COXYDE at 7-30 a.m. on the 18th inst.

(Sd.) O.J. Sutton,
Capt. & Adjt.,
1/9th Bn. Manchester Regt.

DISTRIBUTION :-
    Normal.

WAR DIARY Vol XXVIII App. 7.

Copy No.

1/9 Bn Manchester Regt Orders
No 57.                    Nov. 18/17

Ref. Maps. BELGIUM 1/40,000 DUNKERQUE
            "    "   HAZEBROUCK
      BELGIUM + FRANCE 1/10,000 Sheet 19

1. The Battalion will move by march route to NORMHOUDT AREA "A" on the 19th inst, + will pass the starting point (CROSS ROADS half mile South of FORT LOUIS) at 9.18 am.

2. Distances of 200 yards will be kept between Companies and 20 yards between every six vehicles. The transport will count for this purpose as a Company.

3. The usual hourly halts will be maintained. In addition there will be a halt from five minutes to the half hour until the half hour, and a mid-day halt from 12 noon until 1.30 p.m.
   A. Knowledge.

                        O. Sutton
                        Capt. Adjt
                        1/9 Manch R

1/9 Bn Manchester Regt Orders
No 51   ADDENDUM 1.        No 1.18

1. The Battalion will move off at
8 am. Fall in on Canal Bank
just East of transport lines
in column of route facing
East in the following order. HQ.
B.C. + D.

2. Transport, etc.   All officers'
valises will be returned to
transport lines by 7 am.
Mess Cart will be sent to HQ
Mess (Billet 41*) at 7 am.
Ride horses will be at
the falling in place at 7.45 am.
Cookers will join the transport
at 7.15 am.

3. Dress.   Marching Order Greatcoats
in packs.  Leather jerkins
will be carried rolled & tied on
belt.

4. Route.   Capt Butterworth will
reconnoitre route to FORT LOUIS
& will report to Adjt at 7.50 am
& act as guide to the Battalion.

O. Sutton
Capt Adjt
1/9 Manch R

18.11.17.

WAR DIARY Vol XXVIII

APP. 8
O.O. 51 A

O.C. Coys  B
           C
           D
           R.S.M
           Q.M. M.
           T.O.

1. Coys and Headquarters will move to new billets in RIETVELD this afternoon independently. Billeting NCOs will act now and act as guides. Coys will move out of their present billets between 1 & 2 pm. H.Q. will close at WORKHOUSE at 1.30 pm & open again at RIETVELD at 2 pm.

2. Transport. Blanket valises will be collected by Q.M. at 11 am. & will be returned to transport lines. Cookers will proceed with Coys. Tea urns will be sent at 1.15 pm. Mess Cart will be required at 1 pm.

Ride horses at 1 P.M.

3. Shentr Officer commanding Coys will certify that their billets are left clean and sanitary & that no claims are outstanding against them for damage done to billets & fields. This applies to every change of billets, however temporary.

4. Billeting Lists for the new area will be sent in to-night. 2/Lt HUNT will collect these lists from orderly room, compile billeting list for Battalion & take this billeting certificate to Area Commandant at ZERMEZEELE. He will also obtain certificate of clearance from the Area Commandant.

C/ Sutton
Capt Adjt
20.11.17     1/9 Manch R

WAR DIARY. Vol XXVIII APP 9.

1/9th Battalion MANCHESTER REGIMENT Orders No. 52.

Copy No ...

NOVEMBER 20/1917.

Reference Maps FRANCE, Sheet 27, 1/40,000
HAZEBROUCK 1/100,000

1. The Battalion will march to STAPLE near WALLON CAPPEL to-morrow. Route for "B" & "C" Coys & H.Q. will be by the road running South from Battalion H.Q., joining the WORMHOUDT-CASSEL Road about 3,000 yards South of RIETVELD. "D" Coy will join the Battalion at this point.
The order of march will be as follows - H.Q., "C", "B", "D" Transport. H.Q. and "B" Coy will pass the gate at Battalion H.Q. at 7-45 a.m. "C" Coy will join en route and "D" Coy. as stated above.

2. Transport. Blankets and Officers valises will be collected at 6-30 a.m., except those from Battn. H.Q. which will be collected at 7-15 a.m. Mess Carts and Maltes Cart will be loaded at 7-15 a.m. Teams for Cookers will be sent to Coys at 7-20 am "C" & "D" Coys Cookers will join the transport en route. Ride horses will report at 7-30 a.m.

3. Advance parties will proceed as ordered.

4. 2/Lieut. G. HUNT will complete billeting arrangements, and obtain certificate of cleanliness from Area Commandant, ZERMEZELE. He will report to Adjutant before the Battalion moves.

5. Sick parade will be held at the destination.

ACKNOWLEDGE.

(Sd.) O. J. Sutton, Captain and
Adjutant,
1/9th Battn. Manchester Regt.

DISTRIBUTION :-
Normal.

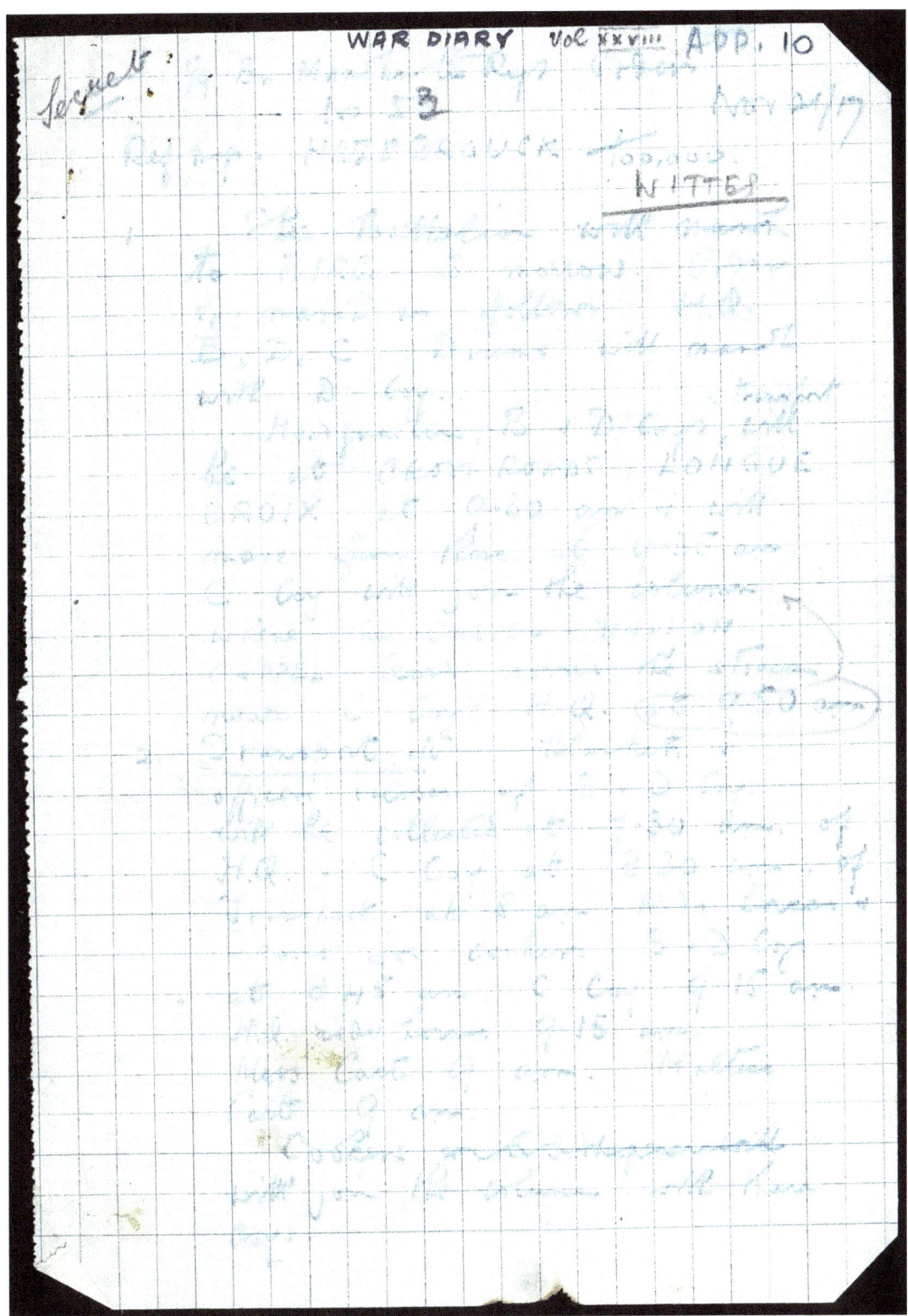

Date ormulas will in future be well camouflaged by any on the convoy. They must be offloaded at the hourly halt.

3. Cpl BARDSLEY will complete the following certificates + other "carpets of clearance" from the AREA COMMANDANT STAPLES.

4. Sgt Parade 7:30 am Altmark(?).

O. Sutton
Capt Adjt
1st Bn ManchR

Blankets + other items must be turned in without delay on arrival of L/Upper
Sgt

111

1/9th Bn. Manchester Regt.

Summary of Officers, O.R.s Killed, Wounded, Missing and Sick to Hospital for Month Ending 31st March, 1917.

| Officers | | Other Ranks | |
|---|---|---|---|
| Total Killed | } NIL | Total Killed | } NIL |
| " Wounded | | " Wounded | |
| " Missing | | " Missing | |
| " Sick | 1 | " Sick | 59 |
| Total | 1 | Total | 59 |

R.B. Howth, Major
for Lieut. Colonel
Commanding 1/9th Manch. Regt.

31.3.17

SECRET.                                          Coy No..
            1/9th Battn. MANCHESTER REGT Orders No.54.
                              a              November 26th, 1917.
    Ref.Map 36   1/40,000   BETHUNE, 1/40,000

QM.

1. **MOVE.** The Battalion will move by march route to ROBECQ on the 27th inst., and MT. BERNENCHON on the 28th inst. The 126th Inf. Bde will be in Divisional Reserve in the BETHUNE Area.

2. **MARCH.** During the march, distances of 100 yards will be kept between Companies, and between Units and their transport. 100 yards distance will be kept between all units except battalions in rear of whom 500 yards distance will be xxxx left. The usual hourly halts will be maintained. There will be no halt at the half hour.

3. **BLANKETS & VALISES.** Blankets and valises of "B" Coy and Battn. H. Qrs will be dumped at Q.M. Stores at 7a.m. Those of "A", "C" & "D" Coys will be collected by Battalion limbers at 6-30 a.m. at Coy. H.Q., and sent to Q. M. Stores by 6-45 a.m., where they will be reloaded by Q.M. on G.S. Wagons. Blankets must be rolled and tied in bundles of 10.

4. **TRANSPORT 1st LINE.** Maltese Cart, Mess Cart will be loaded at 8 a.m. Teams for Water Carts and Cookers will be sent at 8 a.m. Ride horses will be required at 8-15 am. Baggage Waggons and Supply Waggons. The Q.M. will send guides for Baggage and Supply Waggons to 430th, A.S.C. for 6 am. These waggons will be used for drawing rations from refilling point. They will remain with the Battalion during the move and will be returned to 430th A.S.C. at LA HAMEL by 9 a.m. on the 29th inst.
   **Motor Lorries.** 3 Motor lorries will be used for conveying surplus baggage to a dump at BETHUNE. Q.M. will send guide for the lorries to Bde H.Q. for 6 a.m., 27th inst. After loading, the lorries will rendezvous at the road junction H.2. Central, and will proceed to BETHUNE as one convoy in charge of 2/Lieut. J. BROADBENT.
   O.C. "A" Coy will detail an unloading party of 3 ORs to report to Q.M. at 7-15 a.m. and travel on the lorries. This party will be rationed for the 27th, 28th, & 29th inst. The dump will be formed in the Ecole Garson at BETHUNE, and the Officer in charge of the convoy will report to the Town Major, BETHUNE for the exact site. These lorries will be returned to AIRE as soon as unloaded, and must be used for one journey only. The dump will be cleared on arrival in the new area with 1st Line Transport.

5. **BATHS and CLOTHING STORE.** The main clothing store in the new area is at GORRE, Sheet 36b F.5. Central. Baths will probably be supplied with clean clothing.

6. **ADVANCED PARTIES** (a) Advance party of 2/Lieut. W.K. CRICK, 1 N.C.O from H.Q, 1 from each Coy will rendezvous on road near "C" Coy H.Q. at 5-30 a.m. and will proceed to the Church at ROQUETOIRE for 6-30 a.m. from whence they will proceed by motor lorry to BETHUNE Area under Lieut. HAZLEWOOD.
   (b) Advance party of 1 N.C.O. from H.Q. and 1 N.C.O. from each Coy and 1 OR from transport, under 2/Lieut. W.L. PICKFORD will meet the Staff Captain at the Church at ROBECQ, (Sheet 36d ?.29.c.2.5.) at 7-30 a.m., 27th inst. This party will sleep at Q.M. Stores to-night and will meet 2/Lieut. PICKFORD there at 5-30 a.m. The party will be mounted on cycles.

X

                                                  (Continued over)

X This party will report to 2/Lieut. CRICK tonight and sleep at "C" Coy. No cycles required.

                                                        P.T.O

ORDERS No 54 ( Continued )          2.

7. **DADOS**      D.A.D.O.S. is moving to LOCON on the 28th inst.

8. **FIELD CASHIER**.      Office at LESLOBES.

9. **SANITATION**.      Special steps must be taken to leave all billets thoroughly clean, as this Brigade are the first British troops occupying this area for some months.

10. A party of 25 OR will be attached to the 251st Tunnelling Coy, and will proceed by motor lorry from the Church at ROBECQ at 7 a.m. on the 28th inst. This party must be rationed up to and including the 29th inst. The party will be composed as follows:- 1 NCO from "C" Coy, 6 OR from each Company

11. **BILLETING**.   2/Lieut. H. S. HUDSON will complete billeting certificates and obtain clearance certificate of cleanliness from the Sub-area Commandant, ROQUETOIRE.

12. The Battalion starting point on the 27th inst will be road junction, N.10.b.0.8. ( near Smithy ). Time 8.45 a.m. Move in following order - H.Q., "C", "D", "A", "B", Transport. Drums in front of "D" Coy.


**ACKNOWLEDGE**.


(sd) O. S. Sutton,
Captain & Adjutant,
1/9th Bn. Manchester Regt.

**DISTRIBUTION** :-

Copy No. 1 to 4   O.C., Coys.
         5   Q.M.
         6   T.O.
         7   File
       8 - 9   War Diary

WAR DIARY Vol. XXVIII APP. 17

1/9 Bn Manchester Regt Orders
No 55
Nov 27/17
Ref Map. 36ᴬ 1/40,000 "BETHUNE on bas:"

1. The Battalion will move by march route to Mt BERNENCHON on the 28th inst. & will pass the starting point at 10.30 am

2. Starting Point will be @ P 23 c 8.3 Road junction near D Coy's billets.

3. March. Distances of 100 yards will be kept between Companies.

4. Blankets & Valises. Blankets will be collected from Coy HQ & Batt. HQ at 8 am. Officers' valises will be collected at 8.30 am. G.S. Waggons will be used for this purpose. Each Coy will detail an Officer to superintend the loading of Waggons. Blankets must be rolled & tied in bundles of 10.

5. Transport. Maltese Cart & Mess Cart will be loaded at 10 am. Teams for cookers will be sent at 9.45 am. Rite Horse Limbered Gun will be sent at 10 am. All transport will move with the Battalion.

6. Party for Tunnelling Coy. The party to be attached to the 257th Tunnelling Coy

will be composed as follows. 1 NCO from A Coy and 6 O.R. from each Coy (and not as stated in O.O. 54"). This party will be returned up to & including the 29th inst. It will rendezvous at the road junction near D Coy H.Q. at 6.30 am. 2Lt BATES, the Orderly Officer, will assemble the men & march them to the Church at ROBECQ where they will be picked up by motor lorry. 2Lt BATES will return after seeing the party (complete) to the Church. This party will be taken by motor lorry to MOEUX-les-MINES to report by 10 am. O.C. A Coy will give the NCO written instructions stating the number of the Demolition Coy to which the party is to be attached.

Billeting. 2Lt HUNT will complete the Billeting certificates & obtain clearance certificate from the Town Major, ROBECQ.

The Battalion will move in the following order Battn HQ., B, D, C, A. Guns in front of D Coy.

Acknowledge.
O/S ——
Capt OC
2/9 Manch R

WAR DIARY, Vol. XXVIII. APP. 12

1/9th Battalion MANCHESTER REGIMENT.

SUMMARY of Casualties for month ending November 30th 1917.

| NATURE | OFFICERS | OTHER RANKS |
|---|---|---|
| Killed. | – | 2 |
| Died of Wounds. | – | 1. |
| Missing. | – | – |
| Wounded. | – | 12. |
| TOTALS. | NIL. | 15. |

30-11-1917.

*O J Sutton*
Lieut.-Colonel,
Commanding 1/9th Battn. Manchester Regt.

Confidential

WAR DIARY
1/9 MANCHESTER REGT.

Vol XXIX

December 1917

Army Form C. 2118.

# WAR DIARY
## *or*
## INTELLIGENCE SUMMARY.
*(Erase heading not required.)*

Instructions regarding War Diaries and Intelligence Summaries are contained in F. S. Regs., Part II. and the Staff Manual respectively. Title pages will be prepared in manuscript.

| Place | Date | Hour | Summary of Events and Information | Remarks and references to Appendices |
|---|---|---|---|---|
| | | | | |

A5834  Wt.W4973/M687  750,000  8/16  D. D. & L. Ltd.  Forms/C.2118/13.

# WAR DIARY
## or
## INTELLIGENCE SUMMARY.

(Erase heading not required.)

Army Form C. 2118.

1/9 MANCHESTER REGT.

Vol. XXIX
Page 1.

| Place | Date | Hour | Summary of Events and Information | Remarks and references to Appendices |
|---|---|---|---|---|
| MT BERNENCHON | Dec 1-3 | | Ref. Maj. FRANCIS BETHUNE COMBINED. Battalion engaged in Platoon Training & Musketry. | |
| | Dec 3 | | President of M.M.G. addressed by Brig. Commander S.357220 PG 4141175 CAPS Van SGT Brigade. Composite Coy under Capt HANDSFORTH paraded for the decoration at MAIRIE LES BETHUNE. | |
| | Dec 4-8 | | Platoon & Company training. Recreational training during the afternoons. Examination held on 7th & 8th by Divisional Gas Officer. | |
| | 9 | | Church Parade. Service in SCHOPTOWN, MT BERNENCHON. Coy Commanders attended Lecture. | |
| | 10 | | Bn relieved 1/5 LANCASHIRE FUSILIERS in the CANAL RIGHT Sector (See Sketch Map) Coys disposed as follows. B,C,D in the Line. A Coy in support. C Coy 67/15 REGT in Lines REGT in close support on the left. 11 MARYLEBONE LODGE LE BRUNIN (5th Lincoln Regt) on right. 1/10 MANCHESTER REGT on left. | APPENDIX 1 B.O. 36 APPENDIX 2 SKETCH No.6 |
| RIGHT Bn HQ BRADFITT POINT A24C 2.8 | 10/11 | | Bethlehem on night. Left guides arrived night of August on 1/13 & Maryleb? who suffered about to complete. Rob. 9. A Coy sent to Kop ? Gerard | |
| | 11 | | 2nd LT TAYLOR & T.M.TODD Joined. Coy on the line has 3 or 4 officer - about 80 OR. | |
| | 11/12 | | Patrols & out from 10 - 16 feet, the Lith & examined wire area near Hammam both sides. Some machine gun fire. | |
| | 12 | | Major R.B. NOWELL proceeded on leave to U.K. | |

# WAR DIARY
## or
## INTELLIGENCE SUMMARY.
(Erase heading not required.)

Army Form C. 2118.
1/9 MANCHESTER REGT.
Vol XXIX A.
Page 2

| Place | Date | Hour | Summary of Events and Information | Remarks and references to Appendices |
|---|---|---|---|---|
| BRADFELL POINT | Dec 13 | | Ref. Map FRANCE 1/40,000 Support System LABAISE 36c NW1 S3.10.A | |
| | | | Gas was projected into Enemy Trenches on our night 25 at 8.30 p.m. Enemy retaliated with | |
| | | | Gas Shells. Gas masks were frequently during night 24. Enemy ran 2 M.G.s | |
| | | | Rifle Grenades against our front line. One man killed | |
| " | 14 | | Major HOWARTH to R.Y.C. Course for Senior Officers | |
| | | | Major RAYNER 1/5 R. WARWICKS att'd 1/7 Lanc. FUSILIERS came to T.B. for temporary | GS |
| | | | command during absence of Lt. Col. BELLOYD at 38th H.Q. | |
| " | 13/14 | | Patrol from no 1 Post (B.Coy) reconnoitred POLLUX, POLLO & SAXON entrances | GS |
| | | | Wiring & wrecking carried on with | |
| " | 15 | | 2nd Lt. BELLOYD took over temporary command of Brigade during absence of | GS |
| | | | Bde Cmdr on leave. | |
| " | 16 | | Permitted shelling of Hennid & D Batt H.Q. + BRASSERIE BATTH - MULE DUMPS | GB |
| | | | Canals & Trenches | |
| " | 16 | | Battalion moves into Brigade Support (the Disposition arch) between going into rest H.Q. | GA |
| | | | Previous Support Batt H.Q. at A.14.c.0.6 abandoned, many to bed of Crosspoint | APP. 3 OO.57 |
| | | | accommodation. Large collection of Battalion chests (Jam Tin or Hards) removed from | APP. 4 MAP |
| | | | Support Batt H.Q. by B to places in Reserve Battalion Mess at LE PEEL. S | |
| | | | New H.Q. & Dugouts in GLASGOW ROAD | |
| | | | Relieved in Front Line by 1/4 East LANCS Regt. 3 Front line coys at 10 am Support coy at 6pm. | GP |
| | | | Support Battalion in new support near WOBURN ABBEY A 20 B G 3 | |

Army Form C. 2118.

BEATTY
Page 3

# WAR DIARY 1/9 MANCHESTER REGT.
## INTELLIGENCE SUMMARY.

(Erase heading not required.)

Ref Map LABASSEE 10,000 36 CNWI.

| Place | Date | Hour | Summary of Events and Information | Remarks and references to Appendices |
|---|---|---|---|---|
| WOBURN ABBEY A.20.b.6.3 | Dec.17 | | For disposition of Coys see APP 4. B Coy support to Rifle Battalion, D Coy support to Left Battalion, C Coy provide garrison for 4 Keeps. A Coy in Reserve with H.Q. near POTIJZE NORTH. | (G)S |
| - " - | Dec 17-21 | | Each Coy provide working parties daily under R.Es for upkeep of trenches, construction of concrete shelters & carrying of material. Garrison of Keeps found with men then in posts. Small parties sent to YPRES occasionally for bathing. | (G)S |
| - " - | 20 | | A Coy take over 2 of 12 Keeps, BRADDELL KEEP & MOUNTAIN KEEP, thus allowing C Coy to keep the strong force the Garrisons of ORCHARD + SPOIL BANK KEEPS. A Coy H.Q. moves to dugout in VILLAGE LINE A.20.9.5. | (G)S |
| - " - | 22 | 10 am | Battalion relieves 1/4 East Lancs Regt in the Right Sector, 10 am. Work & trench constructs on wiring the front line. Enemy & Heavy front trench mortars rather difficult. Gas alert is repeated & strengthened. Snow fell on night of 22nd with most flat pictures on easily seen & enemy snipers are detected frequently. Raiding party driven off by Lewis Gun & Rifle Fire from No 21 Post. | APP. 5 O.O.58 (G)S (G)P |
| BRADDELL POINT | 23/24 | | | |
| - " - | 24 | | Heavy snow. Gas operations take place on our front & by the Divn on our right. Artillery retaliates by enemy during the Relief, attacks made by E.C. very slight damage to our trenches. | (G)p |
| - " - | 25 | | Quiet day. Machine gun sweep over CAMBRIN where Co learnt 11 wounded. American infantry officer attached for three days. 10 & remaining of the Bn bomb live & on track of snow. | (G)p |
| | | | | 2/Lt BATES wounded |

Army Form C. 2118.

VOLXXX K
Page 4

1/9 MANCHESTER REGT

# WAR DIARY
or
## INTELLIGENCE SUMMARY.
(Erase heading not required.)

Instructions regarding War Diaries and Intelligence Summaries are contained in F. S. Regs., Part II. and the Staff Manual respectively. Title pages will be prepared in manuscript.

| Place | Date | Hour | Summary of Events and Information | Remarks and references to Appendices |
|---|---|---|---|---|
| BRADITH POINT | Dec 26 | | Ref Map BETHUNE COMBINED 1/10,000. C Coy wiring party fired on by rifle, one man wounded. | (G2) (G) |
| | 27 | | D.M. Shells fell between N & S Bank K-ROBERTSONS DUMPS. | (G) |
| | 28 | | E. Aeroplane flew over our line very low (about 100 feet) just before petrol. B. Helm relieved by 1/4 Loyal Lanc Regt. Without incident. B moves to 1/4th and LE PREOL F10, F16. B Coy (Capt KERSHAW) left billets till 4 pm on working parties near R.5. | APP 6 (G2) O.O. 59 |
| LE PREOL | 29 | | C Coy provide working parties. Remainder of Battalion does any in almost up or in complete inspections. Billet from own Christie in later + Rly ab | (G3) |
| | 30 | | Church Parades. + Bathing. 2 Coy provide working parties. Lt Col LLOYD worn from Leave. B.C. | (G3) |
| | 31 | | Section, Platoon training on grounds near billets. | (G3) |
| | | | 6 Officer + 68 O.R. Sent on leave to UK during month. Casualty totals See APPENDIX | APP 7 CASUALTY TOTALS |

Lt Col O.J.
1/9 Manchester Regt.

# WAR DIARY
## or
## INTELLIGENCE SUMMARY.

**Army Form C. 2118.**

HQ MANCHESTER RGT.

MCXXXVI
Page 5

| Place | Date | Hour | Summary of Events and Information | Remarks and references to Appendices |
|---|---|---|---|---|
| | Dec 2 | | Reg Adj. 2Lt W.N.B. BURY struck off strength R.G. Battalion on reports to Heavy Section M.G. Training Centre NOOL 28/11/17 | |
| | 3 | | 2Lt WILKINSON to UK leave | A |
| | | | Capt KERSHAW returns from leave | A |
| | 5 | | 2Lt CARREY attached to 428 Field Coy R.E. | A |
| | | | 2Lt PICKFORD returns from leave | A |
| | 6 | | 2Lt HARKNIGHT to UK on leave | A |
| | 7 | | 2Lt JACKSON to G.H.Q. Gunnery Course | A |
| | | | 2Lt ROWE rejoins from 428 Bn Ty R.E. | A |
| | 8 | | 2Lt BERKELEY to Lewis Gun Course, X1 Corps. | A |
| | | | Hon L/Lt WORMAN from 41st Army Musketry Camp. | A |
| | 9 | | 2Lt BORST rejoin from leave | A |
| | | | 2Lt MELLOR to hospital sick. 2Lt ROTTENAU to Signal School WORBOURN | A |
| | 10 | | 2Lt L.G. TAYLOR & 2Lt TM TOD from on attach from 8 Reserve Battn report to GOC | A |
| | 11 | | Capt REDMOND rejoins from leave | A |
| | 12 | | 2Lt CRICK to leave U.K. 2Lt WAHILLAR rejoins to 1st Divn 2Lt BARLOW, 2Lt ROWE to 136 Ty G Course | A |
| | 13 | | Major NOWELL proceeds on leave to U.K. 2/6 TOZIER rejoins from leave. | A |
| | 14 | | Major HOWORTH to R.F.C. Course, 5th Army. | A |
| | | | Major KNIVETT assumes temporary command of Battalion during absence of Lt Col LLOYD in command | A |
| | 17 | | 2Lt HUDSON to M.G. School England. | A |
| | 18 | | 2Lt BATES, 2Lt TAYLOR to Gas School Leave. 2Lt STONE rej Army School | A |
| | 19 | | 2Lt BAURDON to UK on leave | A |
| | 23 | | Major HOWORTH returns from Course. | A |

# WAR DIARY or INTELLIGENCE SUMMARY

Army Form C. 2118.

1/9 MANCHESTER REGT

| Place | Date | Hour | Summary of Events and Information | Remarks and references to Appendices |
|---|---|---|---|---|
| | Dec 23 | | 2/Lt WILKINSON rejoin from Leave. 2/Lt BARLOW & ROWE rejoin from Course. | |
| | 24 | | 2/Lt SILLIMAN attached for 3 days on H. Sn. | (?) |
| | 25 | | 2/Lts BOOTSLEY, BARTRAM, TAYLOR, BATES rejoin from Course. 2/Lt KNIGHT from Leave. | (?) |
| | 27 | | 2/Lt BATES to O.S. 2/Lt KNIGHT on denial duty with Bde. | (?) |
| | 28 | | Capt STEPHENSON to Z.G. Course LE TOUQUET. | (?) |
| | 29 | | 2/Lt BRODHURST rejoin from Hospital. | (?) |
| | | | 2/Lt CRICK & Major NORTON rejoin from Leave. Capt BUTTERWORTH to gunnery course. | (?) |
| | 30 | | 2/Lt HUGHES to Sniping Course. | |
| | 31 | | 2/Lt HUNT to 1st Bn/R for Course. 2/Lt LLOYD rejoin from Brigade. | (?) |
| | | | 2/Lt BARLOW to U.K. on Leave. | (?) |

R Moray
Lt Col
1/9 Manchester Regt

Confidential

1/9th Battn. MANCHESTER REGT

# WAR DIARY

## Vol. XXX

### January. 1918.

# WAR DIARY or INTELLIGENCE SUMMARY

Army Form C. 2118.

1/9 MANCHESTER REGT. Vol XXX
Page 1

| Place | Date | Hour | Summary of Events and Information | Remarks and references to Appendices |
|---|---|---|---|---|
| LE PREOL | Jan 1 | Ref/Map Bethune Combined 1/40,000 | Training by Companies. Rapid wiring practices. Daily during training. | |
| | | | Lieut E.C. LLOYD proceeds on leave to U.K. | |
| | Jan 2 | | Major J.S. KNNEDY assumes 2i/c duties. Major J.P. HUDSON takes over command. | |
| | Jan 3 | | Training continues. 3/C STONE + Co QR of 2/Cy billets at CAMBRIN (A20½) relieving under Surveilling Coy 34th 7.30pm. Opn. Battalion move to BEUVRY (F14) relieving 1/6 MANCH R. relieved by | APR 1 OO.60 |
| | | | 1/6 MANCH R. 126 Brigade in Divisional Reserve. 3 Coy billets in school with Coy Messy HQt. A Coy billet in huts. Officers billet goot. Inhabitants friendly. Owing mainly owing to the morning cancelled on account of visibility and enemy (Cameron) balloons in air. | ✓ |
| BEUVRY | Jan 12 | | Training by Platoons. Coys + Instructors. Musketry practices stopped on range | ✓ |
| | | | at LE QUESNOY (F8c) | ✓ |
| | Jan 7 | | Working parties found. Brig of men, two on "Rue Coys". Mens Christmas Dinner takes place in Coy Messes. Lieut. E. EDELMAN assumes Cy gift of £104 collected by Lieut J.H. WADE. Party made 2i/c STONE at CAMBRIN relieved. Joins Battalion | ✓ |
| | 14 | | Move to the line cancelled, until Front Line is reorganised. | ✓ |
| | 15 | | Major R.B. NOWELL proceeds to England to report to WAR OFFICE | ✓ |

# WAR DIARY
## or
## INTELLIGENCE SUMMARY.

*(Erase heading not required.)*

Army Form C. 2118.

1/9 MANCHESTER REGT

BEUVRY
Page 2

| Place | Date | Hour | Summary of Events and Information | Remarks and references to Appendices |
|---|---|---|---|---|
| BEUVRY | 16 | | Training & musketry on Range. | |
| | 17 | 10 a.m. | Batten relieves the 1/5 Lancs Fus. in the Right Battalion Sector. GIVENCHY Section. | APP. 2 O.O. G1. |
| | | | Heavy rain all day most of the trenches waterlogged. Everyone wet through. Gum boots taken into use & all precautions made against trench foot. Going to Beuvry ran many off first two fellows & become impassable. 2d Lt D.H. WELLWOOD & 2/Lt H.R. MARTIN from Reserve Batten arrive on post to B.H.Q. Coys respectively. | (G1) |
| Ad 8 5 New WINDY CORNER | 18 | | Enemy shell to in frontline between 2 & 8 P.M. Work during this tour in the line to be concentrated on wiring the posts and areas. Work on closing trenches was imperative. | (G1) |
| | 19 | | Enemy Aircraft activity above normal. Parties from Pioneer Battalion work on further i- offent g- reset improvements. Patrols sent out nightly by each Coy. No life. No artillery active on ourtro & Right Coys. One man 5/4 to Rules J.M. | (G1) |
| | 20 | | | |
| | 21 | | Hostile No action on GIVENCHY RIDGE. Patrol 2/2nd fired on by M.G. | (G1) |
| | 22 | | Capt. AW FARNELL South Staffs Regt. joins battalion as 2nd in Command. | (G1) |
| | 23 | 8 a.m. | Relieved by 1/4 East Lancs Regt. & move to GORRE. (F 3 B) Bygone relief, enemy rifles, T. Sap & T.G. away & 15% away of T.G. and rifle & MG fire but weeps through a source Barrage. Relief reported from 10 a.m. to 5 P.M. | APP 3 O.O. G2. |

# WAR DIARY or INTELLIGENCE SUMMARY

1/9 MANCHESTER REGT. Army Form C. 2118.

Vol XXX
Page 3

| Place | Date | Hour | Summary of Events and Information | Remarks and references to Appendices |
|---|---|---|---|---|
| GORRE | 24 -28 | | Billets in GORRE CHATEAU. All the men provided with wire beds. All Officers except Med. Officer in house in GORRE. Coys training & providing working parties. One Coy provide daily fog carrying to the line. One Coy repairs daily fog small parties & duties. Hostile aircraft pass over about 5.30 P.M. throw nights. | FL (Q) |
| | 28 | | Scout officer goes to C.O. 55 adjutant regarding reorganization of Division. 13 Officers + 279 O.R. to go to 66th Division to be amalgamated with 2/9 Manchesters. | (Q) |
| | | | | APP # OO.63 |
| A.8 d.8.5– West WINDY CORNER | 29 | 10 a.m. | Relieve 1/4 East Lancs Regt in Right Sector. Dispositions B.C.D with A4.b – Support. Patrols leave "K" Sap to reconnoitre ground in front of our machines. Slight activity of Hostile Artillery + T.M's. | (Q) |
| | 30 | 12.10 p.m | Hostile Aeroplane brought down by one of our machines. Lands to the night of our line in MUNITY LEND A16 d 4.4. Patrols again leave "K" Sap on to the night with 2 officers get close to enemy front at A.9.C.4.5. Officers do not consider it possible to make a surprise attack on account of broken ground & cut wire. The other patrol under the Cpl. PRICE found post at A.9.5.3.4 occupied. This post was not occupied the previous night. Patrol discovers that cards & mails | (Q) |
| | 31 | | Gutters down at 3 do an noon with 40 yards to right of K. Post. Bombers & Riflemen off. Party of 6 enter the WITTY 90 out to get information from Post at A.9.C.3.4. Get into Post & find it unoccupied. Enemy attack head, in a few days. | (Q) |

# WAR DIARY
## or
## INTELLIGENCE SUMMARY.

Army Form C. 2118.

1/9 MANCHESTER REGT.
Vol XXX
Page 4

| Place | Date | Hour | Summary of Events and Information | Remarks and references to Appendices |
|---|---|---|---|---|
| LABARRE BETHUNE (O-28-D-88) | Jan 1. | | Strength of Battalion 42 off 769 OR. LOK Wnt 25 off. 497 OR. | |
| | 3 | | Lt Col Lloyd proceeds on leave. Major Canfett reforms 1/5 Lancs Fus | |
| | 5 | | Major J Phoxby 1/5 East Lancs Regt takes over Command. Battalions. | |
| | 6 | | Lt Col Lloyd D.S.O. on ten years honors list. | |
| | 10 | | 2Lts Dowler, Gurst & Todd to 226 I.B School for 10 days course | |
| | 11 | | 2Lt Burrows rejoins from leave | (a) |
| | 12 | | Capt Stephenson, Lt Ruttenau + 2Lt Hunt rejoin from Conran O Instruction | (b) |
| | 15 | | Lt (Major ret) J Broadbent, J Broadbent; Bd Durragh M Officer, proceeds to England to join T.F. Reserve | (c) |
| | 16 | | Major Hogarth rejoins from leave & Lt Ruttenau proceeds on leave | (d) |
| | 16 | | 2Lt Jackson invalided to England 31/12/17. 2Lt Leaver invalided to England 28/12/17 | (e) |
| | 22 | | Major R.B. Montell 2/c in Command proceeds to report to M.O. | (f) |
| | 27 | | Lt Midgley proceeds on leave, UK. 2Lt Barlow rejoins from leave. | (g) |
| | 30 | | 2Lt Hughes rejoins from Course. 2Lt Todd to Musketry Course. | (g) |
| | 31 | | Lt Hellwood D.N. & 2Lt Martin join from Reserve Bn | (g) |
| | | | Major A W Farwell, South Staffs joins as 2/c in Comm. S | (g) |
| | | | Lt Ruttenau rejoins from leave & proceeds to corps signalling School | (g) |
| | | | 26 Readham proceeds on leave UK 2Lt Crick act as T.O. | (g) |
| | | | Lt Wilkinson to corpora School Course | (g) |
| | | | 2Lt Burrows to England for 6 months School Course | (g) |
| | 31 | | Strength of Battn 41 off 734 OR. With Wnt 29 off 504 OR. | (g) |

Out on leave during month 6 off 49 OR.

R Wand

Lt Col C.O.
1/9 Manch R

WAR DIARY. Vol. XXX APP. 1

SECRET.                                              Copy No. 7
                1/9th Battalion MANCHESTER REGIMENT
                      O R D E R S   No. 60.
Ref. Map :- BETHUNE Combined.                        2nd JANUARY, 1918.

1. The Battalion will move to BEUVRY on the 3rd inst.
   Companies will move in the following order, "D","C","B","A", H.Qrs.
   "D" Coy. passing the Drawbridge near Battn. H.Q. at 10 a.m.
   Route, via Road Junction, F.14.b.5.8.    200 yards distances
   will be maintained between platoons.
   DRESS :- Full marching order.

2. WORKING PARTIES, etc.    All working parties will continue work till
   12 Noon, 3rd inst., with the exception of the party working on the
   L.G., "Pop-ups", in WILSON'S TUNNEL, which will be relieved at
   2-0 p.m.    Os.C. Coys will arrange for guides for the parties
   belonging to their Coys.
   O.C. "D" Coy. will supply guide for the party working in WILSON'S
   TUNNEL.    A party of 1 Officer and 60 O.R. composed of
   2/Lieut. A.E. STONE, - "B" Coy. 1 Sergt., 2 L/Cpls., and 28 men to
   include a cook, and a similar party from "D" Coy., will be detailed
   to proceed with D' cooker to relieve a similar party of the
   127th Brigade, employed on work under the 3rd Australian Tunnelling
   Coy.    The party will take over accommodation in CAMBRIN
   occupied by 127th Brigade, and will commence work at 3 p.m., 3rd inst.
   This party will be relieved in 3 days time. 1 limber for this party
   will report at 8 a.m. "D" Coy.H.Q.    Party will proceed at 9 a.m.

3. TRANSPORT etc.    Officers valises and mens' blankets will be collected
   at Cy.H.Q. & Battn. H.Q. at 9-0 a.m.    Maltese and Mess Carts
   will report at 9-30 a.m.    Cookers will proceed with Coys.
   Teams reporting at 9-30 a.m.    Teams for water carts will be
   sent at 9-30 a.m.    Ride horses at 9-45 a.m.
   Baggage waggons from 439th Coy. A.S.C. will report at Q.M. Stores
   at 9-0 a.m., 3rd inst.    Q.M. will send guide to BEUVRY STATION
   (Le Quesnoy), at 9-15 a.m., 3rd inst.    Distances of 200 yards
   will be maintained between every group of 4 vehicles.

4. MOBILE RESERVE.    Q.M. will make arrangements for the exchange of
   mobile reserve with the 8th MANCHESTER REGIMENT.

5. BRIGADE GUARD.    The Brigade Guard will be relieved at 10 a.m. on
   the 3rd inst.    No Brigade Guard will be mounted by this
   Battalion that day.

6. GUIDES.    Os.C. Coys will detail 1 guide per platoon to report
   at Orderly Room to 2/Lieut. G.A. BARTRAM at 10-30 a.m.
   They will proceed to meet incoming Battalion at Drawbridge,
   F.9.b.8.8. at 11-30 a.m.

7. CLEANLINESS.    Certificates of cleanliness of billets and cookhouses
   will be obtained from advance parties of incoming unit, and will be
   sent to Battn. H.Q. by 6-0 p.m., 3rd inst '    Billets will be ready
   for inspection by C.O. at 9-0 a.m.

8. LEWIS GUN POSITIONS.    The 2 A.A., Lewis Gun positions will be handed
   over by "B" Coy.

9. MARCH DISCIPLINE.    Strict attention must be paid to march
   discipline.


   ACKNOWLEDGE.

   DISTRIBUTION :-
   Copies Nos.1 - 4   Os.C. Coys.
              5       Q.M.                    (Sd) O.J. SUTTON.
              6       T.O.                         Capt. & Adjt.,
          7 - 8       War Diary.            1/9th Battn. MANCHESTER REGT.
              9       File.


        ISSUED by........at........

SECRET

WAR DIARY. V01 XXX APP. 2.
Copy No 9.

## 1/9th Battalion Manchester Regiment
### Orders No. 61.

16th January, 1918

Ref. maps:- BETHUNE combined 1/40,000
LA BASSEE 36.c. N.W.1. 1/10,000.

1. The Battalion will relieve the 1/5th Battn. Lancashire Fusiliers in the GIVENCHY Right Sector on the morning of the 17th inst.

2. DISPOSITIONS:- Right Coy "B" relieving "B" Coy 1/5th Lancs Fus.
   Centre Coy "A"  "  "A" Coy  "  "  "
   Left Coy "D"   "  "D" Coy  "  "  "
   Support Coy "C"  "  "C" Coy  "  "  "

3. Companies and Battn. H.Qrs. will parade ready to move at 8-40 a.m. and will move off in the following order "B","D","A","C", Bn. H.Q. "B" Coy moving off at 8-45 a.m. Distances of 200 yards will be kept between platoons to ESTAMINET CORNER after which platoons will be split up into sections.

4. ROUTE:- LE QUESNOY - GORRE - TUNING FORK SOUTH to ESTAMINET CORNER, H.6.a.4.0., where guides will be met at 10 a.m.

5. DRESS:- Fighting Order, groundsheets under the flap of the haversack. Jerkins will be worn outside jacket. Greatcoats rolled and slung round the haversack.

6. PACKS etc. Packs will be stacked near the Coys Billets by 4-30 p.m. to-day, and will be taken to Q.M. Stores by T.O. Blankets, rolled in bundles of 10 and labelled will be stacked at the same place by 7-30 a.m. to-morrow. Officers valises will be stacked at the same place by 8 a.m.

7. LEWIS GUNS. Lewis guns will be loaded under Coy arrangements to-day and will be at ESTAMINET CORNER by 9-30 a.m., 17th inst. Nos. 1 & 2 of each L.G. team will parade at Quarter Guard at 8 a.m. and will proceed to ESTAMINET CORNER to unload limbers. Magazine boxes will be taken into the line and dumped at Coy H.Q. where surplus magazines will be kept.

8. TRANSPORT. Mess cart, maltese cart, and transport for mess, canteen and Orderly Room stores will report at 8 a.m. 17th inst.
Baggage and Supply waggons will report to Q.M. Stores at 7 a.m. These waggons will be used on return journeys by 125 Bde.
Officers chargers will be sent to Orderly Room at 8-30 a.m. Teams for Cookers and Water carts at 8-0 a.m.

9. Q.M. will arrange to collect Coy. Cookhouse Stores, and to send up with rations 17th inst those required by Coys in the line.

(continued over)

Orders (No 61.) contd.    -2-

Rations for H.Q. & "A", "B", "C" Coys will be taken to WINDY CORNER 4-30 p.m. daily, for "D" Coy to ESTAMINET CORNER. Companies will provide their own ration parties.

Q.m. will send 12 petrol tins of water to ESTAMINET CORNER for "D" Coy by 10 am 17th inst. They will be collected by "D" Coy.

10. TRENCH STORES, etc. Trench Stores, Defence Schemes, Air Photos, etc will be taken over. Certificates of cleanliness of trenches dug-outs and Cookhouses will be given if satisfactory. Copies of receipts and certificates will be sent to Bn H.Q as soon as possible after relief.

A.A. Positions will be taken over. All gas equipment must be carefully checked.

11. RELIEF. Completion of relief will be notified by wire by Coys as soon as possible after relief. The code words, ALPHA, BETA, GAMMA, DELTA. will be used by "A", "B", "C", "D", Coys respectively. Relief will also be notified by runner.

12. The following will remain behind at GORRE:-
Q.m's Staff, Drums, Orderly Room Sergt, 1 Clerk, 2 Runners, 4 Coy Storemen.

13. 2/LIEUT. G. A. BARTRAM will hand over billets and obtain certificates of cleanliness of Billets and Cookhouses. He will report to Orderly Room at 8-0 a.m.

ACKNOWLEDGE.

DISTRIBUTION:-
Copies Nos 1-4. O.C. Coys
    5 Q.m.
    6 T.O.
    7 1/5th Lancs Fus.
    8-9 War Diary
    10 File

(Sd) O. J. Sutton.
Capt & Adjt.
1/9th Bn. Manchester Regt.

Issued by_____ at_____

SECRET
ORDERS No. 12

22nd January 1918

1. The Battalion will be relieved in the line by Battalion GIVENCHY Sector by RESCUE on the night of the 23rd inst, and will move into Brigade Reserve at COPSE.

2. Companies will be relieved in the following order:

    | | D A C M bn |
    |---|---|
    | Right Coy B. REBATE | will be relieved by A Coy RESCUE |
    | Centre A | B |
    | Left D | C |
    | Support C | D |

3. GUIDES. Guides will be required as follows:—
    1 per Platoon and 1 from Battalion HdQrs.
    Guides from A, B, C Coys. Battn Hd. will report at WINDY CORNER 9.20 am to 2/c W H CRICK.
    Guides from D Coy to be at point where CHESHIRE Road cuts old BRITISH LINE A.2.a.7.0. at 9.20 am.
    All Guides to have written instructions.

4. Relief complete will be reported by Coys as follows:—

    A Coy — GUN
    B — BOOTS
    C — SOCKS
    D — STRAPS

5. BAGGAGE. Any baggage, cooking utensils, mess stores etc. not taken away tonight will be dumped at ESTAMINET CORNER. Lewis Gun & L.G. magazines will be dumped there by Coys after relief.

6. TRANSPORT. Transport will be at ESTAMINET CORNER at the following times:

    | | A | B | C | D | M bn |
    |---|---|---|---|---|---|
    | Ride horses | 11 am | 11 am | 11 am | 10.30 am | 11.30 am |
    | L.G. Limber | 12 | 12 | 12 | 11 am | |

(Continued)

ORDERS (Contd.)

6. New Draft and transfer party ... at 9 am.
Cookers will be sent for the new draft.

7. TRENCH STORES &c. All Trench Plan, defence & organisation Schemes maps & Aeroplane photos will be handed over and receipts sent to Orderly Room by 6 pm. Gum Boots will be handed into the Drying Room before use.

8. Certificates of cleanliness of Trenches & dugouts will be obtained and handed in to Orderly Room. Receipts with regard to ammunition handed over will be obtained.

9. An Advance Party of 2nd Lieut A.J. BARTON and the Coy. Q.M.Sergts will take over billets. They will report at Orderly Room of Bn East Lancs Regt at GORRE at 8.30 am tomorrow. Certificates with regard to cleanliness of billets & cookhouses will be given and a copy sent to Orderly Room.

10. [crossed out]                                    OPS

11. QM will arrange to have blankets (2 per man, mens packs & officers valises at the billets before the arrival of the Battalion. A hot meal will be ready. 2 Cooks per Company will be sent in advance to prepare this meal.

12. ACKNOWLEDGE.

13. Distances of 200 yards will be maintained between platoons on the march.

14. O.C. D Coy will detail an Officer to superintend loading at ESTAMINET CORNER, to ensure that dumps are made out of sight of enemy balloons, & to prevent crowding.

DISTRIBUTION

Copies Nos 1 – 4   O.C. Coy
           5       QM
           6       T.O.
           7       RESCUE
           8 & 9   Hd Qrs
          10       File

Issued by    LT

O J Sutton
Capt & Adjt
1/5th Manchester Regt

SECRET

<u>WAR DIARY. Vol. XXX. App.</u>

MD3261

Reference <u>REBATE</u> ORDERS No. 62

Para 1   The relief will commence at 5-0 P.M.

Para 3   Guides from A.B. & C. Coys will report to 2/Lieut W.H. CRICK at WINDY CORNER at 4-45 p.m. Guides from 'D' Coy will be at place mentioned (A.2.d.7.4) at 4.45 p.m.

Para 5   Baggage and Lewis Guns etc from A.B. & C. Coys will be dumped at WINDY CORNER.
From D' Coy at ESTAMINET CORNER

Para 6   Transport will be at WINDY CORNER for A.B.C Coys + Hd Qrs at the following times:—

   Ride Horses        7-0 p.m. (HQ. 7·30 pm)
   L G Limbers        8·0 pm
   Mess Cart          6·0 pm
   Maltese Cart       4·30 p.m.

Transport for 'D' Coy will be at ESTAMINET CORNER as follows
   Ride Horses        6·30 p.m.
   L G Limber        6·30 p.m.

Para 14 is cancelled. O.C. 'B' Coy will detail an officer for similar duty at WINDY CORNER

(sd) O.J. Sutton
Capt + Adjt
REBATE

23-1-18.  12·30 p.m.

WAR DIARY. Vol. XXX. APP. 4

**SECRET.**

1/9th Battalion MANCHESTER REGT.    Copy No. 8.
O R D E R S    No. 63.

28th JANUARY.1918.

1. The Battalion will relieve the 1/4th Battn. EAST LANCS. Regt in the GIVENCHY Right Sub-sector on the morning of the 29th inst.

2. DISPOSITIONS. Right Coy. "B" relieving A Coy., 1/4th East Lancs.Regt.
   Centre Coy. "C"    "    B  Coy.   "   "    "     "
   Left   Coy. "D"    "    C  Coy.   "   "    "     "
   Support Coy. "A"   "    D  Coy.   "   "    "     "

3. Companies and Battn. H.Q. will move off at the following times :-
   "C" Coy. 9-30 a.m.,   "D" Coy. 9-40 a.m.,   "B" Coy. 9-50 a.m.,
   "A" Coy. 10 a.m.,     Battn. H.Q. 10-15 am.
   Distances of 200 yards will be kept between platoons to ESTAMINET CORNER after which, if visibility is good, platoons will split up into sections.    No guides will be provided.

4. DRESS :-   Fighting Order, groundsheets under the flap of the haversack, Greatcoats rolled and slung round the haversack. Jerkins will be worn.

5. PACKS, etc.   Packs will be stacked at Q.M. Stores by 5-30 P.M. to-night Blankets rolled in bundles of 10 and labelled, will be stacked at Q.M. Stores by 7-30 a.m., to-morrow.    Officers valises will be taken to Q.M. Stores by 8-0 a.m.

6. LEWIS GUNS.   Lewis Guns will be loaded under Coy. arrangements to-day and will be at ESTAMINET CORNER by 9-30 a.m. to-morrow. Nos 1 & 2 of each L.G. team will parade at Quarter Guard at 8-45 a.m. and will proceed under senior N.C.O. to ESTAMINET CORNER to unload limbers.

7. TRANSPORT.    Mess Cart & Maltese Cart will report at 8-30 a.m. Also half limber for signalling equipment & water tins    Officers Chargers will be required at 9-15 am.    Teams for Cookers and Water Carts at 9-0 a.m.

8. Q.M. will arrange to collect cookhouse stores and to send up with rations 29th inst., those required by Coys in the Line.    Rations for H.Q., "A","B","C" Coys will be taken as before to WINDY CORNER, 4:45 pm daily and for "D" Coy. to ESTAMINET CORNER.
   "A" Coy will carry rations for "C" Coy., and will attach 6 men to "D" Coy. as permanent ration party.    "B" Coy. will provide its own ration party.

9. TRENCH STORES, etc.   Trench Stores, Defence Schemes, Air Photos, etc. will be taken over.    Certificates of Cleanliness of trenches, Dug-outs and Cookhouses will be given if satisfactory.    Copies of receipts and certificates will be sent to Battn. H.Q. as soon as possible after relief.    A.A. Positions will be taken over.    All gas equipment must be carefully checked.

10. RELIEF. Completion of relief will be notified by wire by Companies as soon as possible after relief, using the following code words :-

    "A" Coy. ANTWERP.              "B" Coy. BERLIN.
    "C" Coy. COLOGNE.              "D" Coy. DUSSELDORF.

    Relief will also be notified by runner.

11. SALVAGE.    Each Coy. will detail 1 man to collect salvage.    List of salved material either sent back to Q.M. or used will be sent to H.Q. every ~~Monday~~ Wednesday morning.

12.    The following will remain behind at HOME. - Q.M.S Staff, Drums, Orderly Room Sergt., 1 Clerk, 2 Runners, 4. Coy. Storemen, 1 Cook from Bn. H.Q. and 1 from "B" Coy.

(CONTINUED OVER)

ORDERS No. 63 (Contd.)                  - 2 -

13.   2/Lieut. A.J. BADDELEY will hand over billets and papers and will
      obtain certificates of cleanliness.    He will report at Orderly Room
      at 9-0 a.m. to meet advance party from the 1/4th Bn. East Lancs Regt.
      Billets will be ready for inspection by 9-0 a.m.
      "C" Coy. will leave 2 guides with 2/Lieut. BADDELEY for A.A. Positions


A C K N O W L E D G E .


DISTRIBUTION :-

Copies Nos. 1 - 4   O. s C. Coys.
              5.    Q.M.
              6.    T.O.
              7.    "RESCUE"                        (Sd) O.J. Sutton,
           8- 9     War Diary .                         Captain & Adjt.,
             10     File .                          1/9th Bn. Manchester Regt.


ISSUED by ............at ............

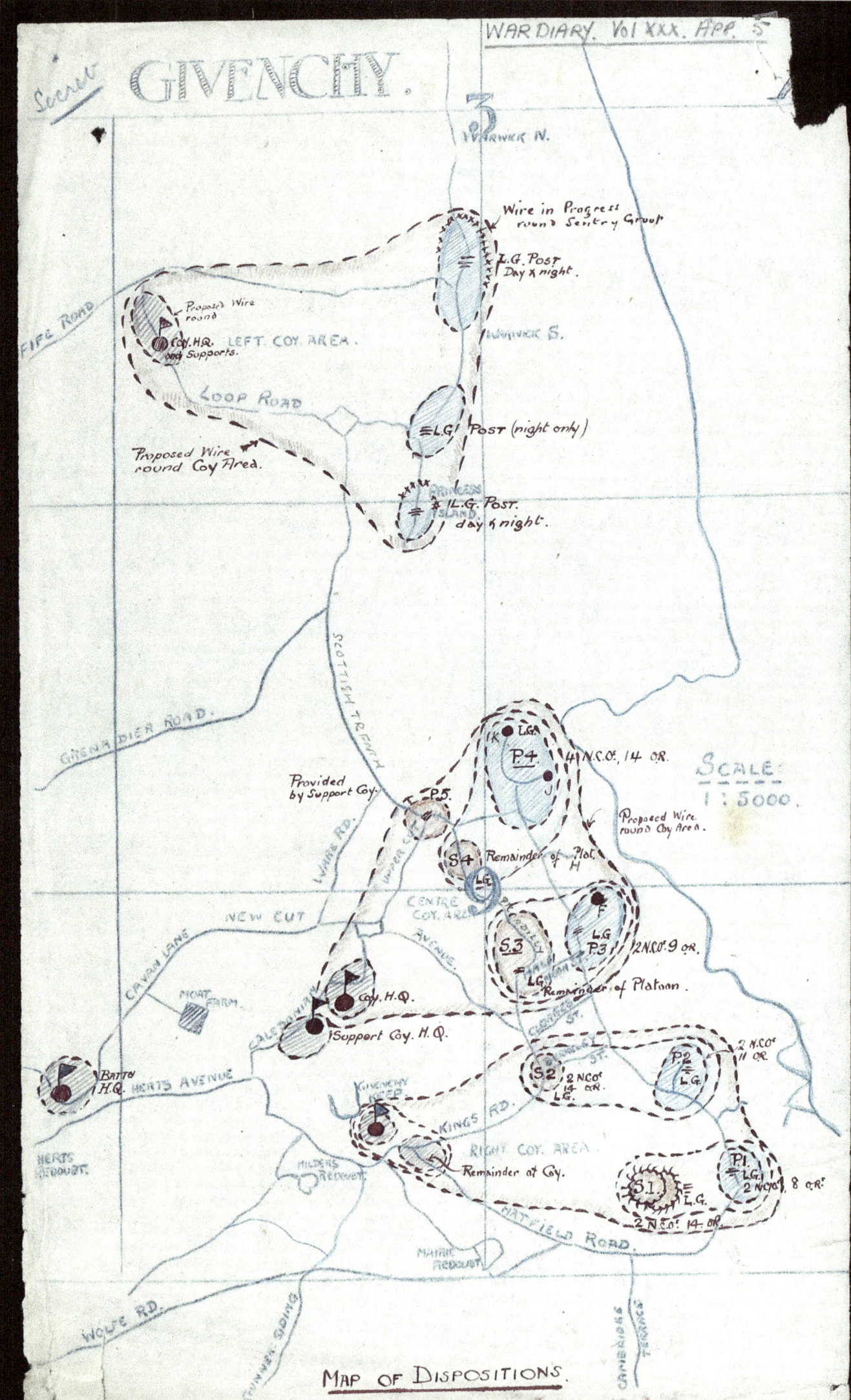

1/9th. Bn. Manchester Regt.

WAR DIARY. Vol. XXX. App. 6.

Summary of casualties for month of January 1918.

| Casualty | Officers | Other Ranks |
|---|---|---|
| KILLED | nil. | 1. |
| MISSING | nil. | 3. |
| WOUNDED | nil. | 2. |
| TOTAL. | nil. | 6. |

31/1/18.

G/Sutton
Capt & Adjt for
Lieut-Colonel.
Commanding 1/9th. Bn. Manchester Regt.

1/9 Manchester Rg 4/126

Vol 13

February 1918

6

Secret & Confidential

# 1/9th Bn. Manchester Regt.

# WAR DIARY

## Vol. XXXI
## February 1918

# WAR DIARY
## INTELLIGENCE SUMMARY

Army Form C. 2118.

1/4 Manchester Regt

DCXXXI
Page 1.

| Place | Date | Hour | Summary of Events and Information | Remarks and references to Appendices |
|---|---|---|---|---|
| A 3 C & B 5 Quir Bn HQ GIVENCHY | Feb 1/2 | 10.30pm | Party of 28 =28- HUGHES Gave 1 Sub (See sketch with not marked xxx) to hunt enemy trenches and capture prisoners. Going on line at 10.25pm. They remain out till about 2 am attempting to get through wire over obstacles in rain. | |
| " | | 5 a- | Enemy patrol outside F Sap driven off by rifle & L.G. fire. One of our men wounded in F sap by enemy bullet. | |
| " | Feb 2/3 | | Quiet night. Slight amount of MG fire from enemy. Otherwise no activity. Patrol under Lt DONNER — sent HUNT reconnoitred no mans land in front of left Coy & reports wire | GS |
| " | Feb 3/4 | | report no quiet, running through A3 Central & in enemy wire. GS | GS |
| " | Feb 4 | 1:pm | Battalion relieved by the 1/4 East Lancs Regt move into Bde Support with HQ near WINDY CORNER. A & C Coys are Reserve give Coys are WINDY POST, MOAT FARM, HILDERS REDOUBT, GIVENCHY KEEP, MAIRIE KEEP – HERTS REDOUBT. B Coy are in obstructed line in support of Left Battalion (Lee Mys & &&&). Manro Q on billets at WINDY CORNER. One Coy of 1/10 Manr R B Coy (Capt Stephen) move to GOREE CHATEAU for special training in preparation for a raid. 15 O.R & A Coy are attached to G.S.Q for this training A & C Coys & C Coy 1/10 Manr P.R furnish working parties for R.E. & furnishing fatigues. Lt-Col E.C. LLOYD Takes over temporary command of Bn. during Major FARNELL. Mr SEYMOUR. 2nd in command returns from Course. | APP 2 List of working Partys GS |

Army Form C. 2118.
1/9 Manchester Regt
Vol XXXVI
Page 2

# WAR DIARY or INTELLIGENCE SUMMARY.
(Erase heading not required.)

| Place | Date | Hour | Summary of Events and Information | Remarks and references to Appendices |
|---|---|---|---|---|
| WINDY CORNER A.14.a.9.9 | Sept 5 | | Ref Map LA BASSÉE 10,000. 2 Coys commence training engaged at GORRE over ground types out will replace of German trenches in A.3.d. 2/Lt Lloyd supervised the training. (OPS) | |
| | 6 | | 2/Lt BURROWS struck off strength on proceeding to England. (OPS) | |
| | 7 | | Working parties provided as usual during tour in trenches or support. 2/Lt GORST proceeds to England on six months tour of duty as instructor. Special parties of Officers & NCOs were sent over ground in No Mans Land to be crossed by raiding party. (OPS) | |
| | 8 | | 2/Lt CE LLOYD returns from 126 Bde HQ. (OPS) | |
| | 9 | | Wire cutting commenced by artillery on raiding parties & the junct. Bn.(End)(a) & objective. The 1/4 East Lancs Bn Regt. Nth Section of Trench over to 11/5 Lancs. (OPS) | |
| | 10 10am | | SLGTS shelling DEF PLANTIN during morning. Raid to take place at 6pm. portions of Supp in the wire. Artillery doing nothing of interest. One Coy of 1/4 East Lancs over in support. (A2c) | APP. 3 O.O. 65 |
| A6d86 | 11 E | | 2 Coys move up from GORRE during the afternoon and assemble about 5pm, with Coy more up to firing line. The raid taken place exactly as ordered (See APP. 4) ready for raid. After an Lens bombardment of the enemy trenches at 7.45pm everything remained quiet for the night. (OPS) 2/Lt HUNT slightly wounded & James bayonet & unarmed at Duff. 5 O.R. & party slightly wounded. Ans 3 O.R. of 14th Lancs blown to line would of still fine. | APP. 4 O.O. 1. APP. 5 Report on Raid |

# WAR DIARY or INTELLIGENCE SUMMARY

Army Form C. 2118.

1/9 Manchester Regt
Vol XXXV
Page 3

| Place | Date | Hour | Summary of Events and Information | Remarks and references to Appendices |
|---|---|---|---|---|
| AESCS | 12 | | Hostile D.M's active. Our D.M's attempt to put out enemy snipers. | |
| | | 10 a | B Coy go through the rail again over on the training ground. | APP 6 |
| | 13 | | Relieved by 1/6th K.ings Liverpool Regt & move to billets at BEURRY except 5 Battalion previously. H.Q. Coy to hospital sick | O.O. 68? |
| BEURY | 14 | | Move to new rest at BUSNETTES. Capt KERSHAW proceeds to England for six months from D. Inf. Arrangement provided will be to breaking up of D. Battalion. H.Q. 1/5th + 250 strength to go to 66th Div. for employment with 2/5 K Manchr Regt. Lt. Col. QUINNEY repeats from 12.6 Mn. to present with Batt'n gr Beurry | APP 7 OO 67 (?) |
| | 15 | | | |
| | 16 | | Draft of 10 officers + 200 other ranks sent to 1/5th MANCHESTER REGT & 1/6 MANCHESTER Rgt. Also drafts of 12 OR to 42 Div Wing. Capt MONDRATH go'n to 1/5 MANCHESTER REGT Major ANTROBUS to 1/6 MANCHESTER RGT. | APP 8 Roll of Officers |
| | 17 | | Bathing + inspection. Medical Officer return to 2/9 DIV. | (?) |
| | 18 | | Clearing up of transport which is to remain with batt. until A/O Div in surplus transport for 127 Bde. Lt. CRICK + complete transport personnel remain with transport Entrainment of batt. on 19/5 am | (?) |
| | 19 | 10 — | Batt'n for 16th Bn entrain at CHOQUES depot billets in hutt for 14th East Lancs. Arrive GUILLAUCOURT 8.30 pm | APP 9 Nom Roll |

FORET.   "REBATE"  Orders N. 64    Copy N. 9

WAR DIARY - Vol. XXXI - Appendix I

3rd February 1918.

1. The Battalion will be relieved by RESCUE in GIVENCHY Right sub-sector on the morning of the 4th inst.

2. RELIEF OF COMPANIES.
Right B. Coy. REBATE will be relieved by A Coy. RESCUE
Centre C Coy.    "    "    "    "    "    D    "
Left D. Coy.    "    "    "    "    "    C    "
Support A Coy.    "    "    "    "    "    B    "

No guides required. Relief will commence about 10. am

3. After relief, the Battalion will move into Brigade support. H.Q. A.H.a. 9.7. One Coll. C.C.7. Companies of REBATE taking over from certain Coys of REAL. Dispositions will be as stated in following orders below:-

A. Coy.  1 Platoon GIVENCHY KEEP. 1 Platoon MAIRIE KEEP. Coy. H.Q. near WINDY CORNER.

B. Coy.  H.Q. WINDY CORNER KEEP. and Coy. in billets round WINDY CORNER.

C. Coy.  H.Q. & 2 Sections HERTS KEEP. 1 Platoon MOAT FARM KEEP. 2 Sections HILDERS REDOUBT.

D. Coy.  OLD BRITISH LINE. H.Q. about A.2.B.3.4.

4. GUIDES. No guides will be furnished by REAL. O.C. Coys will make own arrangements.

5. GUMBOOTS. All torn and wet gumboots will be handed in to Drying Room before relief.

6. An advance party of 1 Officer per Coy. and 1 N.C.O. from each Coy. & Bn. H.Q. will report at the respective Coys of Bn. H.Q. of REAL at 8-0 am 4th inst. to take over Trench & KEEP Stores, etc.

7. TRENCH STORES etc. Trench Stores, Defence Schemes, Air Photos, Plans, Schemes of Work in Progress, A.A.L.G. positions will be handed over to RESCUE and taken over from REAL. Receipts of Posts & Stores will be sent to Bn.H.Q by 4 pm, 4th inst. Separate receipts will also be obtained for Anti-Tank S.A.A. – A.T. Minenkerfer etc – Gas Blankets. A careful check will be made of all Trench Stores & Certificates of Cleanliness in trenches, dug-outs & Cookhouses will be obtained from RESCUE and sent in at the same time.

8. REPORTING RELIEF. Relief complete will be wired to present Battn. H.Q. by the code word "WAR."
Each Company will report to new Battn. H.Q. when they have taken over their new positions by using the code word "SAVINGS"

(C...d)

Orders (contd).

9. **RATIONS.** Rations will be sent up at the same time & places as before. Q.M. will arrange to send Blankets (2 per man) with rations on the 4th inst.
O.C. Coys will make own arrangements for mid-day meal 4th inst, and for removal of Stores etc. to new HdQrs.

10. **WORKING PARTIES.** Working parties will be required as per Working Party Table issued to Companies, with the exception that B. Coy. will provide 25 O.R. on Item 5 at 7.30 am instead of 1 pm, 4th inst.
O.C. "D" Coy will ascertain in advance the nature of work to be done by his company.

11. ACKNOWLEDGE.

Distribution:-
Copy No 1-4  O.C. Coys
       5.    QM
       6.    T.O.
       7.    2/4 E. Lancs R
       8.    L⁰
       9.    1st War Diary
       11    File

C/Sutton

Capt & Adjt
REBATE.

SECRET  Amendment to       Copy No.
         ORDERS No. 64
                    3rd February 1918.

Para 3. B Coy will move to O.B. LINE
        as for items A, 2, 3, 4.
           The whole of D Coy will move
        to GORRE CHATEAU and be billeted
        there by O.C. 1/6th Bn Manchester Regt.

Para 9 RATIONS. Rations for A, C
        and Bn. HQ will be brought to
        WINDY CORNER — for B Coy
        to ESTAMINET CORNER —
        for D Coy to GORRE CHATEAU

Para 10 WORKING PARTIES. Items No 1
        2, 3, 4 and 7 remain unchanged
        Item No 8 will be performed by
        B Coy.
          Items No 5 & 6 by Companies of
        1/10th Bn Manchester Regt.
        billeted at WINDY CORNER

           Attached men return to their
        own coys tomorrow morning.

        Distribution :—
           As per B.O.N. 64
                                O.C. Smith
                                Capt & Adjt
        P.2.18.                  REGIMENT

WAR DIARY Vol. XXXI Appendix II

App 2.

## DAILY WORKING PARTIES.

| ITEM. | WORKING STRENGTH. OFF / O.R. | | FOUND BY. | UNDER SUPERVISION OF:- | PLACE. | TIME. | REMARKS. |
|---|---|---|---|---|---|---|---|
| 1. | 1. | 30. | "C" Coy. | 251 Tunnelling Coy. | mined dug-out A.9.c.4.4. | 12 noon 1/4 mi. day of relief. | mid-day meal before leaving (dinner) on return |
| 2. | 1. | 30. | "A" Coy. | — do — | — do — | 6.0 p.m. | Dinner before leaving tea on return. |
| 3. | 1. | 30. | "C" Coy. | — do — | — do — | 12-0 midnight | Tea before leaving breakfast on return. |
| 4. | 1. | 30 | "A" Coy. | — do — | — do — | 6.0 a.m. | Breakfast before leaving mid-day meal on return |
| 5. | | 25. | Coy. of 1/10 th Manch R. | 429 Fld Coy R.E. | R.E. Dump WINDY CORNER | 9-30 a.m. 1/2 mi. day of relief | mid-day meal before leaving (day of relief) Dinner on return |
| 6. | | 25. | Coy of 1/10 th Manch R. | 1/4 th E.E.R. | A.8.d. 85, 45. | 9.0 a.m. after day of relief | An Officer to report to O.C. 1/4 th Batt landed on the afternoon of Feb 4th to ascertain work and arrange meals etc |
| 7. | 1. | 11. | H.Q. | 251 Tunnelling Coy | BRASSERIE PONT FIXE | 6-0 p.m. | |
| 8. | | | "B" Coy | work on localities O.B. 1 to 4. | | | |

NOTE:- O.C. "A" & "C" Coys must arrange that 50% of the garrison of the KEEPS are kept on the KEEPS.

3 - 2 - 18.

Batt. + Coy. REBATE

WAR DIARY. Vol. XXXI. App. III.

SECRET.   "REBATE" ORDERS No 65   Copy No 10.

9th February 1918

1. The Battalion less "D" Coy will relieve "RESCUE" less "B" Coy in the Right Sector on the morning of 10th inst.
Coys will relieve simultaneously moving off at 9.30 a.m.

2. Dispositions will be as follows:-
Right "B" REBATE taking over from "A" Coy RESCUE & handing over to "C" Coy RESCUE
Centre "C"    "    "    "   "   "D"   "   "   "   "   "A" Coy RESCUE
Left "A"      "    "    "   "   "C"   "   "   "   "   "D" Coy RESCUE

"B" Coy RESCUE will remain in Support and will leave 12 ORs attached to Left Coy as ration and carrying parties.
One Coy of REAL will take over from "C" Coy REGAIN.
"C" Coy REGAIN will move off under orders of O.C. REGAIN.

3. No guides will be required. "A" Coy will move out via WOLFE ROAD.

4. Advance party to take over Keeps, etc will report at Coy H.Qrs at 8.0 a.m. 10th inst.

5. Trench Stores, Aeroplane Photos, Sketches, lists of R.E. material etc in Keeps will be taken over and handed over, and copies of receipts sent to Bn. H.Qrs together with certificates of cleanliness. A.A.L.G. rations will be handed over and taken over. "C" Coy REGAIN will send copy of receipts for stores handed over and copies of certificates of cleanliness to H.Qy REBATE. Gum boots will be handed over and taken over.

6. Blankets will be tied in bundles of 10, labelled and dumped by 8.30 a.m. 10th inst. "A" & "C" Coy at WINDY CORNER - "B" Coy at ESTAMINET CORNER. One man will be left with each dump until blankets are removed by G.M. on returning ration limbers on the 10th inst.

Orders No 65 contd

7. "C" Coy RESCUE will arrange to have some gum boots at their Coy H.Qrs for the use of garrison of No.3 Post moving in.

8. Relief complete will be wired to Battn. H.Q. by the code word "TOMORROW"

9. Rations for B. & C. Coys & Bn HQ. to be brought to WINDY CORNER as before. "A" Coy Returns to ESTAMINET CORNER

10. ACKNOWLEDGE

Distribution:-
Copy No. 1 - 4   O.C. Coys
            5   Q.M.
            6   T.O
            7   O.C. RESCUE
            8   O.C. REAL.
            9   O.C. REGAIN
       10 - 11  War Diary
           12   File

Issued by _____ at _____

Capt & Adjt
REBATE

Operation order No. 1
By
Lt. Col. E.C. Lloyd Comdg 1/9 Manchester Regt

Ref. Maps
VOILAINES (4) 1/10,000
Aero photo. 2 A.E. 4. 96. 6.1.16.

1. The Enemy trenches front and support lines in MACKENSEN TRENCH between the following boundaries (both inclusive)
   (1) C.T. running from A 3 d. 63.70 (F.L) to A 3 d 68.76 (S.L)
   (2) C.T. running from A 3 d 47.87 (F.L) to A 3 d. 55.88 (S.L)
   will be raided prisoners captured and any existing dug outs destroyed Machine Guns brought back and T.M's rendered useless.

2. The raiding party will consist of the following
   O.C. Enterprise Capt. STEPHENSON
                                    1/9 Manch R.
   with 2 other officers Lt Towler & Hunt
   2 Sergts
   13 N.C.O's
   76 men
   1 N.C.O and 6 R.E with mobile charges for destruction of dug outs

The party will be subdivided as follows

FRONT LINE PARTY under Lt Dowler
    2nd in Command Sergt ROBERTS.
  1 N.C.O and 6 men RIGHT BLOCK
  1 N.C.O and 6 men LEFT BLOCK
  2 N.C.O and 16 men front line moppers up
  3 N.C.O and 14 men C.T. Parties.

SUPPORT LINE PARTY under Lt Hunt.
    2nd in Command Sergt THICKETT.
  1 N.C.O 3 men RIGHT BLOCK
  1 N.C.O 3 men LEFT BLOCK
  2 N.C.O's 16 men Eastern C.T.
  2 N.C.O's 12 men Support line Moppers up

Covering Parties
    2 L.G. Sections
    2 Rifle Sections

3. The Raiding party will form up in NO.MANS.LAND. outside our wire in two waves
  1st Wave. SUPPORT LINE PARTY
  2nd Wave. FRONT LINE PARTY.
Each wave will be in two Columns in single file.
  The Officers and Sergts will lead their columns. The interval between Columns. The interval between Columns will be the distance between the two gaps

The enemy wire previously cut by our Artillery.

The distance between the waves will be 30 yards.

The whole will advance to within 100 yds of the enemy wire and be in position behind the ditch running N. and S. through A.3.d. by ZERO minus 5 minutes.

As soon as the barrage on the front line lifts. i.e. ZERO + 3 both waves will advance and enter the trenches by the two gaps in the wire.

The first wave will proceed direct to the enemy's support line keeping the same intervals. on reaching the trench the right and left Blocks will proceed outwards and form Blocks to their respective flanks 30 yards beyond.

The Moppers up will work inwards.
The Eastern C.T. Blocks will move as follows
S.E. C.T. Block will at once work down the Trenches leading E. from the Support line and joining at A.3.d. 60.87 where they will establish a block in the junction

N.E Block will act similarly with regard to the two exploited drains joining at A.3.d. 60.90.

The 2nd wave will close up with the 1st wave. so as to enter the enemy trenches on the heels of the latter.

The action of Moppers up will be The same as for the 1st wave.

The 3 C.T. parties will at once find their respective ~~parties~~ C.T's and work down them towards the support line.

4. Time of withdrawal ZERO + 20. The signal for the withdrawal will be White to Green. The method of withdrawal will be as follows

The 1st wave withdraws first block fall back in the centre and ~~when~~ all are collected, the 1st wave falls back thro' the 2nd wave.

Simultaneously the C.T. parties withdraw to the 2nd wave and the 2nd wave acts similarly after the 1st wave has passed thro'

5. Each party of moppers up will have two men told off as escort to prisoners. all prisoners will be passed back as soon as they can be collected, care being taken that they are organized as parties, so as not to dribble away men in escorting single prisoners.

1 Officer or N.C.O & 6

6. R.E. will accompany the 2nd wave and will confine themselves to destroying dug outs & works in and off the enemy front line

7. The Artillery will open an 18 Pdr barrage at ZERO on the enemy front line & Support line including the Objective and selected targets 200ˣ on either flank.

At ZERO + 3 the barrage will lift off Front & Support line off objective and 150ˣ to either flank will form a box barrage round the Objective.

This barrage will continue until ZERO + 30 and will then cease

8. Every man of the raiding party will carry 50 rounds ammn: and 2 bombs and will discard bayonet scabbards and entrenching tools

9. A field telephone will be carried forward and line layed to forward H.Q. Reports of entry into Enemy Trenches and summary of events will be transmitted

All reports which should be frequent and concise should be sent to Bn H.Q. A runner relay post will be established at junction of CHESHIRE RD & O.B.L

10. Bn Medical Officer will arrange for a forward dressing station N. of PRINCES ISLAND to which all cases will be sent and passed back.

11. Zero Hour 6 p.m. 10.2.18.

12. Watches will be synchronized at 2 P.M 10 Feb 1918

13. A large white flag will be placed in gaps in wire to facilitate exit from the enemy trenches.

**WAR DIARY Vol. XXXI Appendix V**

Report on a Raid carried out by
D Coy 1/9 Manchester Regt on the
night 11/12 Feb 1918. Zero Hour 6.15pm.

I attach the reports of the officer
in Command of the Enterprise and
the officer in Charge of R.E.

The original plan and orders were
carried out to the letter and I
consider the success of the Operation
due to the excellent barrage put down
by the Artillery, the element of
surprise as well as to the spirit
displayed by the Raiding party who
had previously drilled over an exact
replica of the area to be raided
traced on the ground from aeroplane
photographs. Each individual was
supplied with a copy of the trenches
and his approach and the place which
he was to go to marked on it.

Individuals as well as parties were
made to practice their part as well as
the Company as a whole both by day
and night. I beg to add that the
discipline, vim, and keenness could not
be bettered and that everything went off
to time. I am forwarding the names
of officers, NCOs and men who beg to

bring to your notice. Three unwounded and five wounded prisoners were brought in and at least 25 Germans were killed in their own lines. Apparently most of them were a ration party which had just arrived.

Our casualties 1 officer and three men wounded of the actual raiding party, all slight. One man of the covering party wounded and two men missing who are not yet accounted for.

Two German Machine Guns were captured, one was brought in, the other got entangled in the German wire by its belt and was left behind.

11 Feb 1918

E Lloyd Lt Col
Commdg 1/9 Manchester Regt

SECRET     WAR DIARY. Vol XXXI Appendix VI    Copy No. 8
          REBATE Order No 65-A
                                   12th February 1918.

1. **RELIEF.** The Battalion will be relieved in the Line by the 4th K.L.R. on the 13th inst. and will move to BEUVRY. On the 14th inst. it will move to BOSNETTE.

2. **ROUTE.** 13th inst. GORRE – LE QUESNOY – BEUVRY
     14th inst. LE QUESNOY – Road Junction E.11 & 7.8 – thence via CANAL BANK to E.5.a.90.60 – LES QUATRE VENTS – Road Junction W.27 & 8.9 – LANNOY – ANNEQUIN – BOSNETTE.

3. The following distances will be maintained between Units on the march.
    (a) East of LE QUESNOY. 200 yards between platoons and groups of four vehicles.
    (b) West of LE QUESNOY. Five hundred yards between Battalions 100 yards between Coys and 100 yards between Battalion and transport.

4. Party attached to 173 Tunnelling Coy R.E. will rejoin on the 13th inst.

5. A.A. L.G. positions must be carefully handed over. All trench stores, defence schemes, aero photos, secret trench maps etc. will be handed over and receipts obtained. Also programmes of work. The binoculars with A. B. C. Coys will be returned to Bn H.Q. and also all A.A. L.G. sights and mountings taken over.

6. **GUIDES.** Five guides per Coy (one for each platoon of relieving Battalion and one for Coy H.Q.) and one from Battn H.Q. will be at ESTAMINET CORNER at 9-45 am 13th inst. These guides will be provided with written instructions & will report to Officer T.M. Tod at ESTAMINET CORNER ✱ Coys in the Line will be relieved by sister coys of 4th K.L.R. B. Coy by B East Lancs Regt. will be relieved by D Coy 4th K.L.R.

7. **BAGGAGE.** As much heavy baggage as can be spared will be returned on ration limbers tonight. The remainder will be dumped at ESTAMINET CORNER tomorrow morning and moved by T.O.

8. **TRANSPORT.** L.G. limbers will be at ESTAMINET CORNER at 12-30 pm. Mess cart and Mallow carts will be at ESTAMINET CORNER at 11 am. Ride horses for A, B, C Coys at ESTAMINET CORNER at 11-30 am. Ride horses for Bn H.Q. at WESTMINSTER BRIDGE 12-30 pm.

                                           (Contd)
                                             over.

✱ Guides for posts will wait at Coy H.Q.

Orders (cont.) 2.

9. O.C. "D" Coy will detail an Officer to proceed in advance and take over billets at BEUVRY for the Battalion.

The Battalion will move off from BEUVRY at 11 a.m. 14th inst.

Instructions to Q.M. and T.O. for move on the 14th inst will be issued separately.

10. Hot water will be left in Soyers stoves for incoming units on the morning of the 13th inst.

ACKNOWLEDGE

Distribution
Copies Nos 1-4   O.C. Coys
       5.   T.O.
       6.   Q.M.
       7.   Bde & E.L.R.
       8-9. "War Diary"
       11   File

Issued by _____ at _____

J. Sutton
Captain & Adjutant
9th Bn Manchester Regt

SECRET　　WAR DIARY. Vol. XXXI Appendix VII
　　　　　19th Bn. Manchester Regt.
　　　　　　　ORDERS No 66　　　Copy No 8

　　　　　　　　13th February 1918.

1. The Battalion will move by march route to BUSNETTES on the 14th inst.

2. ROUTE. LE QUESNOY – Road Junction E.11.b.3.8. thence via Canal Bank to E.5.a.30.62 – LES QUATRE VENTS – Road Junction W.27.d.2.7. – LANNOY – GONNEGNEM – BUSNETTES. Lieut. W.L. PICKFORD will reconnoitre route before hand.

3. DISTANCES. The following distances will be maintained on the march.
   (a) East of a line N η S through F.7.a Central. 200 yards between platoons and groups of four vehicles.
   (b) West of that point. – Five hundred yards between Battalions, 100 yards between Coys, and 100 yards between battalion and transport.

4. ORDER OF MARCH. Bn HQ, D Coy, Drums, A, B, C Coys. HQ will move off at 11 am.

5. BLANKETS, VALISES &c. Blankets will be rolled in bundles of 10 and properly labelled & dumped at Coy. Billets by 9-0 am to be collected by QM.

　　　　　　　　　　　　　　(Contd.)

ORDERS (Cont'd)   2

Para 5: Officers valises will be dumped at
Cont'd. Quarter guard By 9 am.
Mens Packs B. C. & D. Coys will be
dumped near the School by 8 am
A Coys. Packs will be dumped near the
Packs of other Coys (Jerkins to be in Packs)
Coy Storemen will be in charge of the
Packs until collected by Q.M. Packs
will be conveyed by Motor Lorry on
its second journey.

6. TRANSPORT. Mess Cart will be required at
H.Q. at 10.30 am Maltese Cart at 10-30 am
Teams for Cookers & Watercarts at same time
Ride horses will be required at 10.45 am
Coy Cooks will be prepared to make tea
en route.
L.G. Limbers will be properly loaded
under Company arrangements.
Transport will form up in F.J. a
by 11-30 am, and await arrival of
Battalion.

7. DRESS. Fighting Order. Greatcoats to be
slung round haversack. Steel Helmets
will be worn.

8. BILLETS will be ready for inspection
by 9.30 am.

*[signature]*

DISTRIBUTION:-
Normal.
Captain & Adjutant
1/9th Bn. Manchester Regt.

ADDENDUM to 1/9 Manchester Orders
No. 66

Feb. 13/18

1. During the march to-morrow to the BUSNES AREA the following procedure will be carried out in farewell to the 1/4 East Lancs Regt and 1/6 Manchester Regt on their leaving the Bde.

The 1/5 East Lancs Regt and 1/10 Manchester Regt will line both sides of the road close up SE of the Road Junction N.14.c.00.25 thus protecting it. The Battalion will march between the two ranks. The head of the column will pass the road junction N.21.c.3.8 at 1.50 pm.

2. OC C Coy will detail one officer, 1 NCO + 2 men to remain behind to ensure that all billets are left clean. The officer will obtain certificate of cleanliness from the Area Commandant + will hand it to the Adjutant as early as possible. The Officer will also complete the billeting returns.

3. Transport. When the Transport moves off with the Battalion a distance of 25 yards between each group of two vehicles will be maintained. No pr[eceding] Baggage must be allowed between any vehicles. Cookers will march in a formed body behind the last Cooker. O.C. C. Coy will detail one platoon to march in rear of the Transport.

4. Mid-day Meal. Rations for mid-day meal will be taken. No hot Tea will be made en route + will be issued just before reaching LAMMOY. Q + A Coy will provide tea for Batt. HQ. B + C Coys for transport details.

        [signature]
        Capt Adjt
        [signature]
15.2.18

WAR DIARY. VOL. XXXI. APPNX. VIII

## 1/9th Battn. The Manchester Regiment.

Nominal roll of Officers on the strength of above Unit showing Units to which posted on re-organisation.

### 66th Division.

Act. Lieut-Col. E.C. Lloyd. D.S.O.

Capt. & Adjt. O.J. Sutton, M.C.

Lieut. & Qmr. W. Tarpey.

Major. T.e. Howorth.

Capt. D.B. Stephenson.

Lieut. N. Wilkinson.

Lieut. W.W. Quinney.

2/Lieut. H.G. Willis.

2/Lieut. W. Hughes.

2/Lieut. W. Witty.

### 1/5th Bn. Manchester Regiment.

Capt. G. Makin.

Lieut. S. Ruttenau.

Lieut. O.S. Needham.

Lieut. d.n. Wellwood.

Lieut. M.J. Dunlop.

2/Lieut. E.E. Towler.

2/Lieut. W.L. Pickford.

2/Lieut. A.E. Stone.

2/Lieut. C. Barlow.

2/Lieut. L.G. Taylor.

### 1/6th. Battn. Manchester Regiment.

Lieut. H.H. Knight.

2/Lieut. A.J. Midgley.

2/Lieut. J. Carrey.

2/Lieut. J. Broadbent.

Lieut. J. R. Tommis.

2/Lieut. R.J. Baddeley.

Continued.

Roll of Officers. (Contd.)
--------------------------------

### 1/6th Bn. Manchester Regiment. (Contd.)

2/Lieut. A.E. Rowe.

2/Lieut. H.R. Martin.

Act. Major. A.W. Farwell.

### Surplus.

2nd. Lieut. G.A. Bartram.   To 1st. Corps Reinforcement Camp.
                     (Pending Transfer to M.G.C.)

Capt. CHS. Redmond. (R.A.M.C.) Rejoined 1/2nd. E. Lancs. F.A.

Capt. (Rev.) H. Burrow. Wes. Chaplain.   To 1/10th. Manr. Regt.

2/Lieut. W.H. Crick. Transport Officer, remaining with Brigade.

Capt. G.W. Handforth.  To 1st. Corps Reinforcement Camp.

WAR DIARY. Vol XXXI. Appendix IX

# MOVE ORDERS.
## BY
## LIEUT - COLONEL E.C. LLOYD D.S.O.
## Commanding I/9th. Bn. MANCHESTER REGT.

Copy No. 8

18th. February 1918.

Para 1.  The party of 12 Officers and 250 O.Rs for 2/9th. Bn. Manchester Regt., will entrain at CHOCQUES about 9-30 a.m. 19th. inst.

Para 2.  The party will parade on road facing Orderly Room at 8-15 a.m. ready to move off in the following order - H.Qrs, "A", "B", "C", "D".

Para 3.  Blankets will be tied in bundles of 10 and dumped at Q.Ms stores by 7-0 a.m. Os C. Coys will ensure that no blankets are left in billets. Q.M. will count these blankets before loading.

Para 4.  T.O. will collect Officers valises and Coy Mess Boxes from Bn. H.Qrs and Coy H.Qrs at 7-30 a.m.

Para 5.  Billets must be left scrupulously clean, Os C. Coys will render certificate of cleanliness to Orderly Room by 8-0 a.m. 2/Lieut W. WITTY will obtain similar certificate from Town Major and will complete billeting certificates.

Para 6.  Q.M. will arrange for loading of stores by 7-30 a.m. T.O. will collect Orderly Room boxes at 7-30 a.m.

Para 7.  Q.M. will be in charge of the entraining.

Para 8.  Unexpended portion of days rations will be issued to the men before departure, rations for 20th inst will be carried by Q.M.

Para 9.  Dress - Marching order, jerkins rolled and fastened on the back of the belt, steel helmets will be worn.

Para 10.  Ride horses for C.O., Adjt., & Major HOWORTH will be required at 8-0 a.m.


ACKNOWLEDGE.


(Sd) O.J. SUTTON.
Captain & Adjutant.
I/9th. Bn. Manchester Regt.

Distribution :-
Copies No. 1 to 4. Os C. Coys.
          5. Q.M.
          6. T.O.
       7. & 8. War Diary.
          9. File.

Issued by............ at.........

Addendum No. 1.
to
MOVE ORDERS

Feby 16/16.

1.   The Battalion will parade at CHOCQUES Station at 8-30 a.m.  It will move off at 9-0 a.m. and not 8-15 a.m.

2.   All other times as in Move Orders will be put forward 15 minutes.

3.   All st.een flags must be taken.

4.   "D" Coy will provide loading and unloading party and train guard.

5.   Mess-cart will be required at 7-30 a.m. at H.Qrs.

6.   Transport will move to 127 Bde and will be clear of BUSNETTES by 9-0 a.m.

7.   Os.C. Coys will see that Cookers are left clean and complete.  Os.C.Coys will render a certificate to that effect to Orderly Room by 8-0 a.m.   T.O. will arrange to collect Cookers.

C d O J Sutton
Captain & Adjutant.
1/9th. Bn. Manchester Regt.

1/9th Battn. The Manchester Regiment.

SUMMARY OF CASUALTIES FOR THE MONTH OF FEBRUARY, 1918.

|  | OFFICERS. | OTHER RANKS. |
|---|---|---|
| KILLED. | - | - |
| WOUNDED. | 1. | 9. |
| MISSING. | - | - |
| TOTAL. | 1. | 9. |

28-2-18.

OPERATION ORDER No. 97.

by

Copy No.....

Lieut.Col. W.R. Pike. D.S.O. **IV** Commanding.

----------------------------------------------------------

1. The Battalion will be relieved by the 1/7th. Manchester Regt. on the night 18/19th. On completion of relief the Battalion will be in Brigade Reserve.
   Divisional

2. Coys. will be relieved as follows :-
   "A" Coy. 1/10th.Man.Regt. by "C" Coy. 1/7th.Manchester Regt.
   "B"  "    "        "    "   "B"  "    "        "         "
   "C"  "    "        "    "   "A"  "    "        "         "
   "D"  "    "        "    "   "D"  "    "        "         "

3. "C" & "D" Coys. will send one guide per platoon to report to Batt: H.Qrs. at 1 p.m. in order to guide in the relieving Coys.
   "A" & "B" Coys. will send one guide per platoon to meet relieving Coys. Guides will report at Batt: H.Qrs. by 8-30 p.m. 18th. inst.

4. An advance party of 1 Officer and 1 N.C.O. per Coy. will report to Batt: H.Qrs. at 9-30 a.m. 18th. inst. and proceed to their new area where they will take over Disposition Maps, Trench Stores, Programmes of work &c.
   "A" Coy. 1/10th. Manchester Regt. will take over from "C" Coy. 1/5th. Manchester Regt.
   "B" Coy. 1/10th.Manchester Regt. from "B" Coy. 1/5th. Manchester Regt.
   "D" Coy. 1/10th.    "      "    from "A" & "D" Coys. 1/5th. "     "
   "C" Coy.   "        "      "    will take over FORT BERTHA.
   "A" & "D" Coys. will send down 1 runner per platoon with their advance party. These runners will return to their Coy. in order to conduct platoons to the new area upon relief.
   All platoons before going to positions of accomodation will take up Battle Positions. Before leaving these Battle Positions O.C.Coys. will ensure that every man has a good fire position.

5. All tools, trench stores, disposition maps, gas appliances, etc., will be handed over to Advance party of 1/7th.Manchester Regt and certificates obtained in duplicate also certificates of cleanliness. These receipts and certificates will be sent to Battalion Orderly Room by noon 19th. inst.

6. "C" & "D" Coys. will carry out with them to their new positions all mess stores, Lewis guns, magazines, Very pistols, Periscopes, etc.
   "A" & "B" Coys. on relief will come down to K.25.b.90.05 (cross roads) where Coy. Lewis gun limbers will be waiting. One brakesman per Coy. will be detailed to go down with each limber.

7. The Transport Officer will arrange for "A" & "B" Coys. Lewis gun limbers to be at cross roads (K25.b.90.05) by 10-15 p.m. and one limber to report at Battalion H.Qrs. at 7-0 p.m.
   The Transport Officer will also arrange for the water cart stationed at Rear H.Qrs. to supply one load each to "C" & "D" Coys. new area by 5 p.m. 18th inst.
   Officers valises for H.Qrs. "A" & "B" Coys. will be sent up to new position under arrangements to be made by the Q.M.

8. O.C. "A" & "B" Coys. will arrange for evening meal to be issued at their present position and O.C. "C" & "D" Coys. in the New area.

9. An advance party of the relieving unit of 1 Officer and 4 N.C.O's per Coy. will report to "A" & "B" Coys. H.Qrs. by 7 p.m. this evening.

10. After relief Battalion H.Qrs. will be at J.34.b.2.6.

11. Completion of relief will be wired to Battalion H.Qrs. by code word "ISA" and also on arrival in new area by runner.

July 17th. 1918.

for Captain
Adjutant.

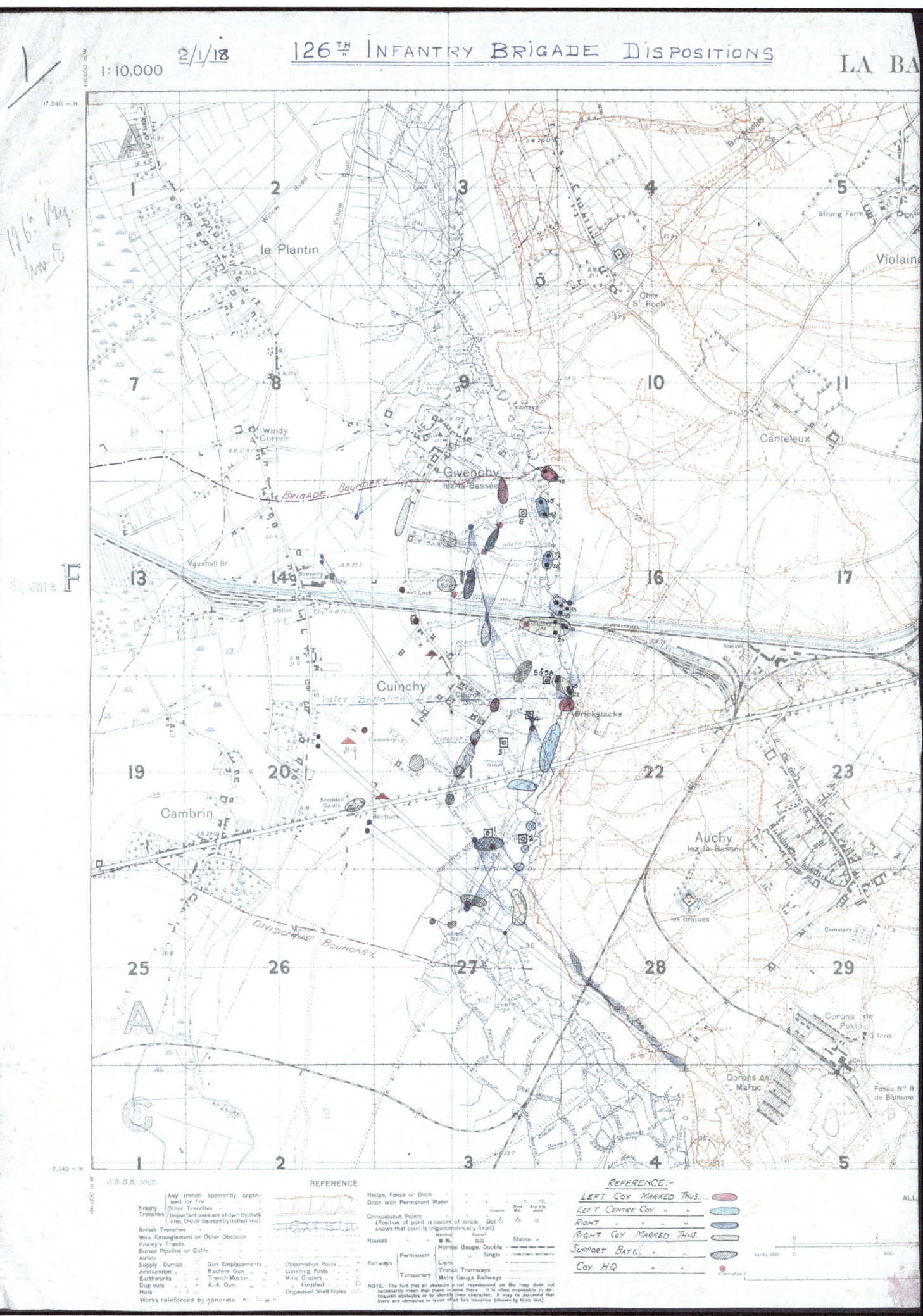

# TRENCH MAP.

## LA BASSÉE.
### 36c N.W. I.
EDITION 10. A

Scale 1:10,000.

INDEX TO ADJOINING SHEETS.

| Nacelle | Ferry. |
|---|---|
| Orme | Elm. |
| Orphelinat | Orphanage. |
| Osier-Belle | Osier-bed. |
| Ouvrage | Fort. |
| Ouvrages hydrauliques | Water works. |
| Papeterie | Paper-mill. |
| Parc | Park, yard. |
| " à pétrole | Petroleum ground. |
| " à charbon | Coal yard. |
| " à essence | Petrol store. |
| Passage à niveau P.N. | Level-crossing. |
| Passerelle, Pas.lle | Foot-bridge. |
| Pépinière | Nursery garden. |
| Peuplier | Poplar tree. |
| Phare | Light-house. |
| Pilier | Pier. |
| Place, Pl. | |
| Plaine d'exercice | Drill ground. |
| Pompe | Pump. |
| Pompeau | Culvert. |
| Pont | Bridge. |
| " levis | Drawbridge. |
| Poste { de garde | |
| Station côtière | Coast-guard station. |
| " de T.S.F. | |
| Poterie | Post, Pottery. |
| Poudrière, Poudre | Powder magazine. |
| Magasin à poudre | |
| Prise d'eau { artésienne } | Water supply, |
| { de sondage | Pit-head, Shaft, Well, Artesian well |
| Puits | Ventilating shaft. |
| | Boring. |
| Quai { aux bestiaux } | Quay, Platform, |
| { aux mar. ses | Cattle platform, |
| { des ..... | Goods platform. |
| Raccordement | Junction. |
| Raffinerie | Refinery. |
| Raperie de sucre | Sugar refinery. |
| | Beet-root factory. |

| Remblai | Embankment. |
|---|---|
| Remise { des Machines } | Engine-shed. |
| { aux ..... | |
| Réservoir, Rér | Reservoir. |
| Route cavalière | Bridle road. |
| Rubanerie | Ribbon Factory. |
| Ruine | |
| Ruines | Ruin. |
| En ruine | |
| Ruins = o | |
| Sablière | Sand-pit. |
| Sablonnière, Sablon.re | |
| Sapin | Fir tree. |
| Saule | Willow tree. |
| Soierie | Silk-works. |
| Scierie, Sc.ie | Saw-mill. |
| Sondage | Boring. |
| Source | Spring. |
| Sucrerie, Suc.rie | Sugar factory. |
| Tannerie | Tannery. |
| Tir à la cible | Rifle range. |
| Tissage | Weaving mill |
| Tôlerie | Rolling mill |
| Tombeau | Tomb. |
| Tour | Tower. |
| Tourbière | Peat-bog, Peat-bed. |
| Tourelle | Small tower. |
| Tuilerie | Tile works. |
| Usine à gaz | Gas works. |
| " électrique } | |
| d'électricité } | Electricity works. |
| " métallurgique | Metal works. |
| " à agglomérés | Briquette factory. |
| Verrerie, Verr.ie | Glass works. |
| Viaduc | Viaduct. |
| Vivier | Fish Pond. |
| Voie de chargement | |
| " déchargement | |
| " d'évitement | Siding. |
| " formation | |
| " manœuvre | |
| Zinguerie | Zinc works. |

www.ingramcontent.com/pod-product-compliance
Lightning Source LLC
Chambersburg PA
CBHW080900230426
43663CB00013B/2590